The Opening of
the Apartheid Mind

Perspectives on Southern Africa, 50

The Opening of the Apartheid Mind

Options for the New South Africa

Heribert Adam
and Kogila Moodley

UNIVERSITY OF CALIFORNIA PRESS
Berkeley · Los Angeles · London

Map of the Republic of South Africa courtesy of the British Broadcasting Corporation, copyrighted by David Harrison, 1981.

University of California Press
Berkeley and Los Angeles, California

University of California Press, Ltd.
London, England

Library of Congress Cataloging-in-Publication Data

Adam, Heribert.
   The opening of the Apartheid mind : options for the new South
   Africa / Heribert Adam and Kogila Moodley.
      p.   cm. — (Perspectives on South Africa)
   Includes bibliographical references and index.
   ISBN 0-520-08199-4 (alk. paper)
      1. Apartheid—South Africa. 2. South Africa—Politics and government—1989–
I. Moodley, Kogila. II. Title. III. Series.
DT1757.A33 1993
968.06′4—dc20   92-36443
                                                CIP

Printed in the United States of America
9 8 7 6 5 4 3 2 1

The paper used in this publication meets the minimum requirements of American National Standard for Information Sciences—Permanence of Paper for Printed Library Materials, ANSI Z39.48-1984 ♾

For Kanya and Maya
in lieu of letters

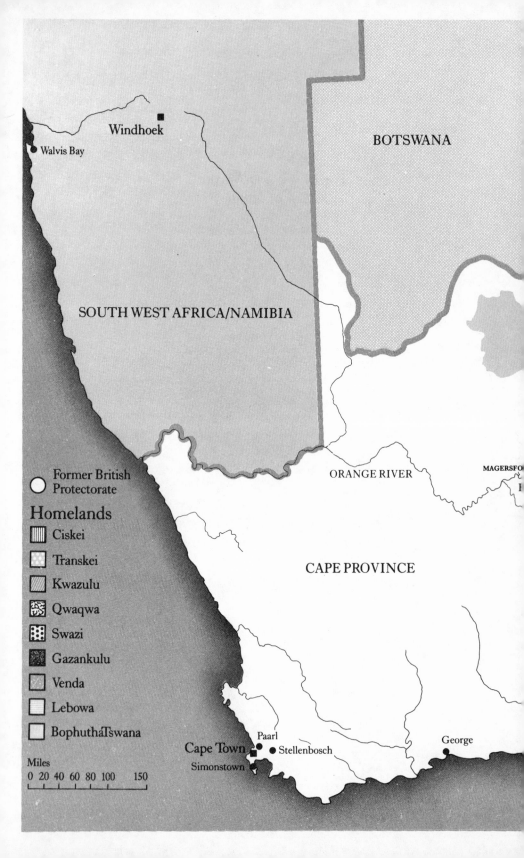

Windhoek

Walvis Bay

BOTSWANA

SOUTH WEST AFRICA/NAMIBIA

Former British
Protectorate

Homelands

Ciskei

Transkei

Kwazulu

Qwaqwa

Swazi

Gazankulu

Venda

Lebowa

BophuthaTswana

Miles
0 20 40 60 80 100   150

ORANGE RIVER

MAGERSFO

CAPE PROVINCE

Paarl

Cape Town
Simonstown

Stellenbosch

George

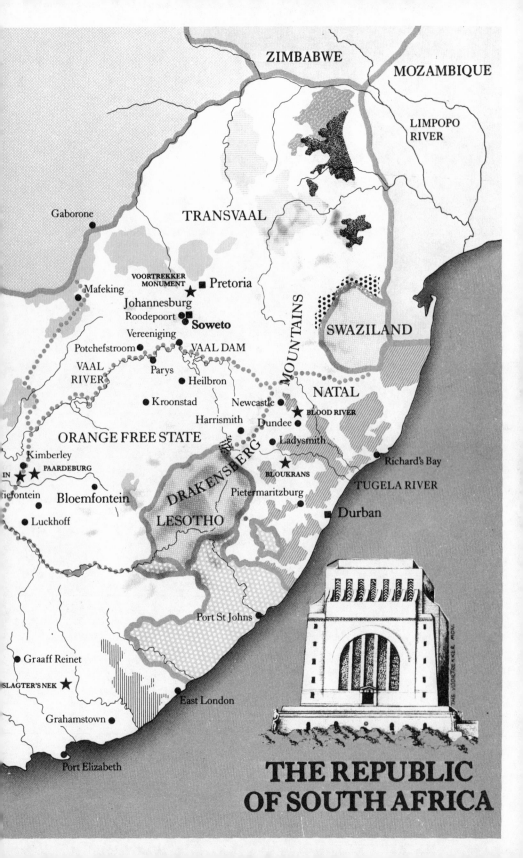

THE REPUBLIC
OF SOUTH AFRICA

Contents

Acknowledgments

Our reasoning has drawn liberally on the insights of many colleagues. First and foremost, we benefited from numerous conversations with two longtime South African friends, Van Zyl Slabbert and Hermann Giliomee. Slabbert's political savvy and Giliomee's sensitivity toward Afrikaner nationalism, as well as our disagreements over the nature of ethnicity, stimulated much of our writing. We had frequent political discussions with Jenny and Alex Boraine, André du Toit, Hamish Dickie-Clark, Pieter and Ingrid Le Roux, Wilmot James, Helen Zille and Johann Maree, Michael Savage, Oscar Dhlomo, Franklin Sonn, Allister Sparks, Solly Benatar, Vincent Mapai, Pierre van den Berghe, Mamphela Ramphele, Theo Hanf, Motti Tamarkin and Tony Williamson.

Jeffrey Butler and David Welsh read the manuscript for the publisher and made valuable suggestions, as did our students in Vancouver and Cape Town. All the research associates who collected data in Canada and South Africa during the past four years, as well as the dozens of busy respondents who allowed themselves to be interviewed, deserve thanks.

We could not have asked for more thoughtful copyeditors than Pamela Holway and Amy Einsohn in Berkeley. The end product would not be in a presentable state without the meticulous attention of Anita Mahoney, Jan MacLellan in the Dean of Art's Office at Simon Fraser University, Peng Wong in the Multicultural Liaison

Office at the University of British Columbia, and Gila van Rooyen at the Graduate School of Business at the University of Cape Town. The Canadian Social Science and Humanities Research Council (SSHRC) continued to support our research.

Cape Town, January 1993
Heribert Adam
Kogila Moodley

Abbreviations and Acronyms

AHI	Afrikaanse Handelsinstituut
ANC	African National Congress
Assocom	Association of Chambers of Commerce
AVU	Afrikaner Volksunie, a splinter faction of the Conservative Party
AWB	Afrikaner Weerstandsbeweging (Afrikaner Resistance Movement)
Azapo	Azanian People's Organisation
BCM	Black Consciousness Movement
BOSS	Bureau of State Security, predecessor of NIS
CBM	Consultative Business Movement
CCB	Civil Cooperation Bureau, an undercover agency of the SADF
Codesa	Convention for a Democratic South Africa, a negotiating forum of nineteen parties established in 1991
Contralesa	Congress of Traditional Leaders of South Africa
Cosatu	Congress of South African Trade Unions

CP	Conservative Party
DET	Department of Education and Training
DMI	Department of Military Intelligence
DP	Democratic Party
EPG	Eminent Persons' Group
FCI	Federated Chamber of Industries
FLS	Frontline States, the eleven states of Southern Africa that are members of SADC
Fosatu	Federation of South African Trade Unions, predecessor of Cosatu
HNP	Herstigte Nasionale Party, an extreme right-wing splinter party led by Jaap Marais
Idasa	Institute for a Democratic Alternative for South Africa
IDT	Independent Development Trust
IFP	Inkatha Freedom Party
JSE	Johannesburg Stock Exchange
KZP	KwaZulu Police
LRA	Labour Relations Act
MDM	Mass Democratic Movement
MK	Umkhonto we Sizwe, the military wing of the ANC
MNR	Mozambique National Resistance, also known as Renamo
MPLA	Popular Movement for the Liberation of Angola, led by José Eduardo dos Santos
Nactu	National Council of Trade Unions
Nafcoc	National African Federated Chambers of Commerce
Nats	Members of the National Party
NECC	National Education Crisis Committee

NIS	National Intelligence Service
NMC	National Manpower Commission
NP	National Party
NSMS	National Security Management System
NUM	National Union of Mine Workers
Numsa	National Union of Metal Workers
OAU	Organization of African Unity
OFS	Orange Free State
PAC	Pan Africanist Congress
PFP	Progressive Federal Party, predecessor of the Democratic Party
PWV	Pretoria-Witwatersrand-Vaal Triangle
Renamo	Resistência Nacional Mocambicano, a South Africa–supported rebel movement against the ruling Frelimo party; also known as MNR
SABC	South African Broadcasting Corporation
Sabta	South African Black Taxi Association
Saccola	South African Consultative Committee on Labour Affairs
Sacob	South African Chamber of Business
SACP	South African Communist Party
SADCC	Southern African Development Coordination Conference; renamed SADC (Southern African Development Community) in 1992 under terms of the Windhoek Treaty
SADF	South African Defence Force
SAIRR	South African Institute of Race Relations
Samcor	South African Motor Corporation
SANCO	South African National Civic Organisation
SAP	South African Police
SBDC	Small Business Development Corporation

SSC	State Security Council
Swapo	South West African People's Organisation, the ruling nationalist movement in Namibia
TBCV	Transkei, Bophuthatswana, Ciskei, and Venda, the nominally independent homelands
UDF	United Democratic Front
UF	Urban Foundation
Unita	Uniâo Nacional para a Independência Total de Angola, the U.S.- and South Africa–supported movement led by Jonas Savimbi
Uwusa	United Workers' Union of South Africa

Methodological Approaches and Political Values

The most repugnant form of lying is to tell, all of it,
whilst hiding the soul of facts.
> Breyten Breytenbach, *Die Suid-Afrikaan,*
> no. 36, 1992

Reluctant reconciliation is taking shape in South Africa. The ambivalent alliance between the two major contenders for power, the National Party (NP) and the African National Congress (ANC), results from a balance of forces where neither side can defeat the other. It is their mutual weakness, rather than their equal strength, that makes both longtime adversaries embrace negotiations for power-sharing. Like a forced marriage, the working arrangement lacks love but nonetheless is consummated because any alternative course would lead to a worse fate for both sides.

The emergence of multiracial domination has surprised those observers who viewed the battle over apartheid as a clear moral issue, the defeat of the last colonizers by a widely acclaimed movement of national liberation. During the 1970s and 1980s the international debate on South Africa was preoccupied with the obvious immorality of legalized racism. The apartheid state was invariably treated as a monolithic racist entity, and internal strategic developments were overlooked or reduced to simple dichotomies between oppressors and victims. This either-or reasoning ignored local contexts and obscured the ambiguities, contradictions, and irrationalities of life under apartheid. Undoubtedly, the grotesque Verwoerdian social engineering was brutal; but it also contained a certain paternalistic benevolence that oiled the system and helps explain why apartheid lasted so long. Incontrovertibly, the system of racially defined privileges designated oppressors and victims, but if we are to understand South African politics, victimology needs to be balanced by accounts of how the seemingly powerless survived, gave meaning to their lives, and acted upon their particular historical circumstances.

Developments in South Africa have also been widely misunderstood owing to the tendency to apply false colonial analogies or popular stereotypes of violent tribalism. Later, the personality cult surrounding Nelson Mandela and the accolades accorded to F. W. de Klerk have further romanticized a conflictual relationship, personalizing it into a literal matter of black versus white, and thereby obscuring the social conditions and constraints under which these leaders act, the passions and interests that drive their interacting constituencies. Criticizing the ANC became taboo among anti-apartheid activists. But it is precisely because the ANC and Nelson Mandela are key players in South Africa's future that they cannot be treated as above criticism or scrutiny. Sympathy for the essential legitimacy of the ANC's claims, and respect for Mandela's moral stature, statesmanship, and pragmatic wisdom do not require progressives to endorse at face value everything the ANC says about itself. Critical solidarity, not cheerleading, is required.

To contribute to a more nuanced understanding of South Africa, this study probes the various competing forces in the ongoing transition. How did the miracle happen that allowed for multiparty negotiations? What are the sources of the continuing violence, which threatens these historic negotiations? What are the prospects for the success or failure of democracy in a society characterized by such extremes of affluence and poverty? How can the legacies of apartheid be overcome without creating new injustices? Can postapartheid South Africa, the most industrialized society in a war-ravaged continent, serve as the engine of growth for all of Southern Africa? What are the options for international assistance in the postapartheid era?

In a referendum held on March 17, 1992, a surprising 68.7 percent of South Africa's whites supported a negotiated abolition of their minority rule. The same cabinet ministers and Afrikaner National Party that presided over the implementation of apartheid in defiance of world opinion, were now, with the support of two-thirds of their constituency, to act as democratic reformers. The approval of the referendum has been universally hailed as unprecedented in the annals of politics. Whites, however, did not vote to transfer power *to* the black majority, as the media reported, but only to share power.* They

---

*The use of racial and ethnic labels is not meant to reproduce, uncritically, the legal classifications enacted under apartheid. Racial and ethnic groupings are, of course, always socially constructed and therefore contested and ever-changing in their boundaries and meanings. Individual South Africans, like people elsewhere, have often identified themselves in

agreed to democratize a system in which they themselves will neces-sarily remain major stakeholders. Though strong in symbolic support, the ANC is weak in bureaucratic resources, military capacity, and economic leverage. Real power will therefore remain in the hands of the present establishment; even if Nelson Mandela becomes president of South Africa, the economy, the civil service, and the army will have to rely on white skills, capital, and goodwill for a long time to come.

Faced with the threat of a beleaguered siege economy, the ruling group thus opted for an inclusive ideology that may in the future even win substantial support from like-minded black conservatives. More-over, by not insisting on guaranteed racial group representation, as white Zimbabweans had, the dwindling white minority in South Africa set in motion the prospect for a broad coalition government of national unity in which whites could emerge as a powerful legitimate force.

The goal of transformation through negotiation corresponds to neither the revolutionary nor the reformist agenda for South Africa. Socialist adherents of the former always falsely assumed South Africa to be the only developed capitalist country "[that] is not only 'objec-tively' ripe for revolution but has actually entered a stage of overt and seemingly irreversible revolutionary struggle."[1] The reformist agenda, on the other hand, was falsely predicated on selective co-option as the most effective method to buy off dissent while preserving political inequality. The multiparty negotiations, however, will neither leave the status quo intact, as the reformers had hoped, nor utterly reverse all power relations, as revolutionaries had expected. Instead, the negotiations grant all major forces a stake in a historic compromise by which each party stands to gain more than it would lose by continuing the confrontation. Most likely, economic and bureaucratic power will remain largely in the hands of the present establishment for some time, even as political power increasingly passes into the

---

terms other than—or contrary to—state-imposed classifications. Nevertheless, given the history of South Africa, one cannot avoid using such problematic labels as "Coloureds," for people of mixed historical origins, about 9 percent of the population; "Indians" or "Asians," for descendants of indentured laborers and traders from the Indian subcontinent, now 3 percent of the population; and "Africans" or "blacks," for the Bantu-speaking majority, about 76 percent of the population. In political discourse "blacks" also refers to members of all three "nonwhite" groups who are conscious of their discriminated status. The restrictive use of "Africans" for the indigenous majority does not imply that others have not also become Africans through longtime residence and subjective identification, as both the African Na-tional Congress and, to a lesser extent, the Pan Africanist Congress recognize.

hands of the formerly disenfranchised. The negotiations concern the precise terms of such a deal.

As a widening consensus on constitutional and economic visions emerges, the prospects for peace depend on more than the designs of political leaders. The continuing political violence serves as a reminder that social conditions and unrecognized ideologies can wreck any official accord. Although the political violence is often simplistically characterized as the result of a power contest between the ANC and Inkatha, and inflamed by state agencies, the dynamics of the urban-rural divide and the hostel cultures explain the daily atrocities far better.

In the former Soviet Union we have seen how liberalizers can be swept aside by the liberalization they unleashed. But de Klerk's situation differs notably from Gorbachev's: Under rising pressure from below, de Klerk preempted revolution from above. De Klerk also has the advantage of presiding over a reasonably functioning industrial economy that, although severely depressed, is potentially buoyant, with a highly developed infrastructure and an established pool of managerial skills. Nor is de Klerk confronted by powerful secessionist forces. Perhaps most important, he enjoys what Gorbachev did not: a democratic mandate from much of his constituency for his commitment to reform.

Political Approaches. It may be useful to situate our approach more clearly within the existing research on South Africa. The recent literature may be crudely classified into four categories:

(1) The vast majority of publications are *descriptive* accounts or running commentaries on the latest events. Granted, journalistic narratives by perceptive authors often contribute valuable insights, particularly when produced by such skilled hands as Allister Sparks (1990), Marq de Villiers (1987), Joseph Lelyveld (1985), Ken Owen (1992), or Rian Malan (1990). But works in this genre tend to focus on personalities as movers of history: comparisons between de Klerk and Gorbachev abound; books on Mandela's life, loves, and trials still proliferate. Such personal accounts add a richness and flavor typically lacking in abstract theoretical conceptualizations of social formations, classes, and structures. But individual biographies cannot explain complex political developments, and academic interpretations must go beyond the conventional wisdom of editorials. While the particular outlooks and idiosyncrasies that result from a public fig-

ure's personal history undoubtedly inspire the style and sometimes even shape the course of politics, political leaders always act within massive constraints. Leaders, however charismatic, can only be effective when circumstances are ripe. Consequently, political analysis is at its most astute when it focuses more on the social conditions and other forces that propel or circumscribe individuals than on their personal characteristics.

(2) Many publications, notably histories of protest and activism, are essentially polemics: they are *accusatory* accounts. Frequently with the best intentions, their authors aim at advocacy—but this approach easily degenerates into a propagandistic exercise. Writing on South Africa by certain authors has become utterly predictable, even when significant shifts in policy call for a fundamental reevaluation. Nothing has changed in the apartheid state; apartheid will be dead only when its entire legacy of inequality has been removed. So runs the tired refrain of that supposedly radical critique.

(3) Less partisan but equally one-sided are the many *prescriptive* accounts. These offer with great persuasion detailed solutions, be they a free market in a Swiss canton system (Louw and Kendall 1986) or a Japanese "high road" (Sunter 1987). More sophisticated analyses in this genre, by outstanding academic writers on divided societies, prescribe power sharing in a consociational grand coalition (Lijphart 1985) or an alternative system of voting (Horowitz 1991).

Similar rather single-minded preoccupations used to dominate the vast Marxist literature, which was concerned with changing modes of production and the various crises of capitalism. Only recently have analysts on the left begun to address current and future transformations more systematically and pragmatically (for example, see Gelb 1991), instead of chronicling a familiar pattern of conquest, exploitation, and heroic resistance. Conceptually more diverse, liberal authors have mainly preoccupied themselves with detailing a rich history of oppression and manipulation, often to the extent of ridiculing the "backward" Afrikaners caught in stale mythologies (Thompson 1985). Most activists in the anti-apartheid church network also fall into this group, writing above all with a moral outrage and a normative insistence.

(4) In their search for a politically feasible means to incremental progress rather than the elusive grand design, pragmatically oriented authors move into an *analytical* realm of strategic debate. We would like to align our work with this approach, while adding a healthy dose

of eclecticism. Politically we write as social democrats who identify with the underdog but lack the enviable certainty of orthodox Marxists or liberal moralists about the best solution. By aiming at the second-best compromise, social democrats usually earn the distrust of ideologues on the left and neoconservatives alike. However, with the conclusion of the cold war, and the resulting ideological confusion, history has not ended. Instead, it has become more fluid and amenable to pragmatic solutions. When the former staunchly socialist governments of Mozambique and Zimbabwe embrace structural adjustment programs and free-market policies; when Afrikaner nationalists praise a thoughtful Stalinist like Joe Slovo, who appears regularly on the state-run television; when former apartheid ideologues renounce their racial exclusiveness and leading African nationalists advocate inclusive policies of sharing in place of turning the tables—who is to say who betrayed whom?

The tradition prevalent among social scientists of predicting gloom and doom on the evidence of perpetual crises or the deficiencies of human nature overlooks a self-fulfilling danger: such predictions can promote the very conditions so deplored. This defeatist stance also evades the basic fact that people learn and adapt. Radicals may deliver witty, cynical, despairing commentary, but in so doing they reveal how far they have reconciled themselves to their marginality in influencing the course of events. Equally trapped, however, are the perpetual optimists who naively claim linear progress by ignoring its obstacles, who substitute mere exhortation for sober evaluation.

The most sophisticated social science position, one that avoids both pitfalls, is best illustrated by Jürgen Habermas's theory of communicative action, in which the focus of philosophy is shifted from consciousness to communication. In this approach, actors' interpretations of the world are discursively negotiated through reasoned argumentation. Rather than leading to a false consensus dictated by power relations, such communicative rationality aims at a common understanding. Although Habermas fails to specify how conflicting claims of validity are adjudicated—how we decide which is the "better" argument—his emancipatory project holds out the greatest promise for arriving at a common meaning. In contrast to the abdicating relativism of the postmodernists, modernity is retained as a universal potential, constructed not to totalize but with the ability to particularize. We write in the spirit of this vision.

Research Methods. This study is based on a critical evaluation of the vast body of social science work on South Africa, including an on-going debate over policy in which we have actively participated through several publications. *Modernizing Racial Domination* (1971) developed the concepts of a "pragmatic oligarchy" and a "democratic police state" at a time when most writers assumed the irrationality of a fascist-like Afrikaner racism. The possibility of internal liberalization and reformist adaptation was further explored in *Ethnic Power Mobilized* (1979), coauthored with Hermann Giliomee. This volume traced the rise and fall of Afrikaner power not in terms of Calvinist ideology or frontier isolation from the Enlightenment but in light of the changing condition of South Africa's political economy. At the height of South African revolutionary fervor we published the revisionist *South Africa without Apartheid* (1986), a work that both predicted the negotiations now underway and argued the case for accommodation in an integrated, economically interdependent consumer society. Our skepticism about the revolutionary outcome so widely assumed at the time was stoutly rejected by those who believed in the likelihood and feasibility of a socialist transformation of racial capitalism. At the same time, an unexpectedly warm letter from Pollsmoor prison in 1987 revealed that Mandela had read our book. So, it turned out, had two cabinet ministers. The fact that our theoretical studies were taken seriously by both sides in this fierce ideological battle was to us a cherished vindication of the idea that an academic analysis can make a practical contribution toward shaping perceptions of alternative policies. Rather than the inevitable unfolding of predetermined antagonistic class or racial forces, history now seemed far more open-ended, susceptible to intelligent intervention by progressive actors.

It was against the backdrop of the repressive 1970s and 1980s that we tried to make this contribution. During the 1960s we had both taught at universities in South Africa, where K.M. was born and educated and where our extended family still lives as part of the Indian community in Durban. After being forced into exile and refused visas in the 1970s, we nevertheless persisted, eventually succeeding in upholding our right to visit our family in South Africa. During regular annual visits during the 1980s we continued our field research as insiders rather than outsiders. During 1986–87, at the height of P. W. Botha's emergency, H.A. was acting director of the Centre for

Intergroup Studies at the University of Cape Town. Our daughters attended a local high school, and K.M., who was attached to the Faculty of Education, addressed parent meetings and teachers groups as frequently as she did her academic classes. We mention all this because these wide interactions over several years gave us many of the insights into South African attitudes and social conditions that inform the present analysis.

Since the inception of this study in July 1989 we have spent several months each year in South Africa, based at the University of Cape Town. We individually conducted interviews with a variety of South African politicians, journalists, academics, community leaders, union activists, and businessmen. These included six ANC executives and seven cabinet ministers, as well as the former state president P. W. Botha at his retirement home in George. In addition, two research assistants tape recorded interviews with key individuals in the legal profession and opinion makers on the Afrikaner right wing. H.A. participated as one of the few foreigners at the historic ANC-Afrikaner meeting in July 1987 in Dakar, led by F. van Zyl Slabbert and Alex Boraine, and, in October 1988 in Leverkusen, Germany, at a similar Idasa-sponsored conference, with Soviet academics, executives of the ANC and the South African Communist Party, and liberal Afrikaners. Together with contacts from numerous other conferences on South Africa around the world, we developed a network of friends and acquaintances on both sides of the ideological divide.

Apart from these conventional research methods we engaged in participant observation of relevant events in South Africa. We attended dozens of political meetings, rallies, funerals, political trials, and workshops in order to add rich atmospheric texture to our readings and formal interviews. We make no apologies for our strong views and even biases—which, of course, all analysts exhibit, whether explicitly or implicitly. All knowledge is socially and historically shaped, and the contingent character of the social "sciences" has long been exposed. This may explain our skepticism when some of our colleagues pontificate about transformation, about the need for sacrifices in the South Africa where our relatives live. Reconciliation and negotiation remain the priorities, although the economic restructuring of a skewed racial capitalism cannot be put off indefinitely. Inasmuch as economic redistribution implies further destabilizing confrontation, transformation will have to be postponed if anything is to survive to be transformed. The less outsiders interfere in negotiations at this point or try to impose their solutions or choose their winners and losers, the better for the domestic legitimacy of the outcome. In any case, given the West-centric bias about political developments in the Third World so typical of moral imperialists of all hues, they are hardly in a position to render counsel. South Africa's critics should be guided by the particularities of historical experience, rather than by universalist formulas or false analogies with developments elsewhere. In short, context-sensitive historical analysis is called for.

Celso Furtado, one of the leading economists of Latin America, has argued that the vast political problems developing countries now face reflect historical circumstances substantially different from those the already-industrialized states passed through in the early phases of their development. Describing these different conditions as "beyond the ideological rationales derived from the experience of classical capitalism" (1970, xxv), Furtado insists that solutions must be developed within the countries themselves. Much the same could be said of the sociopolitical experience of South Africans. What passes as a democratic compromise will depend on South African consensus far more than on international norms. We may hope the two will coincide—but a hope is not a prediction, nor is it a moral stipulation.

CHAPTER ONE

Colonialism, Communalism, and Democracy

*South Africa
in Comparative Perspective*

THE GLOBAL RELEVANCE OF SOUTH AFRICA

It is now conventional wisdom that after the end of the cold war, Africa as a continent has become marginalized to the extent of sliding into what a French official called the "conservatory of the ills of humanity."[1] Benign neglect of a seemingly hopeless irrelevancy characterizes outside attitudes. Even the long overdue World Bank–induced redemocratization of the continent does little to solve the problem of establishing order, stability, growth, and civility in weak states; in fact, the removal of tyrants may make life worse when successors fight each other in endless civil wars. After the abolition of the apartheid system, for example, the number of political killings in South Africa has tripled and the economic decline has accelerated.

Yet it is precisely the immensity of the problems of the "forgotten continent" that makes Africa relevant globally. The category "Third World" may indeed have had meaning only in the context of the global cold war division, as some scholars argue.[2] With the former Soviet Union descending into political and economic chaos, a more relevant classification groups the affluent, economically stable states (North America, Western Europe, Japan, and the newly industrialized Asian countries) into one competing trading bloc. A second bloc consists of states with some resources and potential for growth as well as kinship ties and ideological affinities with the first-tier states; this second bloc includes most of Latin America, some states in the Middle

East and Asia, and South Africa. Relegated to the third category are politically volatile countries without resources and claims on or hopes for Western assistance: sub-Saharan Africa, the southern Balkan states, the Caucasus, and most of South Asia. They are increasingly left to their own misery, at best the recipients of mere charity.

This new North-South division ignores former ideological contests and is characterized by access to the dominant economic resources (credits, markets, and political support) of the first bloc. Yet the powerful North neglects the powerless South at its own peril, for the importance of the South lies in its very weakness, in its capacity to destabilize the entire globe. The worldwide effects of environmental degradation, the streams of economic refugees into the islands of comparative affluence, the spread of AIDS and other diseases, the slaughter enacted in the name of religious or nationalist fundamental-ism—what happens among the have-nots eventually affects the haves. It is this potential to cause chaos, or what Dieter Senghaas refers to as *Chaosmacht,* that constitutes the power of the powerless.

South Africa embodies the North-South conflict in one country, albeit with a decisive difference. Unlike Western Europe, South Africa cannot build new iron curtains to keep its haves insulated from the have-nots. The highways and railways leading out of Cape Town, Johannesburg, or Durban cut right through the huge slums of Khaye-litsha, Soweto, and Kwa Mashu. While the violence of deprivation can be deflected on its victims, their struggles increasingly spill over into the fortifications of the affluent, who cannot enjoy their privileges when the murder rate in Johannesburg is three times higher than that of the worst American city. Especially when the stability and security of the white minority depends directly on the cooperative labor of the majority, its brutalization cannot be contained beyond the factory gates.

South Africa thus constitutes a laboratory for the new global com-promise between the North and the South, whether in race relations, multicultural education, or economic cooperation between capital and labor. The society will either bring forth new forms of coopera-tive development and legitimacy or will disintegrate through ethnic violence and costly repression. Europe increasingly perceives the South as burdensome; begging strangers are to be held at bay. Because the people of South Africa share a common citizenship, history, and economy, they cannot retreat from or postpone the challenge. South Africans cannot divorce each other through partition without destroying their source of wealth. Unlike the centrifugal ethnoregionalism in the rest of the world, centripetal forces in South Africa bind the antagonistic segments into a common state. The poorer regions are dependent on transfer payments. It is out of this imperative that the world's most backward political system of legal segregation could perhaps develop into an advanced model for the gradual solution of the North-South cleavage through unitary federalism with regional autonomy.

In global terms, given the ecological limitations, the North cannot sustain unlimited economic growth in the future, nor can the South ever hope to emulate or catch up with the environmentally destructive Northern examples. The new forms of cooperation needed worldwide to preserve the ecosystem and enhance the quality of life could receive decisive impetus from the one country that combines virtually all the starkest contradictions and predicaments within its borders. This elevates the study of South Africa beyond an esoteric regional problem.

Is South Africa now a hopeful country in the second block or one on the verge of becoming a disintegrating state in the third category? Is the conflict between the ANC and Inkatha a forerunner of the same unnecessary war that happened in Zimbabwe between Mugabe and Nkomo, between Frelimo and Renamo in Mozambique, or between the MPLA and Unita in Angola before they agreed to a ceasefire of sheer exhaustion? Are the material and ethnic divisions that have emerged after apartheid was suspended so deep that the accelerating political and criminal violence ruins all prospects of growth? In short, is South Africa permanently trapped in a transition without development? Why has a seemingly inevitable black-white racial conflict been replaced with much more widespread intrablack violence?

In socioeconomic terms, the violent conflicts among blacks are essentially between insiders and outsiders. The cleavage between the early urbanized and the latecomers constitutes the most fundamental faultline in black society. Privileged insider status had historically been confined to people with Section 10 rights, those legally resident in "white areas" and entitled to work there. The other half, the mass of illegal jobseekers and shack dwellers, were harassed and kept in check by apartheid laws, were discarded and left to starve in the countryside. With the abolition of influx control and apartheid repression, the competition over scarce goods became an intrablack affair. The conflict was transformed from one between illegals and the police to an all-out struggle for space and survival between old-time residents and those desperately seeking access, now unconstrained by the state. Ironically, the termination of unfeasible state regulations to control entry unleashed violent clashes within black society.

This socioeconomic conflict assumed its political overtones through the historic alignment of old-time residents with the ANC and the civic associations. In areas where the majority of the outsiders were migrant workers or squatters of Zulu origin, Inkatha voiced their interests. At the root, however, lies neither a "tribal" conflict nor an ANC/Inkatha feud. In the Western Cape townships that have no Zulu migrants, the violent competition between insiders and outsiders developed with equal intensity at times, beyond the ANC's or the civics' ability to control it.

The politicization of ethnicity (nationalism, tribalism) occurs everywhere in the world not only because ethnic exclusiveness provides scapegoats and explanations for hardship but also because it eliminates competitors by exclusion. If one segment manages to restrict scarce goods (land, taxi routes, houses, schools, clinics) to its members only, it has objectively increased its advantages in the general competition. Only in this respect is tribalism a "natural phenomenon." Exclusion has little to do with historical animosities, which are often invented, manipulated, and exploited by political mobilizers to gain an edge. This advantage then is further reinforced by the new emotional cohesion of the group, as well as by the individual psychological satisfaction and enhanced identity that successful competition provides. In times of transition and crisis, symbolic rewards of a proud identity compensate for material deprivation and general insecurity.

Indeed, ethnonationalism must not be reduced to material interests only. Culture also embodies a moral order by which its members give meaning to their lives and derive rules of behavior. In the competition for status and power, however, common culture and history seldom predetermine political identification, particularly in South Africa. Afrikaners are deeply split about their strategies for survival. Zulu speakers, too, identify with opposing political movements, despite their shared appreciation of Zulu tradition. It is this conflicting definition of political interests that matters. The focus on ethnicity by analysts such as Hermann Giliomee[3] overemphasizes common cultural conditioning at the expense of dissident redefinitions of identity, which soon gain majority support. In postapartheid South Africa, both whites and blacks are reassessing their political interests and identities now that circumstances entice inclusive instead of exclusive policies.

Obviously, democratization, accompanied by political equality for all citizens and the promise of greater material justice, can lay the foundations for a more stable and less violent political order. Yet the black constituency expects the government to negotiate itself *out* of power. However, Pretoria intends to negotiate itself *into* power in a future dispensation and in the meantime clings to control. What kind of power sharing would satisfy all parties and allow the leaderships in all camps to sell the compromise to their constituencies? Will they accept a controversial elite compromise, which is likely to rely on shared authoritarian control rather than democratic input from below, in order to shortchange the impossible demands of a vast excluded underclass?

What is unlikely to pass as legitimate compromise is the current strategy of privatizing apartheid. In such South African codewords as "upholding standards," "protecting community values," and "guaranteeing freedom of association," new de facto discrimination is being entrenched. Private discrimination is immunized from government intervention and exempt from public accountability. The unacceptable result would be that politically empowered citizens would be disempowered in such semipublic institutions as schools, hospitals, restaurants, and large business.

Once the government of national unity shares in the spoils of power, it will have also normalized domination. As that sharp conscience of the rulers-in-waiting, Albie Sachs, has wryly reminded his comrades: "We have achieved a great victory. We have de-racialized oppression. We have done something that Apartheid never succeeded in doing—we have legitimized inequality."[4]

TRANSFORMING MILITARY REGIMES AND SETTLER STATES

South Africa's transition from authoritarian rule differs from the examples of Southern Europe and Latin America, which are analyzed in a seminal study by Guillermo O'Donnell, Philippe C. Schmitter, and Laurence Whitehead (1986). First, although South Africa is no longer a colonial problem, it has a colonial history. It is widely perceived as a settler state where alien intruders conquered and exploited indigenous people and colonial relations prevail, even though the settlers have become natives. Second, South Africa constitutes a divided society of a special type. State-sponsored, in some cases state-manufactured, ethnic groups were legally allocated differential rights and privileges. This imposed group membership distinguishes South Africa from such divided societies as Northern Ireland, Israel, or Nigeria. Moreover, despite the high visibility of racial group boundaries, there are common languages and religions; there is a considerable geographical interspersal, and, above all, there is thorough economic interdependence. These factors combine to produce different intergroup relations in South Africa than in countries with distinct nationalities each in their own territory. Third, deep socioeconomic cleavages—largely coinciding with race—give processes of liberalization and democratization a sharp edge of class warfare in South Africa. No democratization can succeed without some degree of tangible equalization; enfranchisement without redistribution remains meaningless. Yet in South Africa, a special form of democratization is being attempted in order to block too radical an equalization.

Finally, unlike states that endured military dictatorships and one-party rule, South Africa always had a functioning democracy, albeit restricted to whites. Despite the long rule of the National Party, regular free elections were held among whites and the government was accountable to parliament, a relatively free press, and other institutions of civil society. This distinguished South African racial authoritarianism from political totalitarianism, where no opposition or dissent are tolerated. In South Africa it is a question of extending democracy and political equality to all citizens, not of creating democratic institutions from scratch.

Unlike Chile, Brazil, and Argentina, white South Africa has always pretended to be a civilian government with the military under the control of the politicians. The extraordinary influence of the security establishment notwithstanding, particularly during the reign of former Defence Minister P. W. Botha until 1989, the generals never took charge formally and disbanded the institutions of white democracy. Therefore, "civilianization" in South Africa never became an issue. In any case, the Afrikaner establishment that runs the country politically and bureaucratically has been so closely intertwined through the National Party, the Broederbond, and the civil service, including the security apparatus, that the Latin American distinction between a castelike military and a civilian democracy does not apply.

The challenge that the South African transition shares with its Latin American counterparts and particularly with the successor states of the Soviet Union lies in establishing democracy in the face of a declining economy and threats to personal security. The extreme economic deprivation and deteriorating standard of living in the former Soviet states have led to nostalgia for the old dictatorship, or what Russian observers call a "posttotalitarian depression." Combined with the unrealistically high expectation about what democracy could deliver materially, compared with the unjust monopoly of the ousted ruling clique, the critical transition is undermined at the very moment when it is about to be born. Nostalgia for colonialism has already gripped apolitical populations in many disintegrating African states. It is also visible among a majority of Coloureds and Indians in South Africa, who turn to the National Party for protection instead of embracing majority democracy under African auspices.

However, unlike the states of the former Soviet Union under conditions of extreme economic deprivation, the new South Africa at least inherits a developed market economy, together with a civil society of state-independent institutions (trade unions, churches, media outlets, community structures and business associations) in both black and white segments.

In this chapter we probe the interrelated themes of colonialism, communalism, and equalization, in a broad comparative perspective in order to sketch the unique features of South Africa. By placing South Africa in a broad historical context and comparing its situation with those of other countries, we hope to point out the flaws of arguments that rely on conventional analogies.

During the 1970s and 1980s the dominant view in informed liberal and left academic opinion held that "nothing short of violent revolution and guerrilla warfare with outside support has realistic prospects of destroying Apartheid" (van den Berghe 1979, 13). These observers ruled out evolutionary change, since "the South African government cannot make any real changes without precipitating its own downfall" (p. 15). At the most, they expected a postponement of "the day of reckoning" through tightening repression, resulting in "a permanent garrison state." In the escalating insurgency, van den Berghe predicted, most of the whites "can be expected to emigrate" until the regime "would collapse with a final rush of whites for the ships and aeroplanes" (p. 16).

Though Pierre van den Berghe has offered many stimulating analyses of ethnicity, he and other academics derived their apocalyptic scenarios from false colonial analogies and from American images of the U.S. departure from Vietnam. As we now know, the apartheid regime did liberalize itself, and whites overwhelmingly supported power sharing in a referendum, because they wished to stay and cooperate with the black majority. And contrary to van den Berghe's assumption, no Western government saw "support for white emigration as a relatively inexpensive solution to a dangerous problem" (p. 16). In fact, most Western states not only imposed punitive sanctions but actively supported a negotiated transition to democracy in South Africa partly in order to forestall another exodus of unwelcome refugees. Van den Berghe, like most academic analysts of decolonization, failed to grasp the potential for internally motivated transformation because the concept of settler state, or *Herrenvolk,* blurred his political analysis.

The concept of settler society is both useful and misleading in understanding South Africa—or Northern Ireland or Israel—in its historical context and in terms of the global political economy. "Settler colonialism" represents a refinement of the orthodox Leninist theory of imperialism but also shares some of the crude generalizing of the Marxist theory of colonialism that does not apply to specific cases. In response to those deficiencies, the South African Communist Party developed the concept of "colonialism of a special type," or "internal colonialism," but this term also misses crucial distinctions in the processes of decolonization. It, too, obscures the interdependence of internal colonizer and colonized as well as the relative independence of indigenous settlers from outside control. Nor can the traditional concepts of colonial departure and subsequent neocolonial sovereignty explain what is taking place in South Africa.

Nonetheless, it is useful to distinguish between settler colonies and colonies of exploitation. In the latter, the much more common form of pure exploitative colonization, imperial powers controlled a territory through a relatively small group of administrators, soldiers, and missionaries. These colonial representatives returned home when their contracts ended, and they were replaced by new male European personnel who clearly perceived themselves as sojourners. European women—with the exception of Catholic nuns and "society ladies"—seldom made the hazardous journeys to the exotic colonies. Some colonial powers, particularly Portugal, even encouraged intermarriage between colonizers, natives, and imported slaves in order to provide the colonial administration with a distinct mestizo class, an additional source of loyal personnel. Other colonial powers, such as France, pursued a policy of assimilation for a small educated native elite, while Britain generally frowned on social integration and preferred indirect rule and control through local traditional institutions. In all these colonies of exploitation the traditional institutions and customs were left largely intact, as long as they provided the expected services, slaves, markets, and access to the desired local products. In many instances—for example, in the climatically inhospitable West and Central Africa—the European colonizers hardly penetrated the hinterland outside the ports and major trading posts. Contact between the rural native population and the colonizers remained minimal and indirect.

Settler colonies differed from colonies of exploitation by attracting a much larger population of European men and women for permanent settlement. Several million Europeans had settled in Algeria and South Africa by the 1950s and 1960s; by 1960 there were 223,000 Europeans residing in Southern Rhodesia, 76,000 in Northern Rhodesia, and 68,000 in Kenya.[5] Both France before the Algerian war of independence (1958–1962) and Portugal under Salazar (1932–1968) considered their colonial territory in Africa an "integral part" of the motherland. Portugal made plans to increase massively the 500,000 Portuguese in Angola and the 220,000 non-Africans in Mozambique before granting independence in 1974.

In South Africa, above all, much of the surplus extracted was not exported back to a metropole, as occurred in colonies of exploitation. Instead, the local reinvestment of mining profits laid the foundation for the only truly industrial economy in Africa. In recent decades the South African economy has increasingly moved away from extractive industries and agriculture to manufacturing and a service sector, which now has to compete with the rest of the world. This competitive requirement, together with the political isolation, capital outflow, and lack of direct investment, has plunged the South African economy into a deep structural crisis. Nonetheless, South Africa's First World industrial opportunities, comparatively high wages, and pleasant climate continuously attracted new immigrants for unfilled skilled jobs, from which the native population was excluded.

Several features of the historical origin and later characteristics of settler states deserve to be highlighted. In the era of decolonization, metropolitan capital favored a neocolonial "independent" native state to an entity controlled by white settlers. Political decolonization was hastened by the desire of the metropole to forestall a potential unilateral declaration of independence by the settlers or to risk economic secession by a province from the former colony, as threatened, for example, in Katanga. Settlers were not mere agents of a mother country but developed their own identity and interests.[6] Though cut off from outside support, settlers remain part of the technologically more advanced First World and are also ideologically linked to powerful segments of the former metropole. Despite the overall conflict and the desire to curtail the political and economic power of the settlers, the former metropole is reluctant to see its settler kith and kin defeated militarily. In 1965 British Prime Minister Harold Wilson, by his own admission, could not risk using the British military to quash the Rhodesian Unilateral Declaration of Independence for fear of mutiny.

In terms of settler-native relations, settler rule was usually much harsher and more oppressive than traditional colonial domination. The settlers were isolated from liberal public opinion in the metropole, which, for example, pressed for the abolition of slavery. When settlers determine the law of the land, their interests dominate, rather than those of a distant Crown and Church from which the natives could expect some symbolic legal protection.

On the other hand, the numerically weaker settlers also had to come to terms with the natives. Dependent on the labor, taxes, and trade of the indigenous population, settlers could not imitate the genocidal practices of traditional colonists. In the Americas, in contrast, the European intruders either did not need or failed to coerce the labor of the conquered and they destroyed the fragmented and vulnerable native hunting-and-gathering societies. In South Africa, though, the Europeans had to accommodate themselves to the larger, better-organized herders and peasant societies. Not until the late nineteenth century did the Europeans in South Africa succeed fully in using superior weaponry to subjugate all indigenous resistance; one recalls that the British colonial army suffered its only major defeat at the hands of the Zulus.

It has often been stressed that the colonial analogy does not apply to South Africa for three reasons. First, during several centuries of residence the settlers have become indigenous. White Africans share the land as citizens legitimately with other groups, and blacks have recognized this right provided it is applied equally and without exclusion and racial privilege.[7] Second, historical settlers cannot return to a homeland upon decolonization. Because the ties to the countries of origin have long been broken, the majority of South Africa's five million white settlers are not willing to emigrate; nor are any countries ready to receive them as citizens or refugees. Third, because the anticolonial native movement had been defeated at the time of state independence, settler sovereignty attained worldwide legitimacy. No metropole controls South Africa administratively, and the country is not as dependent on military or economic outside assistance for its survival as traditional colonies were. Indeed, the Afrikaners pride themselves on having fought the first anticolonial war of liberation against the British at the turn of the century. Even more than Jews in Israel, white South Africans consider themselves an indigenous people. In fact, a higher percentage of South African whites have resided for much longer in the conquered territory than Jews in the current Israel. Even if the continued presence of a Jewish minority in Palestine since the destruction of Jerusalem two millenniums ago is acknowledged, the "resettlement," founding, and populating of Israel is a comparatively recent historical event. Zionism is a twentieth-century nationalist movement. To be sure, so is modern Afrikaner nationalism, but nevertheless it can claim a longer evolution, though not a return to an ancient homeland.[8]

The acquired indigenous status of settlers notwithstanding, they usually behave toward the natives as colonizers, and they are perceived as such by the natives. The state the settlers created is an ethnic state, dominated by the symbols and political power of one group. Only members of this group are allowed to immigrate. Others are declared ethnic outsiders and tolerated at best, or relegated to second-class citizenship, or denationalized in homelands, or, at worst, completely disenfranchised. The policies of victorious settlers have ranged from paternalistic tutelage to assimilationism, from crude repression of traditional cultures in North America, to segregation, retribalization, and denationalization in South Africa. In response to such policies conquered native populations have advocated various resistance strategies, from secession to military defeat, from counternationalism to the boycott or destruction of the foreign invaders.

In South Africa a stalemate developed. Neither side could defeat the other, but each could prevent the other from ruling alone. At the same time the cost of the escalating confrontation weakened both sides. The internationalization of the regional conflict and the sanctions of stronger global forces heightened the need for compromise. With the end of the cold war, the antagonists had lost their value as proxies. Accommodation became not only advantageous but imperative for both sides.

It is the prospect of social-democratic compromise that critics of the negotiations denounce as accommodation with colonialism. The possibility of a reforming South African state is denied, and the obvious resistance of whites to surrender all accumulated privileges at once and for all time is considered proof of the persistence of internal colonialism. For the advocates of all-or-nothing, the "transfer of power from the enemy" (Pallo Jordan, *New Nation*, November 13, 1992, p. 14), not power-sharing, should be the goal of liberation. Eventual seizure of power in a "final showdown" is advocated. A compromise is ruled out because the assumption of continued colonialism makes the defeat of the colonial order by the democratic forces imperative: "It has been the ANC view that since the colonial state and the colonised people cannot be spatially separated, there is no possibility of the two co-existing. This necessarily means that the struggle must result in the destruction of the colonial state," Jordan asserts. However, those who reject compromise fail to specify how the colonial masters are to be defeated, except through exhortation to more destructive struggle.

Given the stalemated balance of forces, continued struggle is justified with fallacious victories. The ANC "compelled the enemy to seek negotiations"; the ANC compelled "the de Klerk regime to accept our terms," in Jordan's perception. At the same time, Jordan admits, "we have not defeated the regime." He astutely diagnoses Pretoria's co-optive capacities, contrary to the traditional colonial intentions invoked previously: "While quite prepared to make room for Blacks to enter the political domain, the regime is determined to so condition what power the majority acquire that it will frustrate any attempts to tamper with these essentials of White power." Lack of trust in the ability of enfranchised blacks to gradually overcome colonial privileges accompanies a romanticized exaggeration of past victories.

In Jordan's view, negotiation is merely another "aspect" of struggle, not a strategy by itself through which democratic advances can be secured as a process. Instead, in a national liberation struggle against colonial domination, "one or the other party to the dispute must go under," Jordan contends: "Negotiations, in such a situation, are aimed at the liquidation of the antagonists as a factor in politics."

However, it is precisely the geographical interspersion that Jordan invokes as the reason that the antagonists cannot coexist, together with their economic interdependence, that forces reluctant reconciliation on the adversaries, regardless of their intentions. The alternative is joint suicide. Fortunately, the ANC leadership decided for negotiations and against confrontation. This will not make the emerging arrangement between the contenders free from serious conflict and competition; but it will widen the area of cooperation in an ever fluctuating pursuit of common as well as separate goals.

The necessity of accommodation with local or surrounding native majorities always required settlers to devise a sophisticated ideology to legitimize their conquest and continued domination. The credo was then served up for domestic consumption as well as against external opposition. Apartheid stands out as the most comprehensive blueprint to entrench racial domination economically, politically, and ideologically. At the same time it deepened ideological cleavages among the ruling establishment regarding the most expedient tactics for dealing with the natives. The cohesiveness of the minority was affected by immigration, secularization, urbanization and, above all, the changes created by the requirements of a more skilled labor force to build an industrial economy. Though the settlers were never a monolithic group, the more they succeeded in reaping the fruits of domination, the more they sowed the seeds of new divisions. English capital interests were set against the desires of the Afrikaner state bureaucracy, and relatively autonomous factions within the state vied for dominance over competing departments. Farmers were deprived of subsidies and the remnants of the white working class were dropped from state protection in favor of a new Afrikaner bourgeoisie that forged alliances with its English-speaking counterparts and later with an emerging black bourgeoisie.

In settler states, an extreme legalism keeps these cleavages in check and regulates the high degree of state interference in the economy. While settler nationalism is not the "ethnic socialism" its liberal free-market critics charge, nonetheless it relies on patronage and massive racial privileging. State and society are deeply intertwined because only through the domination and manipulation of the political realm can the settlers' privileges be maintained. Political enfranchisement threatens centuries of colonial accumulation, for the numerically stronger natives could restore entitlement, empower themselves legally, and redistribute land and other spoils of conquest. Therefore, settler states are, above all, embroiled in deep political conflicts. Unlike depoliticized Western liberal democracies in which civil society exists independent of the state, hardly any sphere in settler states escapes politicization. The public and the private merge.

SOUTH AFRICA AS A COMMUNAL CONFLICT

Among South African social scientists, Hermann Giliomee (1989a, 1989b) and Lawrence Schlemmer stand out for their insightful comparisons of South Africa with communal conflicts elsewhere. At the theoretical core of their writing lies the warning that ethnic identities and nationalism be taken seriously. Giliomee and Schlemmer, applying lessons from intercommunal strife elsewhere, inveigh against reducing a communal competition to a class conflict. People have not only material interests but ideal interests as well, the authors advise, and status concerns, emotional security, or "powerful white identity needs" could interrupt and interfere with the democratic transformation in South Africa. For Giliomee and Schlemmer, much of the political debate denies or obscures "the essential reality of the conflict, namely, that it is primarily a struggle between Afrikaner and African nationalists" (1989b, 211). African nationalism, of which the ANC is seen as a vanguard, "would promote cultural homogeneity . . . and would impart to the state an African character to which all personnel would have to subscribe, whether they be Africans or not" (p. 213).

Such an assumption about the dominant opposition movement is doubtful. The ANC promotes an inclusive South Africanism, not an exclusive nationalism. Nonracialism is the antithesis of communalism and nationalism. To be sure, nonracialism has not yet been tested and may well not last if it fails to be effective. While mere promises and policy statements should not be taken at face value, they should also not be cast aside as untenable propaganda, adopted under the pressure of external recognition. Nonracialism is not an "unbreakable thread," as the author of an idealistically titled collection implies.[9] It has to be constantly striven for against many odds. Nonracialism also does not imply colorblindness, which would be a naive assumption after a long history of apartheid. Nonracialism merely holds out the promise that the state will not recognize or tolerate race as a criterion of exclusion, private racism notwithstanding. In practice, South Africa resembles a multiracial rather than a nonracial society.

Contrary to Giliomee's assertion that the ANC/PAC split

amounted to a mere leadership quarrel and that both are nationalist, a fundamental ideological cleavage still exists between nationalist Africanists in the PAC and the nonracial, inclusive Charterists in the rational Enlightenment tradition. One of the more remarkable developments in resistance politics is the recent hegemony of the ANC's view over the Africanists'. A counterracism would have great emotional appeal among a frustrated black township youth. Yet despite the dormant PAC and the more serious Black Consciousness challenge in the 1970s, the inclusive nonracialism of the ANC has so far carried the day. This happened not because of outside expectations or because nonracialism offered better strategic benefits to an exiled movement dependent on foreign support, as ANC critics charge. ANC members, particularly those in the internationalist SACP tradition, have generally internalized a deeply felt universalism, welcoming anyone who shared their ideological convictions. Intolerance toward proponents of ethnic nationalism extends among whites and blacks (Inkatha) alike. There is no evidence that Xhosa culture has been elevated to an ethnocentric ideal, although it would only seem natural that people enjoy speaking their mother tongue and display pride in their cultural heritage.

Giliomee and Schlemmer hold the inevitable affirmative action programs of any postapartheid government as proof of racial group preferences. But having the nation's ethnic diversity reflected in the senior civil service or corporate culture does not constitute reverse discrimination, merely the restoration of equity. It is also not unreasonable that after centuries of denigration the black majority would expect its historical presence to be respected and represented among the state symbols. Such symbolic recognition of majority culture may indeed require a black African rather than a white or Indian as president of a ruling ANC party—but that would not contradict the principle of nonracialism. After centuries of racial discrimination, nonracialism cannot mean colorblindness. Identical treatment of the races could itself be discriminatory because it would leave apartheid's legacies intact by focusing only on equality of opportunities rather than equality of results. Colorblind equality of opportunities without state intervention merely continues to favor those who monopolized the opportunities in the past.

It is unlikely that postapartheid society will produce "a liberated nation of and for Africans" where "everyone will have to defer to African symbols" (1989b, 239). Obviously, the present Afrikaner symbolic monopoly will have to be broadened with African values, Giliomee and Schlemmer would readily admit. Die Stem will give way to Nkosi Sikeleli Africa, Jan Smuts airport will become Mandela airport, and there will be many June 16th streets across the land. However, the Voortrekker monument is unlikely to be blown up, Dutch Reformed churches will still be well attended, and education in Afrikaans will continue, although the biased history curriculum will have to be rewritten. The ethnic character of most small towns and neighborhoods will hardly change, even after the Group Areas Act will have long been repealed. Giliomee and Schlemmer predict that "the numerical preponderance of blacks will unlock the symbolic ideal of a liberated African state" (1989b, 240), yet paradoxically admit at the same time that "almost all white fears of majority rule are based on myth."

Given the record of ethnic strife around the globe, Giliomee and Schlemmer plead for open recognition of the "communal and national identities" (1989a, 238) that have given rise to turmoil and bloodshed elsewhere. While such an admonition is well placed for the truly communal, nationalistic conflicts in divided societies, the assumption that South African whites will have enduring nationalist symbolic needs remains questionable. Schlemmer, more than Giliomee, recognizes that "white identity" differs from legitimate national self-determination elsewhere, because it is built around race privilege: "It is not so much culture in the sense of deeply imbued values and rituals but 'material culture' which has been constructed around power" (1989a, 154). The identity of a "first-world community" threatened by the majority boils down to a conflict between haves and have-nots. Schlemmer concedes that among whites "culture of origin and nationalism" is currently obscured. Apartheid racialized ethnicity and nationalized race. Both attempts failed to secure legitimacy, even among the beneficiaries. But cultural nationalism that is no longer burdened with racial discrimination could clearly gain support among many sectors in the future postapartheid competition. Schlemmer fears it as a "latent force particularly among Afrikaners" that "will probably come to the fore under duress" (1989a, 154).

Giliomee's and Schlemmer's skepticism about liberal visions of individualism and the prospects of nation-building are shared not only by a vast mainstream social science literature on the importance of primordialism but also increasingly by Marxist analysts. However, there are important differences in the explanations of and responses to the communal phenomenon.

A vast literature reveals little agreement on whether a common South African nation exists, or whether it should be forged, as well as how the resurgence of ethnonationalism elsewhere in the world affects South Africa. Neville Alexander (1985), a Cape Trotskyite activist, believes, as do most anti-apartheid campaigners in rival movements, that a South African nation will emerge through working-class struggle, reinforced by a common national language and curriculum. Pierre van den Berghe (1991), evaluating experiences elsewhere, considers such programs of nation-building likely rationalizations for nation-killing (ethnocide) by dominant groups in the name of combating divisive tribalism by ethnic competitors. Similarly, Donald Horowitz (1991) detects what he calls a meta-conflict among some dozen vastly different interpretations of what the South African problem is all about. The Russian scholar and South African specialist Irina Filatova (1991), in a thorough and perceptive review of the debate, concludes that all oppositional movements except Inkatha equate nation-building with socialism, "though they mean completely different things by it." After a similar review, the Stellenbosch philosopher Johan Degenaar (1991) recommends that all projects to forge a South African nation be dropped and the focus be placed on building democracy. But can South Africa ignore the forces of ethnonationalism because nationalism has been associated with apartheid?

The difficult task of nation-building without common symbols and a unifying history has been highlighted by the debate about divisive national anthems and flags at sports events. A South African nation has yet to be born. South Africa at present constitutes an economic and political entity, but not an emotional one. Neutral symbols negotiated for the Olympic games are widely considered an unsatisfactory compromise. On home grounds, spectators at national competitions defiantly raise their symbols to the embarrassment of officials on both sides, who hope to use sport to forge a common South Africanism. Thus, the ANC's Steve Tshwete puts the onus on spectators by depicting rugby as either "a reconciler of people or . . . a ritual that celebrates conquest and domination of black people" (*Business Day*, 20 August 1992). Judging by the emotional nature of rugby or soccer matches, they seem to fit neither of these purposes for the sports-loving public. As is true the world over, sports teams provide group identity for atomized individuals who symbolically borrow strength from the victory of their side. This immense psychological gratification has little to do with reconciliation or domination of the colonial outsider. It merely reflects the historical segregation of sports in a divided society where the different segments, on the whole, play different sports: Afrikaners cherish rugby culture, with all its customary tribal machoism, while soccer, with much more multiracial teams but uniracial spectators, has developed into an equivalent obsession in the townships.

Regis Debray, a former revolutionary activist, once wrote that "during every crisis in a capitalist country it has been shown that nationalism is stronger than class identity even among the main mass of the people, the working class." This empirical evidence does not prove Walker Connor's (1984, 5) contention "that the most fundamental divisions of humankind are the many vertical cleavages that divide people into ethnonational groups," let alone van den Berghe's (1979, 58) point that communalism "may well have a genetic basis." Nonetheless, such evidence requires the unrealized potential of non-communal identity to be reconciled with the contrary evidence that ethnic mobilization seems to have been far more successful than interest-based class solidarity in offering meaningful explanations of life experiences.

Ancient tribalism or even evolutionary advantageous genetic conditioning are most often cited as the cause of ethnic friction. In this view, ethnic identity constitutes a self-generated perception, independent of state designs and social conditions. Ethnic antagonisms, however, always occur in specific circumstances. Genetic predilections and references to tribalism, therefore, do not explain the causes of a conflict but merely anthropologize antagonisms as eternal, historical givens.[10] In failing to specify the causes of a particular antagonism, the notion of tribalism also implies that a conflict cannot be solved, only contained. It is this methodological deficit of the concept—rather than its association with Africa and "backwardness"—that makes tribalism as a label, let alone as an explanation, useless and objectionable, regardless of whether it is also applied to European conflicts.

The Northern Irish "troubles," for example, do not constitute a tribal theological war. The doctrinal issues function as symbols for much wider communal cleavages, although virtually all protagonists now identify either with the label Protestant or Catholic. But it was only after 1968—when several people were injured during a civil rights march on October 5 and the present Northern Ireland "troubles" were said to have been revived—that the division of society into Catholics and Protestants became so widely accepted.[11] The largely segregated housing, schooling, workplaces, and leisure activities "tell" the profound difference between Catholics and Protestants, despite the linguistic and phenotypic homogeneity.

In contrast, in South Africa communal divisions, in terms of self-identification, are not as deep. In spite of or, more likely, because of the official classifications in the apartheid state, more people label themselves South Africans first, rather than black or white. Coloureds, Indians, and English-speaking whites in particular (and urban Africans to a lesser extent, but rarely Afrikaners) stress their South African identity before their subgroup. In any case, the two identities are not incompatible and can be held simultaneously, as even Zulu-nationalist Buthelezi has pointed out.

In Northern Ireland it is impossible to be anything other than republican or loyalist, nationalist or unionist, Irish or British—either by choice or by designation of the adversary. In South Africa, however, after apartheid artifically imposed group membership on all citizens, a widespread resentment developed against communal identities and racial categories. Now, nonracialism and common citizenship encourage the demise of racial identities. Black and white can celebrate their common South Africanness because they both stand to benefit from it. In the truly divided Ireland, the communal conflict amounts to a zero-sum game, winners and losers; in South Africa all can be winners if they compromise.

Moreover, in Northern Ireland the adversaries do not even use the same name for their land. Catholics hardly identify with the labels Ulster and British; Protestants eschew the label Irish and vice versa. Each side plays its own sports, and in the one sport popular in both camps (soccer), they support different teams. In South Africa only the small Africanist PAC and Black Consciousness groups prefer the name Azania, and all groups rejoice over the successes of a mixed South African Olympic team, an esprit de corps that Mandela views as one of the crucial mechanisms for nation-building.

The chances of black and white reconciliation in South Africa seem far greater than in Northern Ireland also because of the comparative importance of the two conflicts in the global political constellation. The relative geopolitical insignificance of Northern Ireland encourages terrorism. The president of Sinn Fein may well be right when he claims that without the armed struggle "the issue of Ireland would not even be an issue."[12] While the economic muscle of black workers in South Africa ensures that felt injustices are kept in the forefront even without armed resistance, the democratic veneer of Ulster domination spurs Irish militants into violent venues to press their case. The uncompromising domination of the majority triggers armed resistance, the last resort of the politically powerless.

The communal conflict between Palestinians and Jews in Israel affords another point of contrast. The ANC strives for power; the PLO struggles for territory. The multiethnic ANC aims at an inclusive democracy; the nationalist PLO advocates a Palestinian state that is likely to mirror the ethnic exclusivity of its Jewish counterpart. Both movements represent the majority of an "indigenous" constituency waiting to be liberated from "colonial" conquest, but the ANC has achieved far greater international legitimacy for its claims. Both ANC and PLO have been labeled "terrorists," but the accusation has stuck much more with the PLO than the ANC, whose policy was to avoid civilian casualties and eschew indiscriminate violence against an adversary who was defined in political, not ethnic, terms.

The ominous comparisons of the South African right wing with the IRA or Basque-type terrorism underestimate the even more dangerous characteristics of the Afrikaner nationalists. Afrikaner insurgents are proportionally much stronger numerically and, unlike the IRA, they do not depend on outside funding, expertise, and weaponry. Almost all of their male members have had army training as conscripts, and many have had active battle experience in Angola. It is true that the right-wing groups are all vulnerable to penetration by state agents, but, in turn, the government security apparatus is also thoroughly infiltrated with people with extreme right-wing sympathies. This battle within and about the heart of Afrikanerdom distinguishes South Africa from communal conflicts elsewhere. It is much more an intra- rather than an intergroup struggle, both in the white and black communities.

However, the intragroup pattern of violence could change quickly if, for example, high-profile assassinations or attacks could be successfully blamed on communal sentiments by the other side. An accommodation that rests mainly on the appeal of leaders is fragile indeed. At present, endorsement of accommodation is soft and contingent; it does not command the solid support of a large grass-roots constituency, particularly among blacks. The negotiations have been punctuated by political assassinations, though the state's fluctuating pursuit of accommodation and the legitimation of negotiation by the leadership of the ANC and SACP seem to have deterred extremist elements from attacking the top leadership. To date, the violence has been aimed at undermining organizational strength or enhancing the role of certain political actors, rather than eliminating antagonists.

In "Resurrecting Civil Society," O'Donnell and Schmitter (1986, 48) refer to "the success of most authoritarian regimes in depoliticizing" their respective societies. Such depoliticization entails the withdrawal into private realms of most subjects; people ignore or forget their political identities and tacitly accept the hegemony of the regime, willingly or by coercion. In South Africa, however, apartheid did not allow the easy separation of private and public lives, particularly since the majority of the population could not expect economic benefits from political acquiescence. Under apartheid the private realm—where one lived, where one worked, how much one earned—was circumscribed by politically defined racial identity. Apartheid thus politicized the private sphere to a high degree, even at the height of repression during the 1960s and 1970s. In O'Donnell and Schmitter's analysis, the resurrection of civil society requires "corroding the normative and intellectual bases of the regime" (p. 50). But the regime in South Africa was never based on consensus in the first place. For the excluded, the emperor has always been naked; when blacks obeyed, they complied without consenting. Once tentative liberalization began, therefore, the opposition in civil society could fall back on a shared understanding, rather than having to educate and repoliticize for mass action.

One legacy of the extensive politicization in South Africa is that people now have high expectations that democracy will bring quick material improvements. A new ANC-led government may find itself the victim of the same unrealistic mass expectations that the ANC and other groups encouraged during the period of repression. Should the new regime become discredited but remain in power, democratization itself would be in danger of reversal. Although realistic economic policies may disappoint mass expectations, the incoming ruling coalition surely cannot afford to adopt economic policies that would negatively affect growth rates and labor market conditions in the long run.

CONSTITUTIONAL AND ECONOMIC OPTIONS

There can be no doubt about the moral legitimacy of redistribution in South Africa. Apartheid amounted to a state-sponsored enrichment of whites and state-enforced economic limitations on blacks. Through the Group Areas Act, for example, the urban properties of blacks,

Coloureds, and South Africans of Indian origin were confiscated for small compensation; ideological resettlement threw Africans off ancient communal land. Justice demands restitution for blatant theft.[13]

If democracy is to be meaningful, there can also be little doubt about the political necessity for some rapid material equalization. The debate about constitutions and political democracy aims at who should occupy positions of authority. As theorists of democracy (Przeworski 1986) have always argued, the more substantive question relates to "the uses to which authority will eventually be applied" (O'Donnell and Schmitter 1986, 11). Even the liberal assumption of equality of opportunity presupposes some material empowerment to compete in a market-driven economy. If the claimed competition remains grossly unequal in terms of resources, the stronger individual or collectivity will impose its power on the weaker. Totally free markets only work to the benefit of the strongest; the perception of economic domination and exclusion leads to strife. Ultimately, democratic systems must address the destabilizing inequality, or else abort multiparty representation in favor of authoritarian repression.[14]

Three additional, and specifically South African, circumstances support fundamental economic transformation. First, apartheid has created one of the most unequal societies in the world. Second, this class cleavage overlaps with race to such a degree that even the United States or Brazil look progressive, though inequality was not created only by apartheid. But nowhere else do poverty and race so wholly coincide with each other. Third, the capital concentration and monopoly control by the six major conglomerates in the South African economy are unmatched in any other developed capitalist economy.

Although economic equalization is morally justifiable, it is an entirely different question whether too radical a redistribution is pragmatically feasible. The limitations of the conventional instruments of redistribution have frequently been pointed out in the South African debate.[15] First, sustained redistribution presupposes a growing economy—the very opposite of the current protracted recession. The rate of fixed investment has dramatically declined from 32 percent of GDP in 1975 to 17 percent in 1991. Second, capital mobility quickly responds to perceived risks. The fear of hyperinflation through deficit financing by a new government together with possibilities of nationalization reinforce cautious attitudes by investors. Third, redistribution through taxation is limited by the already high tax rate in South Africa and the fact that the vast majority hardly pay taxes anyway. Yet it is mostly through additional new taxes—particularly a land tax, property tax, and tax on capital transfers—that future social spending can be financed. Fourth, and finally, balance-of-payment constraints severely impede strategies to generate sustained growth. Peter Moll (1991, 125), in an instructive summary of the possibilities and limits of redistribution, therefore, states a widely accepted view: "Racial equalisation at current white levels is impossible at the present time given South Africa's level of economic development. Racial equalisation will have to be achieved at substantially lower levels of expenditure per capita."

It is this prospect of "becoming an African state," to use the code phrase of whites, that scares the white minority. They do not want to lose their standard of living and privileges in education, their health system and public administration—nor do they want to pay dearly for them. With good reason, the white electorate chose to trust the National Party with safeguarding their wealth and power. "Vote yes, if you are afraid of majority rule," read one of the NP slogans during the March 1992 referendum. The National Party's constitutional designs are fully committed to entrench the existing disparities with minor modifications.

The new NP strategy co-opted key demands of the opposition as its own but attached conditions that altered their consequences. Hermann Giliomee astutely defined the essence of the de Klerk administration as "the attempt to seize the strategic initiative by appropriating the form of the adversary's demand and giving it its own substance" (*Cape Times,* February 3, 1991). The core principles of the ANC, nonracialism and universal franchise, were adopted by the NP but tied to minority party protection, veto rights, a consensus mechanism, and a collective rotating presidency. Such a system not only invites paralysis and fragmentation but, above all, it renders majority rule subject to minority agreement far beyond the prescriptions of "contingent democracy." Contingency merely ensures that majorities "will not use their dominance to permanently exclude the losers from gaining the majority . . . and conversely, the losers will accept the right of the winners to govern and take binding decisions" (van Zyl Slabbert 1992, 7). However, the NP designs go much further in circumscribing the rights of the winners by constitutionally entrenching existing interests in the name of fundamental rights and freedoms. Parliament will not be able to override the "rule of law," or at least not without high qualifying majorities. The law is further protected by an independent judiciary that can declare laws passed by parliament unconstitutional if they conflict with the court's interpretation of the constitution.

Insofar as the new South African constitution enshrines property rights, taxation levels, and fiscal responsibilities, it freezes existing economic relations with little chance of a politically motivated transformation later. A particularly devious design in this respect is Pretoria's preemptive privatization. The ANC quite correctly states: "The current privatisation programme is simply transferring wealth to a privileged few and would diminish the stock of assets and resources available to a future government to satisfy a pent-up demand for social services" (*SouthScan,* April 10, 1992, p. 106). The privatization advocates are thus sowing the seeds for future unconstitutional temptations by depriving the postapartheid government of one of the few means to address past injustices. For example, if large tracts of state land are now sold to the few corporate interests wealthy enough to buy, a democratically elected government will come under pressure to expropriate—with or without adequate compensation.[16] The failure of state socialism elsewhere does not guarantee that a vast underclass in South Africa will tolerate its own exclusion and exploitation under capitalism.

Yet South African capitalism, which poses as a victim of Afrikaner nationalism, is particularly hostile to social-democratic corrections of inequality through state intervention. "What we have to fear is not socialism but a kind of crippled capitalism, loaded down with remnants of socialist theory and practice, like Wilson's Britain," writes Ken Owen, the editor of the country's largest paper (*Sunday Times,* February 16, 1992). Such uncompromising sentiments reinforce old-fashioned class warfare from above. Peace and stability, however, will depend on how well and how fast the new government can institute sensible, effective affirmative action programs, enact antitrust legislation, put unused and state-subsidized land on the market for blacks to buy with state loans, upgrade black education, make low-cost housing accessible for squatters, and, above all, create jobs through tax incentives—all measures requiring the fettering of free-market capitalism by democratically determined state policies. Yet, the National Party now strives for a minimal state, which led Roger Southall to conclude: "They seek not so much to control a central government as to abolish it" (*Monitor,* October 1991, p. 90).

It is these issues of future economic control and political power that

lie at the heart of the constitutional wrangling at Codesa. Behind the
rhetorical cacophonies of who should represent which constituency
according to which rules and with which status, the National Party
and the ANC are exploring how far they can live with an economic
compromise that is still to be hammered out. The five working groups
established by Codesa dealt with the creation of a climate for free
political activity; constitution-making process and principles; transitional arrangements; the future of Transkei, Bophuthatswana, Ciskei,
and Venda; and time-frames for the implementation of decisions. The
negotiating groups have yet to tackle the crucial economic compromise and the new economic order, which many falsely assume will
automatically flow from political democracy. The "reasonableness"
of Pretoria in abolishing legal apartheid has put great pressure on the
opposition to respond in kind. International opinion wants South
Africa saved from another failed socialist experiment, and the pro-
longed recession further pressures the ANC to accept far-reaching
concessions. It appears as if the ANC cannot but accept the democratic and constitutional clamps around its options. If the ANC were
again to withdraw from negotiations, as it did in May 1992, it would
have to return sooner or later in order to avoid a descent into barbarism.

Yet for the ANC essentially to agree to the NP's plan would be
suicidal. Just as apartheid redistributed wealth to the white minority,
the new government will certainly need to use state intervention to
benefit the black majority. Decisive will be whether the movement can
stick together or fall apart once ANC incumbents are inevitably en-
trapped by the spoils of office, and when the new government faces
hard choices about who should be favored and who neglected.

The pragmatists among the ANC leadership also recognize that the
Afrikaner civil service and the security establishment need reassurance, not only about pensions and severance benefits but also about
amnesty for past offenses upon disclosure. These pragmatists are
willing to accept limitations on the powers of the majority in any
future government. Joe Slovo even recommends "compulsory power-
sharing" for a certain period rather than straight majority rule. (*The
African Communist*, 3d quarter 1992, p. 40). The compromising ANC
negotiators have abandoned the simplistic notion that political power
amounts to an addition of mere numbers. They recognize that there
are other nonquantitative sources of power, equally if not more important than votes: the power to disrupt and sabotage an accord if the

minority is not included and, above all, the dependence on capital, skills, and expertise if democratic expectations are to be fulfilled and stability is to be achieved.

However, even the ANC pragmatists have a blind spot in that they recognize the interests of their adversaries only in material terms. They hope to preempt the legitimate anxieties of civil servants about Africanization through guarantees and sunset clauses. The non-ANC minorities, from Afrikaner to Zulu nationalists, on the other hand, insist in addition on symbolic recognition of their identities and on the right of some self-determination. The promise of mere equal treatment by an ANC-dominated central government is considered insufficient. It is this recognition of ethnic claims, in which regionally concentrated minorities express themselves, that dogmatic nonracialism and an orthodox democratic vision find most difficult to tolerate. The nonracial ANC has no problems with whites in government, as long as they are ANC-approved whites, while the Afrikaner and Zulu nationalists insist on having representatives of their own groups recognized as equally legitimate political actors in a federal or even confederal system.

It is the populist streak that the ANC represents "the people," who are considered identical with the ANC, which logically tends to reject any outsiders or dissenters as traitors, collaborators, or "non-people." By defining itself as a liberation movement, the organization perpetuates this all-embracing claim against which opposition is by definition nonliberatory and reactionary. Were the ANC to assume the mantle of a political party—which in reality it is—it would forfeit the people's voice because it would clearly speak for only a segment of the people. The same applies to the self-ascribed label "The Democratic Movement" for the tripartite alliance, which by implication defines everyone else as undemocratic.

Thus dissenting voices are not only repressed by Bantustan autocrats and vilified by government but are frequently also not tolerated by overeager ANC loyalists in their sphere of control. A culture of intolerance poses problems for free elections, and the hoped-for replacement of bullets with ballots is said to be a naive dream since electoral competition would exacerbate the violence. In the past, violent protest was directed against an undemocratic regime and its surrogates, but mutual violence in an inclusive electoral contest could not claim to be legitimate resistance against apartheid exclusion. Those resorting to violence nonetheless would be heavily stigmatized.

The problem remains, however, that past exclusion has not only not prepared the disenfranchised for democratic politics, but left a legacy of bitterness that sometimes leads even the self-proclaimed democrats to be undemocratic. Instead of setting an example, the ANC, let alone the right wing or Inkatha, repays the state in its own currency. For instance, in April 1992 more than ten thousand people gathered in Mitchells Plain to welcome de Klerk, but he was shouted down by a group of vociferous ANC supporters who pelted him with gravel and forced him to depart. Such demonstrations of "victory" may backfire by inducing uncommitted voters to turn against the ANC for having violated the proclaimed freedom of speech. The rhetorical support of the ANC or Inkatha leadership for the freedom of speech means little when ANC-aligned student groups will not allow Inkatha representatives to speak at any liberal campus because they charge that they are not allowed to operate freely elsewhere. Many black journalists who are viewed as supporters of a rival party can list veiled threats and intimidation by opponents, and local ANC supporters in the Eastern Cape have burned copies of provincial newspapers for continuously misrepresenting and neglecting ANC views.

With all the major parties having their political armies to enforce dominance in their territory (SAP, MK, AWB, KZP), it will indeed be a major challenge to stage an election free of intimidation. Nonetheless, an election would seem the only way to settle conflicting claims of support and bestow legitimacy on a new government. It would be naive, however, to assume that elections would necessarily guarantee a future democracy. The power struggle, expectations, and emotions engendered by elections could also tempt a multiracial elite of national unity to fall back on authoritarian rule in order to suppress common challengers. Both the National Party and the ANC contain hegemonic strains; their respect for liberal pluralism is neither absolute nor unqualified.

Nationalism avoids such antagonisms by pretending to look after all its kin at the expense of ethnic outsiders. The ANC, however, is not a nationalist movement that represents only insiders. It is an inclusive, all-class, heterogeneous, basically liberal alliance to dismantle apartheid. It is therefore particularly vulnerable to splits and realignments once apartheid has been abolished. Factionalism could even lead to a repetition of the 1930s, when the Communist Party denounced the ANC: "The African National Congress is now openly a servant of the imperialist bourgeoisie and uses its endeavours to damp down the revolutionary activities of the masses."[17]

Other issues will also effect a fragmentation of existing political parties and blocs. A realignment has already taken place in white politics and among Bantustan leaders. The issue of proportional representation is likely to stimulate breakaways and reinforce ideological rifts, because dissenters are no longer faced with the alternative of leaving for the political wilderness. Small parties, centered more around personalities than issues, could exercise disproportional influence as they will hold the balance of power between an ANC and NP bloc in the lower house. While such fragmentation will allow for the representation of many interests, it bodes ill for political stability.

CHAPTER TWO

From Confrontation to Negotiation

What right has the West, what right have the whites
anywhere to teach us about democracy when they
executed those who asked for democracy during the time
of the colonial era?

> Nelson Mandela in Nairobi,
> *International Herald Tribune,* July 14, 1990

REDEFINING THE ENEMY

One of the more striking aspects of contemporary South African
history is that the abolition of formal apartheid, the gradual repeal of
the race laws during 1991, passed almost as a nonevent. In contrast to
what was universally described as Pretoria's "dramatic turnaround"
in February 1990 (the legalizing of banned organizations and the
release of Nelson Mandela), the advent of a new era of legally un-
regulated race relations was scarcely noticed. To understand why, one
must first realize that many apartheid laws had been largely ignored
and unenforced for some time. The reality of integration in some city
housing, in English-language universities and private schools, and
above all in the workplace had rendered the laws obsolete long before
they were formally abolished. No influx-control measures, for example, could stem the flow into the cities of rural migrants in search of
jobs and better living conditions. Repealing the laws simply verified
social trends that had outpaced ossified regulations. Therefore, under
nonapartheid conditions, little or nothing changed.

Given that the disenfranchised enjoyed no formal political power,
the dominant minority remained unthreatened. Many whites now
wondered why they had not supported the policy change earlier, since
the immediate benefits outweighed the potential dangers. On the
strength of their formal rejection of apartheid, South Africans were
admitted to places hitherto closed to them. They could participate in
the Olympics; they could travel more freely as landing rights for South
African Airways were extended. In short, South African whites were

no longer outcasts—a status they had deeply resented. Now they could hold their heads high again. The stigma was gone, and without the sky falling in. The secret to the growing approval for de Klerk among the dominant white minority lies in the hope that they could continue to dominate without costs attached. Normalcy for whites had returned despite the lasting abnormality from the legacies of apartheid. Few ruling groups in history have ever wriggled themselves out of a deadly predicament more elegantly. The world praised and rewarded a change to what should have been normal policies and intergroup relations in the first place.[1]

Nationalists repeatedly made it clear that negotiations would have nothing to do with surrender but would simply concern power sharing. F. W. de Klerk insisted that to "those who arrogantly equate the concept of a new South Africa to a takeover of power, the message needs to be transmitted loudly and clearly that the new South Africa will not fall prey to a section of the population at the expense of the rest" (Cape Times, April 13, 1990). He emphasized that "we will not accept a dispensation in which the quality of existing liberties and rights are dismantled." His constituency, de Klerk asserted, was "not prepared to bow out apologetically from the stage of history"; whites would still play a "key role," he predicted.

How, then, did the apparent political miracle of a privileged minority voluntarily agreeing to give up exclusive political representation come about? The process began much earlier than the March 1992 referendum or even the rise to power of de Klerk and the release of Mandela. Apartheid—the gigantic Verwoerdian dream of social engineering—had increasingly proven a dismal failure, despite all the zealous efforts of its advocates in power. Its rising internal and external costs, both real and symbolic, had led to halting, ambivalent moves to reform since the late 1970s under the hardline Prime Minister John Vorster. His successor, P. W. Botha, essentially continued the policy of reluctant liberalization without being able to break with the racial paradigm and blind anticommunism. But with the end of the cold war, negotiations and compromise between previously implacable ideological foes became not only possible but imperative for both sides. Unlike in the Middle East or Northern Ireland, in South Africa no religious values impeded bargaining over power and privilege. The elites, no longer constrained by dogma, were free to be pragmatic as they adjusted to new realities.

As early as 1986 Pretoria came close to embracing alternatives.

Sections of the National Party and the cabinet, particularly the Department of Foreign Affairs under Pik Botha, had seriously considered the option of negotiations at the time of the mission of the Commonwealth Eminent Persons' Group (EPG) in the spring of 1986. Letters had gone out from Foreign Affairs to Washington and to European capitals saying that Mandela could be released provided the Western powers would back South Africa in any ensuing internal strife. Since 1983 the secret Broederbond under its new head, Pieter de Lange, had circulated a document about the minimal conditions for future Afrikaner survival, which culminated in the sentiment that "the greatest risk is not to take any risks." However, as the scuttling of the EPG mission by the South African bombing of the capitals of the Frontline States on May 19, 1986, proved, in the internal power struggle the hardliners in the security establishment won out over the softliners in Pik Botha's Department of Foreign Affairs and Chris Heunis's Department of Constitutional Development. The time for liberalization was not yet ripe, given cold war mentalities. Until the securocrats were deprived of their ideological weapon—a Moscow-directed ANC-led onslaught—and were themselves party to the transition, P. W. Botha's administration could not travel the final road, particularly not under foreign prodding rather than under its own steam.

Moreover, during the 1980s South Africa's rival intelligence services vied for dominance in the National Security Management System and State Security Council (SSC), on which P. W. Botha relied as his base. The old Bureau of State Security (BOSS) under the megalomaniac General Hendrik van den Bergh had become discredited in 1978 in the wake of the notorious information scandal. In 1979 it was reorganized as the National Intelligence Service (NIS), led by the political science professor Niel Barnard. The NIS differed from the smaller Department of Military Intelligence (DMI), which Botha favored, by defining the main threat to South African security and minority rule as internal to the country. The DMI, in contrast, saw the threat as a communist-led onslaught originating outside the country's borders. The DMI engaged in destabilizing the Frontline States in order to deprive the ANC of forward bases, while the NIS favored a more diplomatic approach, as evidenced by its support of the Nkomati nonaggression accord with Mozambique. It was the special forces within the DMI, its hit squads and its assassins, who lost out in the emerging politics of negotiations.

Already in 1987 the minister of justice had had an unpublicized dinner in his home with the imprisoned Nelson Mandela. After being transferred from Robben Island to Pollsmoor prison on the mainland, Mandela was occasionally taken out on sightseeing trips in the Cape so that state officials could have easier access to their most prominent inmate. He was repeatedly offered release by P. W. Botha on condition that he explicitly renounce violence, but he refused. Prisoners could not engage in free contractual arrangements, he replied, and his release would have been meaningless if the ANC was unable to engage in free political activity.

Leading members of the Broederbond, including the older brother of de Klerk, had since late 1986 met secretly with ANC officials in London, particularly Thabo Mbeki, Aziz Pahad, and Jacob Zuma, then the head of ANC intelligence. In July 1987 a historic and much-publicized meeting took place in Dakar between a large group of South Africans with ANC leaders living outside the country. Organized by F. van Zyl Slabbert and Alex Boraine's Idasa, this meeting set the trend for the next three years and culminated in the lifting of the ban on the ANC in February 1990, by which time even P. W. Botha and F. W. de Klerk had held several meetings with the imprisoned Mandela, after initially threatening the Dakar organizers with charges of treason.

In part, the official denunciations, prior to 1989, of any dialogue with the ANC, as well as the intrigue and rivalry surrounding such dialogue, stemmed from intense bureaucratic competition over who would control the inevitable future negotiations. Access to Mandela, for example, became a highly prized asset. As minister of prisons, Kobie Coetsee refused permission to see Mandela to his senior colleague Chris Heunis, so that Coetsee and his protégés, rather than Heunis's Department of Constitutional Development, could retain control. Barnard's NIS withdrew the security clearance of two senior officials, Kobus Jordaan and Fanie Cloete, both of Heunis's department. They were considered too liberal for having engaged in independent efforts at dialogue with the ANC, as had a host of other organizations, following the successful Dakar example. At this stage, P. W. Botha's administration followed a basic two-track policy: Heunis's department was supposed to find a legitimate internal solution through co-optation of black leaders outside the ANC; if that were to fail, and it became increasingly evident that it would, negotiations with the "real enemy" should be explored with the hope of splitting the movement by concluding a deal with moderate nationalists but not communists.

In February 1990, with the mandate for negotiations received just four months earlier, the government could begin to move boldly without jeopardizing parliamentary seats. In any case, since another election under the tricameral constitution was quietly being ruled out, the government could stake its long-term political chances on the success of negotiations.

In 1990 the world witnessed the extraordinary spectacle of the South African government and the African National Congress socializing, even bantering, with each other for the first time. Not only was the ground irrevocably laid for negotiations and compromises between two deadly rivals, but the antagonists actually established a cordial relationship during the three days of talks at the foot of Table Mountain. They discovered, in Thabo Mbeki's words, that to their mutual amazement they "had no horns." Members of the dreaded Security Police, assigned to guard the ANC delegation, became buddies with their enemies and were soon on a first-name basis. While white and black South Africa wondered about respectable "terrorists" being invited into the official residence of South African prime ministers, a flabbergasted correspondent observed: "When Mbeki began to crack jokes, accompanied by some boyish elbow-tugging with General Basie Smit, the chief of the Security Police, the unusual appeared to become elevated to the sublime."

Politics, however, is about the manipulation of symbols as a precondition for the exercise of real power. This striking event thus needs to be decoded for its psychological implications. The instant love affair between the National Party and the ANC replicates an experience many South African exiles from different political backgrounds have had when they meet abroad. Free of the apartheid framework, they discover their common South African–ness. A psychological explanation of cordial relations between former archenemies would point to the rediscovery of bonds of origin, of a repressed kinship. Children of the same soil come to realize what they have in common. Meanwhile, the forgiveness of the ANC brought renewed legitimacy to a beleaguered regime. The state president could now walk through the front door of the world. Celebrated as peacemakers endowed with strategic foresight, the engineers of apartheid occupied a new moral high ground.

This psychological constellation also explains the surprising cohesion that the National Party displayed during the process of change. Most seasoned observers expected defections to the right if the leadership were "to go so far." Yet the party caucus endorsed the Cabinet's moves unanimously, issuing encouragement and congratulations. Such support was particularly surprising because the caucus was left in the dark about the precise contents of the president's speech of February 2. The crucial last-minute input and consultation took place not within his own constituency but with an opponent in prison. The potential coalition, the government of national unity, was born at this moment. As a result, a sense of relief—even euphoria—swept the land. Finally there was light at the end of a dark tunnel. Both sides frequently stressed the foolishness of not having undergone the exercise of reconciliation years ago.

An even more remarkable feature of the process was the forgiveness displayed by the victims. With no bitterness over decades of suffering, with no word about revenge for horrendous crimes, Mandela publicly declared, "Let bygones be bygones." With this attitude, Mandela did, in fact, manufacture a new myth: that the past no longer matters. But it does. It may be forgiven, but it can't be forgotten.

There is insufficient space to weigh all the causes for this shift in strategy. However, the government's own explanation is interesting. The National Party's mouthpiece, Die Burger, invoked historical character traits—"the Afrikaner's desire for freedom"—as lying "at the root" of this switch: "The knowledge that their own desire for freedom may not involve the permanent subservience of others compels the continent's first freedom fighters now—only 80 years after Union—to take the lead in the quest for the joint freedom of all in the country" (February 5, 1990). There was no perception of defeat or outside coercion, no admission that a new policy had to be adopted in order for South Africa to reenter the world economy (personal interviews of cabinet ministers, 1990). On the contrary, self-confidence reigned supreme among Afrikaner policy planners, who congratulated themselves for grasping a unique opportunity to exploit the end of the cold war.

For above all else, it was the change in the Soviet Union that emboldened Pretoria to unban the ANC. "In the government's perception the ANC without Soviet backing was a containable force," observes Hermann Giliomee (African Affairs 91, 1992, p. 359). With the active encouragement of the ANC to find a peaceful political solution and the simultaneous overtures by Moscow toward Pretoria during the joint negotiations on Namibia, even stubborn cold war warriors in the South African government could not fail to see unique opportunities. The "total onslaught" ideology had become totally discredited. Thus the politics of withstanding threats gave way to the politics of exploiting opportunities. With the increased pressure from below and encouragement from its allies abroad, particularly Margaret Thatcher, the National Party could now project itself as in tune with world trends by liberalizing and promising negotiations for democracy. Even the conservative Afrikaner nationalists were taken aback by the collapse of their "evil empire." Only P. W. Botha in his literal wilderness warned his successor against misplaced trust in the KGB and cunning Americans (personal interview, 1990).

Sanctions were hardly mentioned as a crucial impetus for the change. This attitude demonstrates how much Pretoria's confidence had increased since the scare in mid-1989, when the country's reserves were apparently down to thirty-one days, of obligations. "What was crucial in the Cabinet's calculation was not the threat of sanctions but the government's belief that the economy would beat them and would survive risky political experiments, which the unbanning of the ANC undoubtedly is."[2] However, the theme of the 1992 referendum campaign—that the victory of a negative vote would have consequences "too ghastly to contemplate" in terms of economic decline and renewed social isolation—suggests that outside pressure had a far deeper impact on both sides than was normally recognized. A review of the competing claims can shed light on the complex origins of the historic compromise.

INSURRECTIONISM AND THE MYTH OF VICTORY

Prior to its legalization, the ANC refused to believe that incrementalism could lead to the dismantling of apartheid. ANC intellectuals accepted that there had been some reforms but considered the liberal advocates of gradual reform to be dangerous detractors. Thus in 1989, at an ANC–Soviet Social Scientists' Seminar in Moscow, Rob Davies warned: "The danger is that often those who speak of reforms seek to convey the image of a process which, by small incremental changes, will finally lead to the cumulative result of Apartheid being dismantled" (Proceedings of ANC–Soviet Social Science Seminar, p. 18). However, this was precisely the result of the reform process. Even when the de facto stalemate was admitted, this ANC strategist could only think of other options as a "means of exploiting the transfer of power in a situation of unfavourable balance of forces." The idea of negotiation with an undefeated enemy was ruled out as a sellout.

The current ideological confusion and skepticism of black activists about the new politics of negotiation can be traced to such past indoctrination. The assumption was that the government would make no concessions unless absolutely forced to do so. But that regime almost outradicalized its opposition in adaptive political maneuvering.

As a result, many activists have manufactured a new myth to explain the contradiction: Pretoria had no choice but to capitulate at home because it has been defeated militarily in Angola and economically through international sanctions. At the July 1991 ANC conference in Durban, outgoing President Oliver Tambo received the loudest applause during his lengthy report when he said that the South African Defence Force "met their match" at the battle of Cuito Cuanavale. This reveling in an imagined victory was all the more remarkable since no ANC units were involved in the stalemated siege: the conference delegates were appropriating foreign heroism. Likewise, Andrew Clark, an analyst at the Ottawa North-South Institute, wrote that Pretoria suffered "a sobering military defeat at the hands of Angolan Cuban and SWAPO forces at the Cuito Cuanavale" (1991, 46). Similar assumptions are widely cited in European literature on the left as the main reasons for Namibian independence and the concessions by Pretoria.

Military defeat was also given as the reason for Pretoria's willingness to negotiate by ANC stalwart Elias Matsoaledi, a former Umkhonto we Sizwe commander in Johannesburg: "The government mounted talks with the ANC because it had been 'shaken militarily' " (Cape Times, April 12, 1990). Such explanations are sometimes combined with exhortations in support of military education: "To shoot down the enemy's aircraft you need mathematical knowledge, so get into the classrooms and learn military science," University of Cape Town students told their boycotting peers. Other adherents to the insurrection myth see the "armed struggle" as interchangeable with negotiations: "Whether we enter Pretoria with tanks, mortars and bazookas, or whether it is done via a negotiated settlement, the option is left to the enemy to decide."[3]

Ironically, in the view of the state it was the military victory of the apartheid forces, rather than their defeat, that led to the policy changes and to negotiation with the adversary. "The military successes of the SADF in the late 1980s in Southern Angola paved the way for the political dispensation in South Africa," declared Magnus

Malan on the day of his demotion and reassignment (*Argus,* July 30, 1991). The former commander of special forces tells soldiers of a typical *Dolchstosslegende* (stab in the back): "You did not lose in Angola. You did not lose in Namibia. You were betrayed by politicians acting under foreign pressure."[4] Obviously, for both sides the myth of victory seemed a crucial precondition for realignment. But both cannot be right, and the question remains, Who has the more credible claim? James Barber has appropriately commented: "Although South Africa did not lose the war in a strict military sense, after the stalemated battle of Cuito Cuanavale the cost of continuing the war was considered too high by all sides, including Pretoria."[5]

The South Africans calculated that they could not afford to lose three hundred white soldiers in a full-scale assault on the newly reinforced Cuito Cuanavale. Although South Africa had lost air superiority in Angola, owing to the arms boycott, it is doubtful that "military realities in Southern Angola had been the single most important factor forcing the South African government to the negotiating table."[6] Other developments, such as the increasing cost of the war in a declining economy, together with the end of the cold war and the less adversarial relationship between the Soviet Union and the United States on regional conflicts, would seem far more important causes for the shift. The war in Angola had long been unpopular among those on the far right, who viewed it as an American-inspired adventure. With the ANC weakened—cut off ideologically and financially by its disintegrating East European sponsors—the National Party saw a unique opportunity to gain global legitimacy, especially after the demise of the unpopular P. W. Botha after a stroke.

Cuito Cuanavale has thus been celebrated as the decisive battle that turned around the Angolan war and forced South Africa to give up Namibia. In the perception of the South African officials, however, particularly those involved in the protracted negotiations, quite different calculations tipped the scale. The South African government concluded that the only way to renewed world acceptance lay in improved relations with other African states. Namibia was seen as the major stumbling block to South Africa's open entry into Africa. With respect to Namibia, South Africa was a colonial power, defying international law. A South African official remarked: "African leaders considered Namibia even more important than Apartheid."[7] Kenneth Kaunda called it the South African "testing ground." Getting rid of this liability became a priority of foreign affairs officials in their

perennial competition with the militarists who would have liked to
keep Namibia, despite the costs. By including the head of the military
and intelligence services in the American-sponsored negotiations at all
times, the diplomats coaxed their suspicious adversaries into gradual
agreement and also secured the reluctant support of P. W. Botha for
the Namibia solution.

In addition, the South Africans were very impressed with the
changed attitude of the Soviet Union at the negotiations, which contradicted the image of the communists as the masterminds of the total
onslaught. On the contrary, the Soviet Union counseled its Cuban and
Angolan allies to steer a course of compromise and flexibility. In the
estimation of most participants in the negotiations, a Namibia agreement would not have been reached without the Soviet tutelage of its
clients and the new Soviet relationship with traditional adversaries.[8]

Not surprisingly, there exists a substantial psychological block
against recognizing that the South African anti-apartheid transformation is presently taking place with the willing cooperation of the
former supporters of apartheid. After all, if they "made it happen,"
this would taint the undeniable sacrifices made by activists. To ignore
the decisive impact of the decade-long mass mobilization, or to consider it ineffective, would render all the attendant suffering meaningless. As Farid Essack observes: "Many of our activists are understandably resentful of the way those sacrifices are now rubbished or
dismissed as insignificant in the dismantling of Apartheid" (*Cape
Times*, January 4, 1991).

If all the changes were a result of mobilization from below, with the
help of some hard-won external pressure, then there is no reason why
the ruling class should be rewarded for reluctantly bowing to the
inevitable. In this view, the easing of sanctions "to encourage the
movement underway" would be counterproductive. Instead of speed-
ing up the final abolition of apartheid, it would slow it down, since
it would lessen the outside pressure that is construed as crucial to
change. When ANC grass-root activists, therefore, stubbornly insist
on maintaining sanctions and mass mobilization, this is not only a
device to reserve veto power for the organization at whatever cost to
the opponent, but a strategy that rests on a particular view of the
causes of the historical change.

In order to present a leadership that was in fact engaged in compromise as a militant vanguard, the public resolutions adopted by the
ANC used the strident language of the past and denied that any

relevant changes had taken place. Thus in December 1990, a full ten months after the ANC was legalized and was operating freely in the country, the ANC National Consultative Conference resolved: "We unanimously and unequivocally rededicate ourselves to the four pillars of our revolutionary strategy, believing that there have been no fundamental changes in the political situation which would require a departure from our strategy." At most, the conference conceded, "the regime has its own agenda, that of retaining white domination in a new form." Even though the organization was hardly in a position to resume the suspended ("but not terminated") armed struggle after the return of exiles, the conference issued the threat that "our patience with this regime is running out" for "the transfer of power." The weaker the ANC is, the more it has to present the changes in Pretoria as the result of "the struggle of our people" that has "succeeded in forcing the apartheid regime" to make concessions.

It may be important to psychological equality in negotiations to speak of Umkhonto as "victorious." But the illusion of victory also hampers any predisposition to compromise, inasmuch as it denies the reality of stalemate. By emphasizing the forced "transfer of power," albeit to all South Africans in a democracy and not to the ANC alone, the ANC does not truly prepare its constituency for power sharing. Since power sharing will nonetheless be the inevitable outcome of negotiations—which otherwise would be superfluous—the resulting compromise will necessarily be considered a sellout, especially when compared with the notion of a victorious transfer of power. Thus, by acceding to the illusionary rhetoric, the ANC's leadership also unwittingly undermines its own long-term negotiation strategy. The short-term need to appear militant cannot but backfire, imperiling the legitimacy of a negotiated compromise.

In the light of the widespread popularity of armed struggle among the youth, the negotiating ANC leadership now has to deny that it ever aimed at the military defeat of its opponent. While the leadership never had illusions about the eventual fate of its guerrilla war, it nevertheless had to uphold the myth of military victory—the very myth that it is now demolishing. Thus, "on behalf of the ANC," Terror Lekota reinterprets the goals of the "armed struggle" in terms quite contrary to the mobilizing slogan of "Victory or Death": "When the armed wing was set up it was not because the ANC was in search of a military victory. No, Umkhonto was merely to pressure the government to respond to the demands of the people" (*Cape Times,*

May 3, 1990). Against the ANC Youth League, which argued that the ANC did not start the armed struggle in order to trigger negotiations, Lekota insisted on the primacy of political solutions: "Those organisations which demand a military victory of the ANC have misunderstood the approach of the ANC in the first place."[9] Even the popular Chris Hani openly admitted that his MK troops were not in a position to destroy apartheid. When asked whether MK could have won the war, Hani said, "MK alone without the Mass Democratic Movement would not have caused problems." Although he stressed the ANC's capacity, ultimately "to destroy the will of the government to continue with Apartheid," he added realistically, "but it would have taken a very, very long time" (*Monitor,* December 1990).

In light of these realities one can only be amazed by the claims of foreign academics that "the popular movement in South Africa complements its already broad and impressive range of political tactics with a growing military capacity."[10] When John Saul fantasizes that "the regime itself has nightmares," he reveals a view of South African politics that seems to underlie, albeit in less dogmatic forms, many Western activists' accounts of why the apartheid regime has finally embraced reform.

South African commentators often warn that the accelerating slide into endemic violence seems to be following the pattern seen in Angola. In the opinion of Gerald L'Ange, for example, "Once the objective of ousting the Portuguese had been achieved in Angola, the liberation movements began to fight among themselves for a new objective: political power in 'liberated' Angola" (*The Star,* September 25, 1990). However, the analogy is misleading for three reasons. First, the whites have not been ousted from South Africa, nor are they likely to depart. They constitute a permanent force that, even as a small minority, has the economic and military power to ensure that its needs are accommodated and to guarantee a minimum of coercive stability in the country. South Africa is not a colonial situation. Second, the postindependence conflict in Angola cannot be divorced from the larger cold war context. In 1974, when revolutionary Portugal and the Soviet bloc adopted the MPLA as the only legitimate force, in contravention of the Algarve agreement that promised elections, the United States and South Africa responded by supporting Unita as a counter to Soviet influence in the region. With the cold war over, local South African antagonists will be hard put to find international sponsors for continued warfare. Third, the external pressures for a political settlement, rather than a proxy war, deprive the South African factions of access to the heavy arms that sustained the Angolan fighting. Unlike the Angolan liberation movements that fought the Portuguese inside the country, the armed struggle of the ANC was hardly ever more than a propaganda weapon.

In the absence of the East bloc's sponsorship of the ANC, the South African government maintains a monopoly on the instruments of coercion. The official suspension of the armed struggle by the ANC merely acknowledged its relative military powerlessness (in contrast to the situation in Angola or Mozambique). Winnie Mandela may appear in battle fatigues and threaten "to return to the bush" if negotiations fail but, unlike Savimbi or Frelimo, Winnie Mandela and most South African activists have never experienced bush warfare in the first place—and there is no "bush" in South Africa to fight from. The difference in context belies any facile comparisons with liberation struggles elsewhere in Africa. South Africa remains a unique case, not only because of its level of economic development and mutual interdependence, but because it is qualitatively different from the peasant economies of Angola and Mozambique. As Tertius Myburgh once observed, the diversity of South Africa makes victory impossible for any party, and therefore makes compromise inescapable for all parties.

The concept of a self-limiting revolution was developed by the intellectuals of the Polish Solidarity movement because of the threat of Soviet intervention. Solidarity could have seized power, but had it done so, it would have risked almost certain occupation. In South Africa, by contrast, although the ANC shares the same widespread legitimacy as Solidarity, the option of seizing power simply does not exist, except in the rhetorical fantasies of ill-informed activists. That makes a power-sharing coalition of national unity a matter of necessity in South Africa but of choice in Poland. In the Polish case, the historic compromise resulted from the strength of the opposition; in South Africa it has emerged from the mutual weakness of the antagonists.

John Carlin of *The Independent* has judged that "the ANC's arrogance, as much as its naiveté, blinded it to the fact that the scales were tipped heavily against it." Indeed, the myth that a cunning adversary has finally been bludgeoned by sanctions, armed struggle, and mass action to negotiate a deal for the transfer of power lies at the heart of the ANC's false triumphalism. The ANC has failed to realize that the release of political prisoners, the return of exiles, the normalization of politics, and even the end of formal apartheid were not the real issues at stake. Apartheid would have had to go anyway, with or without the ANC. In the eyes of the dominant enlightened Afrikaner establishment, the political incorporation of disenfranchised subordinates had clearly become the only way for the government to retain power and regain international legitimacy. Contrary to the ANC's belief that "we initiated negotiations," as Chris Hani would have it, the Afrikaner liberals and corporate planners had long prepared themselves for this historical inevitability. By not acknowledging the real causes of the change—by attributing it to the opposition's own efforts, with some small assistance from "de Klerk's integrity"—the ANC has deceived itself into overrating its own power. An organization with such a crucially flawed political orientation must also fail to understand that the skewed economic order established under apartheid will essentially remain intact long after apartheid itself is gone. In this respect the militant slogan "Victory is certain!" more accurately characterizes the other side. But *la lutta continua* cannot offer a suitable guide either, unless the ANC, once in power, wants to turn the struggle upon itself while it is simultaneously constrained by the duties and responsibilities of office. The Maoist dream of a permanent revolution ignores the truth that officeholders necessarily turn into bureaucratic functionaries, despite their past activism. Initially, the ANC has undergone the painful process of resocializing exiles to South African realities. In so doing, it has changed the sociopolitical environment and itself at the same time, its strident rhetoric about the legacies of the past notwithstanding. Liberal democrats can only hold their breath, hoping that the ANC does not become internally ungovernable during the volatile transition.

THE IMPACT OF SANCTIONS

The overwhelming majority of the white South Africans whom we interviewed are amused by the foreign insistence that sanctions made the ultimate difference in bringing Pretoria to the bargaining table. They point to internal reasons as having been far more significant. The more historically minded list the evolution of Afrikaner identity and its redefinition in the Vorster era to include English-speaking whites; the failed co-optation policies of P. W. Botha, which aimed at incorporating Coloureds and Indians through the tricameral constitution; and, finally, the admission under de Klerk that only inclusive citizenship for all South Africans could secure a future for Afrikaners. Overall, then, Pretoria's decision is attributed to the intrinsic pragmatic rationality of Afrikaners, rather than the circumstances in which perceptions are formed and group boundaries are redefined. Yet these new approaches were largely spurred by internal opposition and foreign isolation, which in turn shaped perceptions and mediated policies. The American scholar Robert Price correctly points to the "boosting effect" of internationally imposed economic constraints on the domestic political dialectic (1990, 298). However, if our interviewees are to be believed, Price, like most other foreign analysts, overestimates the impact of outside pressure and engages in economic reductionism when he "directly relates" the risks Pretoria is willing to take with "full black participation" to the "amount of international economic pressure it feels" (1990, 291). Deon Geldenhuys, one of the most respected South African political scientists and author of an acclaimed comparative analysis of South Africa, Chile, Israel, and Taiwan, writes that "I could not find any direct, positive correlation between reform in South Africa and disinvestment from abroad."[11] Geldenhuys points out that the undoubted harm to the South African economy did not automatically translate into political reformism, although he does concede that disinvestment was one among several other factors contributing to the abolition of apartheid.

In this ongoing controversy most of our interviewees agree on the salience of some indisputable historical facts, but they draw different conclusions from these facts. Mass mobilization and spreading unrest in the mid-1980s, while never threatening the existence of the South African state, nonetheless weakened it in unexpected ways. It motivated the Chase Manhattan Bank to recall its loans, which triggered an avalanche of similar withdrawals by other banks. This forced Pretoria to declare bankruptcy in August 1985. In the minds of its originators, this flight of capital was not intended to speed up political change; the political instability in South Africa had simply led to a higher perception of risk, leading to the refusal to roll over short-term loans. It was this economic decision, not the legal sanctions introduced later, that accelerated South Africa's crisis. Between 1985 and 1990, the state lost some 30 to 33 billion rand, mostly in the repayment of foreign loans. The inability to raise new loans—and in any case the various sanctions acts soon made new loans illegal—merely sealed the unfavorable economic assessment of South Africa as a high-risk area.

While, in a much-publicized visit to Lusaka in 1985, South African business flirted briefly with the idea of courting the ANC, it abandoned the overture soon afterward because it caused problems at home. The prospect of a liaison with "communists" was, of course, anathema to the arch-capitalists.[12] In fact, there is some evidence that sanctions reinforced a unity of interests between government and business, each needing the other in order to overcome a hostile environment. Hermann Giliomee, who has always had an astute sense of the shifting currents within the Afrikaner establishment, persuasively suggests that it was the new opportunity rather than economic necessity that brought about liberalization.

> Internal resistance and sanctions exerted constant pressure but they failed to achieve the fundamental requirement for a substantial shift in power: a crack in the regime. No significant section of the ruling bloc went outside for support. In making his decision in late 1989 to unban the liberation organisations, de Klerk did not act at the behest of business or religious elites but on the advice of his security establishment who felt that the ANC had been sufficiently weakened to be a containable force. (1992, 118)

In a speech to the U.N. General Assembly on September 22, 1987, Canadian Foreign Affairs Minister Joe Clark claimed that "the sanctions imposed upon South Africa have been effective" in that "growing numbers of individual South Africans have reached out for reform." However, none of the liberal whites we interviewed even hinted that sanctions had motivated their reformism. On the contrary, almost all of them deplored economic sanctions as counterproductive and ill-advised. South African liberals thus enthusiastically applauded the antisanctions policies of London and Washington, while Ottawa held to its contention that the pressure of sanctions was indispensable for achieving dialogue. Nonetheless, the South African business lobby continued to invoke the threat of more sanctions to stave off further apartheid measures or to advocate incremental liberalization, and it allowed the liberal opposition to warn Pretoria that government intransigence would only provoke more harmful foreign hostility. For example, the Urban Foundation, which advocated the repeal of the Group Areas Act and of forced removal, argued: "Needless to say, even debate on the prospects of such removals at this stage would provoke a local and international political and economic backlash of disastrous proportions."[13]

It would be difficult to assess to what extent such statements amounted to self-serving rhetoric in light of the obvious desire of South African business to circumvent sanctions. It would be even more difficult to ascertain whether or how seriously the South African cabinet heeded the warnings from the business sector about the harmful effect of foreign restrictions. Apart from the advocates of a siege economy,[14] genuine confidence that foreign interference could be overcome alternated with laments about its counterproductive impact and the widely expressed hope that international legitimacy would soon be restored, in order to avoid further economic decline. Hardly any public utterance by a business executive failed to point to a political settlement and a climate of optimism as preconditions for economic growth.

In this respect, the lack of confidence regarding long-term investment decisions proved effective in contributing to a change of perceptions. In the early 1980s conventional wisdom in South Africa held that economic recovery could solve the political crisis. By the end of the decade the reverse was true: political reconciliation was now viewed as the essential first step in dealing with the economic crisis. Everyone from cabinet ministers to industrialists acknowledged that the annual growth of the GNP could be 3 percent higher given international legitimacy and open access to world financial markets.[15] Because of a low level of domestic savings relative to the desired level of investment, the "fundamental constraint on the South African economy" was "the shortage of funding to finance fixed investments" (Garner and Leap, 1991, 1). Lack of confidence and the inability to obtain long-term loans on foreign markets led to a refusal to invest in job-creating industries. The lack of investments in turn created the need to generate large current-account surpluses. In this predicament, South African policy makers had no choice but to maintain high interest rates and restrain growth, even at the cost of high unemployment and declining real incomes.

Several of the authors of a series of incisive papers produced by the Commonwealth-funded Centre for the Study of the South African Economy and International Finance at the London School of Economics caution against overestimating the impact of sanctions. Merle Lipton (1990), who has published the most systematic and comprehensive investigation of this question so far, argues that South Africa's foreign debt problems are neither unique nor solely due to sanctions. She contends that the political effects of sanctions have been "mixed," leading to increased support for an immoral and unsustainable system in some cases, but to an intensified resentment and intransigent in-security in others. In contrast, Joseph Hanlon, the coordinator of the Commonwealth Independent Expert Study on Sanctions Against South Africa, maintains that without sanctions "Namibia would not yet be independent, and Mandela would not yet be free" (1991, v). Yet even Hanlon admits that sanctions were not the most important impetus for either event.

In short, sanctions compounded market forces already at work, especially the flight of capital that began in the mid-1970s, long before sanctions were instituted (Kahn 1991). However, sanctions also pro-vided an additional push to the anti-apartheid movement, by giving outsiders leverage to influence South African developments through psychological blows to business confidence. The apartheid regime was finally caught in a vicious circle: over time, black protest contributed to an increased perception of economic risk, which triggered further capital flight, reinforced by sanctions, which in turn strengthened the protest movement.

A firmly held belief among the black opposition is that the South African government is basically kept in power by its Western allies. Hence, sufficient external pressure—the withdrawal of international support—would force Pretoria to relinquish its exclusive political control. "We believe that you in the U.S., together with your allies, have the means to get the South African government to the negotiating table," read an "Open Letter to the American People," signed by Allan Boesak, Desmond Tutu, Beyers Naudé, and Frank Chikane on the occasion of their Washington visit to the newly elected President Bush (ANC Newsbriefing, June 4, 1989).

Such an assessment, however, perhaps overestimates the intrinsic vulnerability of the South African regime as well as the clout and the political will of Western conservative powers. It has also contributed to a widespread view of liberation as something of a cargo cult, a commodity to be delivered by outsiders. Unfortunately, inasmuch as it has geared protest toward triggering outside pressure rather than challenging the domestic power equation directly, this attitude has reinforced domestic political paralysis.

The effects of sanctions can be summarized in nine more or less controversial propositions:

(1) Of the three basic categories of sanctions measures—disinvest-ment, trade restrictions, and bans on long-term credit—the last has affected South Africa the most. Trade boycotts were relatively easy to

circumvent, albeit at some additional cost, while "disinvestment has not noticeably impeded the functioning of the South African economy" (Lipton 1990, v).

(2) Many foreign firms that have withdrawn from South Africa have maintained their links with the South African market by supplying it with their products through new, independent local outlets (Kodak-Samcor) or from neighboring states (Coca-Cola).

(3) The nominal withdrawal has allowed South African conglomerates to buy out absconding foreign firms at bargain prices. Although this has increased the capital concentration in the South African economy, the process has principally benefited the larger corporations such as Anglo, Barlow Rand, and Sanlam.

(4) The expected pressure by business on government as a result of sanctions has not occurred. In fact, sanctions brought business and government closer together in the patriotic cause of circumventing foreign interference. Sanctions have thus been counterproductive vis-à-vis one important precondition for change: the deepening of cleavages within the ruling minority. Nevertheless, sanctions have undermined business confidence and contributed to the search for alternatives.

(5) The withdrawal has had a negative effect on the social responsibility program and labor codes through which various foreign interests morally rationalized their South African presence. Local management has proven less amenable to fair labor practices.

(6) Sanctions have marginally increased the already high rate of black unemployment. In the general economic recession and the restructuring of firms, the interests of white, rather than black, workers have been protected. Those who hold power have deflected the impact of sanctions onto the weaker sectors. Blacks were dismissed first.

(7) Nonracial unions, although numerically stronger than ever, have been weakened by the growing army of the unemployed. Although the Congress of South African Trade Unions (Cosatu) officially supported all pressure on the South African government, many affiliated unions have been ambivalent about further economic measures, particularly disinvestment. Union officials fear that rising black unemployment will make workers reluctant to take political risks— that it will depoliticize them.

(8) After 1987, although the ANC continued to demand comprehensive mandatory sanctions, the sanctions drive lost momentum in Western public opinion. This perception was reinforced by the failure

of existing measures to change Pretoria's policy as well as by the realization that South Africa was relatively self-sufficient and that the Frontline States depended on the South African economy.

(9) The loss of Western markets for South African products has to some extent been offset by the dramatic development of South African trade links with Pacific Rim countries, particularly Japan and Taiwan. In developing these markets, South African exporters have taken elaborate precautions to disguise the origins of their products, labeling them as made in Mauritius, Swaziland, the Seychelles, or Namibia—a tactic that has proved quite successful.

All in all, then, no general conclusion can be drawn about the success or failure of sanctions against South Africa. The judgment remains an open question, as it depends on an empirical evaluation of the political and economic effects of different measures in specific historical circumstances.

CHAPTER THREE

Prospects for a Historic Compromise

There is no guarantee, however hard we work, that the balance of forces will be more favorable to us in, say two years time, than it is now.

Joe Slovo, *New Nation*, November 26, 1992.

The dramatic change in government policy, accompanied by a striking moral shift and verified by a long-stalled grant of independence to Namibia, caught both the opposition and the international anti-apartheid forces by surprise. Normally well-informed analysts totally misjudged the dynamics of white politics and the determination of de Klerk to introduce a universal franchise, which increasingly gained the support of the white electorate. George M. Fredrickson speaks for many with this false prediction, made in the fall of 1990: "In the unlikely event that de Klerk agrees to move directly to one-person–one-vote, it is almost certain that he will lose the support of most whites and that the right-wing Conservative party will come to power and attempt to reestablish full-fledged apartheid, thus making a racial civil war virtually inevitable. This might happen even if he concedes less than that."[1] The majority of whites did not desert de Klerk, however, nor is the right wing likely to obtain power, despite de Klerk's direct move to a one-person–one-vote system.

In an intriguing comparative analysis Donald Horowitz (1991) detects in South Africa a unique feature: not only a conflict between divided segments as in other plural societies but "a conflict over the nature of the conflict"—what he calls a "metaconflict." But Horowitz overemphasizes the cleavages in South African society. In reality, there are only four irreconcilable positions on the present spectrum of conflict. First, there is the extreme right-wing demand for the secession of a racial white homeland or at least some autonomy for a Boerestaat. While the disruptive power of armed ideologues must not be underestimated, the secessionist project has little chance of gaining mainstream support because it runs counter to business interests in an integrated economy. Likewise, since South African business, including Afrikaner capital, needs to be part of the global economy, on the one hand, and, on the other, is dependent on the willing cooperation of black labor, it would be equally hostile to a military takeover— something that distinguishes South Africa from Latin American regimes.

Second there is the Africanist/socialist position: No negotiations until the regime is defeated and ready to transfer power. This would be a threat only if the present negotiations were entirely to fail. However, power is not a static commodity that is possessed by one party and transferred to another. As Kathryn Manzo (1992, 4) has rightly stressed, it is fallacious to argue "that change in South Africa occurs only when power is handed over from white to black." Such a conceptualization overlooks that blacks are not passive victims, that the "power of the powerless" already exacts a high price from the rulers. It is in this interplay of mutual dependency between the establishment and opposition parties that power is distributed and always contested.

Third, there is the emerging working relationship between the National Party and the ANC, which is more solid than Horowitz realizes. The ANC leadership, including its South African Communist Party members, have moved ever closer to a social-democratic economic compromise.

The fourth option, of course, is a protracted conflict between the ANC and the NP. Given the new international constellation, the pressures and expectations for a settlement, such a course of events would amount to an impossible reversal of all the changes that have already taken place.

According to Stephen Cohen (1991), the process of conflict resolution is a cumulative ladder of four rungs: (1) begrudging acceptance of the adversary as an unavoidable fact, (2) mutual recognition in a legal context, (3) interaction with the other as fully equal in status, and (4) partnership in a common postconflict environment in which defined roles are shared. As of 1993 South Africa has moved into the third phase, with the fourth phase, a semipermanent, interim coalition, in view. Both antagonists no longer see themselves as victims but, in Cohen's phrase, as "creators of new realities." A cluster of fearful attitudes has given way to an aura of hope among those participating in negotiations. Those still clinging to the status quo may wish to join at a later stage, rather than being marginalized, as

the present wavering of many Conservatives and members of the PAC
and the Azanian People's Organisation (Azapo) indicates.

The historic compromise increasingly takes on more concrete features. Economically, the ANC is likely to settle for the representation
of blacks on company boards, participatory management by unions,
progressive taxation, equalization payments, equity ownership, and
joint ventures rather than nationalization. It is only worth capturing
the "commanding heights of the economy" if the heights have not
been flattened by further economic decline. Anything more than a
social-democratic compromise toward redistribution would founder
on the current power of the establishment to withhold economic
benefits from the would-be socialist political victors. All evidence
points to the gradual *embourgeoisement* of the black middle strata.
The ANC leadership acts as their reluctant, posturing, but ultimately
compliant representative, because the spoils of entry into hitherto
closed realms are real. The left wing of the South African opposition
will try to block such neocolonial accommodation, but it will fail to
prevent it. In all likelihood, it will split from the old alliance and form
the new opposition.

Any theory regarding this new alignment has to come to grips with
the now self-evident fact that some of the former victims of racial
discrimination have increasingly joined the realms of power in per-
petuating class domination. In this sense, South Africa has become
normalized: as in other Western societies, exploitation is color-blind.
Instead of a transformation of racial capitalism into nonracial socialism, a new multiracial nomenclatura is likely to emerge, in which the
dominant group shares relative privilege at the expense of an increasingly marginalized underclass. This has been referred to as the 50
percent solution in South Africa, since the other half of the population
is shortchanged in both political representation and influence. The
National Party's constitutional proposal, for example, envisages a
double vote for people who own or rent property. In the ANC executive and voting constituency, migrant workers and the unemployed
are equally underrepresented.

In short, South Africa is heading toward a corporatist state where
business, state bureaucrats, and unionized labor in the form of the
ANC-SACP-Cosatu alliance agree among themselves about the basics
of an unwritten contract at the expense of the unorganized and
weaker sections of the population. This cartel of the privileged may
well find electoral expression one day in the substitution of a series of

appropriately worded and pretested referenda for genuine elections. Such a tactic legitimizes the stake of the major players without risking unpredictable outcomes that could lead to a declaration of civil war by the losing side.

The ANC has been far more open to compromise than its detractors ever expected. In wooing his opponents, Mandela has bluntly invoked the special historical circumstances: "We have to address the fears of whites and we should go beyond the mere rhetorical assurance in order to address structural guarantees which would ensure that this principle will not lead to the domination of whites by blacks." While reaffirming that the political party that wins the most votes should form the government, Mandela assured his Stellenbosch audience, in Afrikaans, that all principles, democratic or otherwise, can be bent: "Having regard to our background it may not be enough to work purely on one-person, one-vote because every national group would like to see that the people of their flesh and blood are in the government" (*Sunday Tribune,* May 19, 1991).

Mandela's stance dovetails with the National Party's notion of the mandatory, constitutionally entrenched participation of minority parties at all levels of political decision making, including a statutory, collective presidency. This does not amount to majority rule in the traditional sense but represents a conception of democracy that rests on a wide participation by major interest groups. In a key strategic discussion paper, Joe Slovo (*African Communist* 3, 1992, p. 40) proposes a "sunset clause" in the new constitution that "would provide for compulsory power-sharing for a fixed number of years in the period immediately following the adoption of the constitution." It is significant that Slovo does not specify the time period—which the Nationalists would like to be unlimited. Slovo qualifies "compulsory power-sharing" only with the stipulation that there should be "proportional representation in the executive," together with deadlock-breaking mechanisms, while the Nationalists insist on parity and consensus in decision making. Whether such an approach will paralyze decision making and thereby preserve the status quo remains to be seen. Undoubtedly, power sharing, as opposed to majority party rule, is the only feasible outcome at present, short of civil war. But those who view the ANC exclusively as a "government-in-waiting" overlook this fact. The ANC could become the sole government only if it were able to defeat its opponent, a capacity that, by its own admission, it lacks. Pretoria is thus under little pressure to surrender, especially since the ANC no longer has the intention to declare war.

As Guillermo O'Donnell (1988) has pointed out, corporatism is not a static concept; rather, it changes from country to country. The semifascist corporatism of Latin America differs vastly from the "corporatist" social-democratic accord found in many Western European states. The precise role of the state depends on the country's historical experience, although the Eurocentric bias of many Western scholars often causes them to miss, or to misconstrue, these particularities beyond the Western horizon. South Africa's main interest groups will thus have to negotiate a unique democratic corporatism in both the economic and political realms. Indeed, in the opinion of Denis Beckett the country has no successful models to follow, "only failures to avoid" (Frontline, May 1991). In short, South Africa needs to pioneer a course of its own, and most indicators show that the country's historic compromise is proceeding slowly but steadily in both the economic and political arenas.

Indeed, the initial flexibility of Pretoria deprived the ANC of an important weapon for mobilization: the intransigence of the opponent. As Simon Barber mused: "An opponent who asks so little in return for relinquishing his monopoly of power is almost too easy. How, if you are the ANC or its 'formations,' can you mobilise against an enemy that suddenly turns out to be so reasonable that he is willing to treat all your demands as negotiable?" (Cape Times, April 3, 1990). More politically romantic and sensitive ANC members like poet Breyten Breytenbach expressed amused bewilderment: "Most people in the ANC don't seem to have any enemies any more. The other day a friend from the national executive committee of the ANC proudly introduced me to a National Party MP, as though he was some kind of friend. I was absolutely horrified" (Weekend Mail, September 14, 1990). This "toenadering" (getting together) was temporarily interrupted by government intransigence at Codesa II in May 1992 and the ANC's walkout from the formal negotiations and adoption of "rolling mass action" instead. Nevertheless, even during the five months' suspension of negotiations and old-time posturing on both sides, forty-three informal meetings took place between the ANC's general secretary, Cyril Ramaphosa, and the government's chief negotiator, Roelf Meyer.

One of the crucial watersheds in the establishment of a corporate state was Cosatu's 1990 decision to join the National Manpower Commission (NMC). This participation, although later temporarily suspended, resulted from the successful negotiation of unions with employers and manpower officials over the controversial Labour Relations Act. The accord they reached, which was subsequently enshrined in law, provided a model for social-democratic compromise. Since the state and employers need the support of unions to ensure stability, the union threat of withdrawal from the National Manpower Commission functions as a powerful bargaining tool, preventing unilateral dictates by state bureaucrats when it comes to drafting labor laws.

For example, the ANC-Cosatu opposition has challenged with increasing success the government's exclusive right to decide economic policy. The two-day national strike over the introduction of a new value-added tax in November 1991 was not called because the unions disagreed with the tax in principle but because they had no say in introducing it. The mass actions were aimed at further undermining the legitimacy of the government by proving that it can no longer rule on the strength of a white vote alone. Since Pretoria has itself admitted that its apartheid constitution is wrong and needs to be renegotiated, it has also contributed to its own caretaker status. If South African business seems determined to learn the corporate contract mentality the hard way, it is nonetheless reluctantly embracing necessity. The more sophisticated companies also discover new allies, and the ANC-SACP alliance is willing to contribute its share to the compromise. To be sure, there are still great obstacles to be overcome and lessons to be learned on both sides.

How much the ANC-SACP alliance wishes to achieve an accord and marginalize groups that oppose its own disciplining structure was demonstrated in what the *South African Labor Bulletin* (November 1990) labeled "the most high-profile dispute of the year." In a bitter strike at the Mercedes plant in East London in 1990, workers opposed their union's policy of centralized bargaining. The ANC, SACP, and Numsa (National Union of Metalworkers) lined up with management in opposition to the strikers' demand for factory-based bargaining. The Mercedes labor aristocracy was rejected as purveyors of "industrial tribalism," with a grateful company rewarding the assistance of the "socialist" mediators. Mercedes is now engaged in abolishing "racial Fordism" in order to involve its workers in more autonomous decision making on the factory floor as well as in the boardroom.

However, before a viable social democracy can emerge, two obstacles need to be addressed: the commitment of middle-level union leaders toward socialism, and the ambivalent relationship between the ANC and Cosatu.

Surveys of Cosatu shopstewards reveal a remarkable commitment to nationalization of key industries—as stipulated in the Freedom Charter—worker control, and redistribution of profits. A nationwide sample of 863 shop stewards conducted in September 1991 asked what economic policy a new democratic government should adopt to change the inequalities of the past. Nationalization was favored by 67 percent; only 16 percent favored government regulation of the economy, and 17 percent preferred privatization (Pityana and Orkin 1992, 67). The authors comment that "this overwhelming support for nationalisation is out of step with the direction the ANC seems to be taking" (p. 67). While the majority of union members would vote for the ANC, viewing it as the only viable vehicle to displace the apartheid regime, there exists simultaneously a far greater loyalty and identification with the union than with the ANC. The Cosatu leadership has always insisted on independence from a future ANC government and rejected the East European model of using unions as subservient agencies of the party in power. The same attitude is adopted by the emerging civic organizations, which increasingly challenge ANC policy although they remain closely allied to the ANC.

Hindsight suggests that it may have been a strategic error to confine Codesa to political parties. Had trade unions, employers' organizations, and other major actors in civil society been included in the negotiations from the outset, the latent rivalry between the ANC and Cosatu would have been minimized. The 1992 mass actions were mainly spurned by unionists who needed to demonstrate their clout vis-à-vis elitist ANC compromisers. Thus suddenly the tail was wagging the dog, and many optimistic ANC executives found themselves caught in the militant sweep rather than leading it. Similarly, the emerging Cosatu-employer pact would most likely not have been sabotaged by the government had it been concluded inside Codesa rather than being concocted as a rival initiative outside the political framework. The statement in the Saccola-Cosatu draft charter concerning the role of political organizations implicitly denies a union role in politics. However, Cosatu has always been proud of its political involvement and resented being shut out, albeit represented by its other two tripartite allies. The future of a social-democratic compromise in the discussed Economic Forum of government, business, and labor will hinge not only on a new relationship between the three major forces but equally on a clarification of roles and policies within each bloc.

In early 1991 Thabo Mbeki indicated that the two adversaries had reached a virtual consensus on the future constitution: "Now that we have arrived at more or less common positions on the basic constitutional issues, there is no reason why the process should take a long time" (*Leadership*, May 1991, p. 62). That judgment may have been premature. The ANC and the government agree on the devolution of power, differing, however, on whether the local and regional units should have authority in their own right or whether they should have rights delegated by the central government. There is consensus on a justiciable bill of rights, a two-chamber parliament, a constitutional court, and, most important, on the voting system.

ANC constitutional experts have embraced proportional representation. Thus, like Mandela, Kader Asmal argues that "there must be recognition that the cultural, social and economic diversity of South Africa requires the adoption of an electoral system at all levels which will enable sectoral groups and political tendencies to be adequately represented in decision-making" (*Transformation* 13, 1991). Asmal, a member of the Constitutional Committee of the ANC, also praises the "virtues of proportional representation," calling attention to the additional advantage that "gerrymandering" will be prevented by voting according to party lists: "The winner-takes-all majoritarian electoral system may have served its purpose in ensuring stability among the whites, but it is a form of stability which a democratic South Africa must reconsider."[2]

The newly found preference of the ANC leadership for proportional voting, however, stems not only from its concern for minority representation but from its desire for control over the political process. Unlike the constituency-based Westminster system, where candidates are selected by and accountable to a local electorate, proportional representation minimizes grass-roots control over candidates. It instead favors the party leadership, since it is primarily the party that decides who is placed on the nationwide list and in what ranking. It is this enhanced central control that made proportional representation attractive to the constitutional planners of the ANC-SACP.

However, South African political culture is so wedded to the Westminster system of voting that proportional representation still appears to many as an undemocratic concession to racial group rights. Thus, in an interview with Harry Gwala (*Indicator*, Autumn 1991), Yvonne

Muthien asks the somewhat misleading question: "Would the ANC consider compromising on their demand for 'one person one vote' by accepting proportional representation?" Gwala responds predictably: "Whose proportions? That suggests group rights, vested interests. Racism serves vested interests." Both fail to grasp that the proportional representation of political parties constitutes a far more democratic and comprehensive way of ensuring participation in decision making than a system that relegates minority parties and candidates to irrelevance.

The National Party, on the other hand, does not consider proportional representation sufficient to guarantee minority political influence. Regardless of the voting system, the Nationalists argue, the ANC can realistically expect to receive more than 50 percent of the vote, and thereby to dominate the political process, unless there are constitutionally entrenched limits on majority rule. Codesa II foundered, among other reasons, over disagreement on the size of the supermajority that an elected constitution-making body would require to adopt constitutional clauses. It is this question of power sharing versus majoritarianism, or "ordinary democracy", as Mandela called it, together with the nature of federalism versus centralism that proved the most obstinate stumbling blocks for a consensus on constitutional principles.

In reviewing the origins of apartheid legislation, Hermann Giliomee has astutely isolated two interlinked motivations: "Without a privileged position the Afrikaners could not survive as a separate people; without safeguarding the racial separateness of the people, a privileged position could not be maintained."[3] The ANC opposition, however, needs neither separateness nor privilege. Free of the insecurities of the few, the majority does not have to mobilize on exclusivist nationalist grounds but can trust in democratic equality to secure its interests.

One striking feature of South African constitutional negotiations is the absence of formal outside intervention, facilitation, mediation, or arbitration. South Africa, unlike Namibia or Zimbabwe during their transitions, is a sovereign state, and the only body that can legally enact a new constitution is the present parliament. If there is to be legal continuity, the present regime will have to legalize its own transformation. This constitutional continuity is clearly recognized by the government agenda, which sees precisely such a process unfolding. The opposition, however, argues quite understandably that the government cannot be player and referee simultaneously. It therefore proposes a mutually agreed-upon interim government and an elected constituent assembly that could also function as the first parliament once a constitution has been negotiated. Pretoria, though, rejects elections before negotiations. From its perspective, elections before a new constitution has been ratified would amount to surrender, a blank check to the majority and an abdication of power rather than negotiation over a new order. Pretoria also insists that lawful government and the administration of the country must not be jeopardized during the period of constitution making.

In adopting these legalistic positions, however, the government consistently confuses sovereignty with legitimacy. Sovereignty Pretoria possesses; legitimacy it widely lacks. It also falsely equates liberalization with democratization. Since de Klerk's rise to power, the South African state has clearly become more liberal, but it has yet to agree upon meaningful democratic participation for all citizens. Liberalization extends rights and opens up new political space. It reduces the costs and risks of individual expression. Democratization aims at the equality of citizens and an improvement of opportunities for everyone. It is the economic democratization that will prove the sticky part—not the transitional arrangement and constitutional accords themselves.

There are two dangers that an interim government of national unity has to avoid. First, if the setting up of such a government were perceived by the right wing as tantamount to surrender, it could easily trigger more violence from this sector and plunge the country into a real civil war. Therefore, constitutional continuity and the legitimacy of any transitional arrangement in the eyes of the majority of whites and black dissidents would seem an important consideration. This danger also points to the need for a constitutional accord to precede the establishment of an interim government. This charter consensus should be as broad as possible and include all forces that can wreck the rules of the game. The subsequent governing coalition can be much narrower, provided the charter coalition, in Jannie Gagiano's useful distinction, is inclusive even of extremist parties. The hesitant participation of white conservatives (AVU), as well as the PAC, in negotiations bodes well for this principle, while the vehement rejection of bilateral accords and Codesa's Declaration of Intent by Inkatha signals the opposite.

Second, for the ANC the danger of an interim government lies in assuming responsibility in the absence of power. While the ANC would have some measure of control over the security forces in particular, it is doubtful that this newly acquired limited power would be sufficient to stop all the atrocities that would now be committed in the name of the ANC as well as the old regime. The ANC would carry the burden of a declining economy but would also be constrained to implement radical restructuring. Disappointed expectations and disillusionment with the ANC are the likely results.

Some of the more astute ANC leaders view with alarm the perception of being co-opted and wisely maintain a distance between themselves and Pretoria. As Chris Hani put it, "We are adversaries—the government and the ANC. The government sometimes acts as if we are part of that government, and yet we are not part of that government." Hani emphasizes the usefulness to the ANC of remaining a symbol of radicalism and militancy. Rather than being concerned with the content of a radical policy, he admits to its manipulative function: "I don't want the ANC to lose that image because once it loses that image, it will lose the support of young people" (*Monitor*, December 1990). How the inevitable ANC participation in government is to be reconciled with its aura of militancy remains to be seen. Nevertheless, when the ANC sets deadlines and declares that "our patience with this regime is running out," everyone knows that the tough talk merely camouflages an inevitable, deeper involvement of the two antagonists.

White South Africa has so far failed to recognize the ANC's need for symbolic victories. The more the ANC is drawn into constitutional politics, the more it loses its moral status as the vehicle of liberation. Vulnerable as a fallible political actor in a powerful establishment, it must show its supporters either that it can deliver on their inflated expectations or that the adversary is as intransigent as ever and that the ANC therefore cannot be blamed. Both choices, however, are detrimental to the need for compromise in negotiation politics. The less leverage the ANC is able to exercise within the narrow constraints of constitutional negotiations, the more the emphasis shifts to socioeconomic issues. Against the establishment's attempt to restructure the economy through preemptive privatization and constitutional guarantees stands the ANC's need to guard against disappointing the economic expectations of its constituency.

The rise or fall of the future South African democracy thus depends on an upturn in the economy. Only an expanding economy will allow both sides to satisfy their supporters, thereby easing the necessary compromises. The fewer the economic options, the more the ANC will fall back on street mobilization to guard its flanks, and the more the establishment will view the necessary long-term redistribution as a zero-sum strategy. It would want to sabotage such attempts in every way it could, including the refusal to reinvest in South Africa. The ANC in turn loses the incentive for entering negotiations if the talks produce neither economic gains nor symbolic political victories. Yet the ultimate paradox remains that economic recovery depends on a creditable political settlement. Negotiations therefore cannot wait for an economic turnaround, for a time when conditions are more conducive to a democratic compromise.

It is sometimes uncritically assumed that if "negotiations stall or break off, then South Africa could find itself back on the path to insurrection" (Price 1990, 296). Yet the disintegration of the Soviet Union, the major outside sponsor of the previous insurrectionist strategy, means that Libya, China, or smaller Stalinist relics like Cuba or North Korea would have to step in. Renewed exile or repression for South African activists is not an inviting prospect for the current ANC leadership, which would rather bend over backwards to reach a compromise than repeat a failed historical experience. For the Afrikaner nationalists, too, there is no option of going back to the repressive era; they are too weak and divided. A renewed consensus on racial repression is simply inconceivable. It would also be suicidal for the white minority.

CHAPTER FOUR

Dilemmas and Contradictions in the ANC Alliance

We initiated negotiations and we are serious about
negotiations. . . . I think we need to have a lot of what I
call revolutionary patience.

Chris Hani, *Monitor,* December 1990

LIBERATION, COHESION, AND HETEROGENEITY

In the process of preparing itself for normal politics, the ANC was confronted with its own shortcomings. It was forced to become more self-critical. As ANC spokesperson Gill Marcus admitted, "The emotional support for the movement is massive, but translating that support into a knowledge and understanding of the ANC's policies, strategies, programmes and tactics is proving to be an unenviable task" (*Natal Mercury,* February 4, 1991). The rival organizations that maintained the liberation posture, standing aloof from the politics of compromise, could much more easily maintain a purist stance on internal problems.

The initial organizational chaos within the ANC reflected badly on its potential for rule and deterred sympathizers and adversaries alike from considering the organization an effective alternative to the present government. "When the movement cannot even clean up the hopeless muddle in its own head office," read an editorial in the National Party organ, *Die Burger* (July 4, 1991), "how does he [Mandela] actually expect that people should trust him to govern a taxing country like South Africa." Other observers focused on the spreading political violence, which had clearly weakened the organization. One South African commentator, Harold Pakendorf, asked in all seriousness: "Does the ANC actually exist—as an organization—beyond the rhetoric and the headlines?" He concluded: "What is apparent is that the ANC does not initiate the violence in the country, does not direct it, does not control it and cannot end it" (*Sunday Times,* August 26,

1990). Blaming the victim was combined with naive dismay that the ANC could not guarantee instant stability.

The international press, too, voiced criticism and disappointment. The *Guardian Weekly* (April 14, 1991) concluded that the ANC "has not had a good year." The writer, Roger Ormond, summarized sympathetically the various obstacles the ANC had encountered, but could not hide disillusionment: "Whatever else the ANC may have in its armoury—international goodwill, the backing of probably the majority of South Africans, and moral force, a magic wand is missing." Other more cynical observers wondered about the temptations of exile. As Simon Barber commented, "The truth perhaps is that the ANC is only truly at home abroad. Abroad, it is treated as the government-in-waiting. Foreigners, especially in the West, fawn obediently, allow it to dictate their policies and grant it the illusion that it has won a famous victory. At home, there is no such obedience but rather a grinding confrontation with unpleasant facts" (*Sunday Times*, September 2, 1990).

The most important criticism of Mandela's first period in freedom deplores his failure to reconcile the ANC with Inkatha. By placing himself squarely within the ANC fold upon his release, he also inherited the organization's feuds and constraints. An alternative strategy would have been to assume the mantle of a reconciling statesman capable of rising above the petty quarrels. Mandela's huge prestige, along with the widespread longing for peace and stability, would perhaps have allowed him to play such a nonpartisan role for a while. However, he would have had to rely solely on his prestige, since he would have sacrificed his organizational power base. By subjecting himself to the collective ANC discipline, Mandela eschewed the presidential role and faith in a fragile charisma in favor of a more democratic mandate and greater organizational clout. That decision is now bearing fruit in Mandela's extraordinarily high prestige and influence within the organization.

The moral stature of its leader notwithstanding, it was in the organizational arena that the self-declared "premier organisation of the oppressed and democratic majority" faced major gaps.[1] Having taken for granted its mass support, the ANC hierarchy gradually woke up to the harsh reality of a fragmented, confused, and skeptical constituency. So disappointing was the first ANC recruitment drive that the organization initially refused to reveal membership figures. Total membership in June 1991 was given as 521,181, well below the

April target figure of 776,000. In contrast, the government minister in charge of constitutional negotiations boasted in all seriousness that the newly inclusive National Party could beat the ANC in a straight election contest. Granted, Gerrit Viljoen may have been engaging in wishful thinking—or perhaps he placed his trust in the manipulative power of the government-oriented television monopoly, whose immense influence on attitudes is still vastly underrated by the opposition.

The ANC certainly did not fare as well as expected. South African politics remains far from a marketplace where groups may compete on equal terms. However, many of the ANC's dilemmas cannot be reduced to weak institutional support for people whose main political qualifications were suffering and commitment in the past. Some problems were of the ANC's own making, the result of ideological contradictions and dubious policy decisions. The ANC argues that it has to remain a liberation movement rather than becoming a political party "because Apartheid is not yet gone."[2] However, there are other advantages to being a liberation movement, regardless of apartheid. Several foreign donors do not fund political parties. A liberation movement can continue to define itself as a broad alliance, while an ANC political party would obviously have to separate from the South African Communist Party. At the same time, though, defining itself as an ideologically heterogeneous liberation movement spares the organization from developing specific policies, since it cannot risk a split. Instead, it must rely more on symbols and myths, of which the notion of Africanization and the image of the defeated enemy are prime examples.[3]

The symbolic Africanization of the ANC, however, hampered its support among other ethnic groups, who either stayed on the political sidelines or looked to the government for protection from a feared black majority domination. At the 1991 Durban National Congress, Mandela acknowledged that the ANC could ill afford to be content with its low level of success in attracting whites, Coloureds, and Indians. "We must ask ourselves frankly why this is so . . . confront the real issue that these national minorities might have fears about the future," Mandela warned. The ANC had to remain a movement representative of all the people of South Africa, both in name and in reality.

Mandela's commonsense emphasis on minority representation runs counter to the colorblind nonracialism of the ANC. For example, while Allan Boesak or Mac Maharaj publicly announce that they are unwilling to represent Coloureds or Indians in the ANC, Mandela's sense of political reality leads him to stress the opposite. In Mandela's old-fashioned recognition of ethnicity, "the ordinary man, no matter to what population group he belongs, must look at our structures and see that 'I, as a coloured man, am represented. I have got Allan Boesak there whom I trust.' And an Indian must also be able to say: 'There is Kathrada—I am represented.' And the whites must say: 'There is Gerrit Viljoen—I have got representation' " (*The Star,* July 18, 1991). The racial representation that Mandela advocates constitutes a dramatic departure from the official doctrine of color-blind nonracialism hitherto propagated by the ANC. Were Mandela's views followed literally, the ANC would embrace the previous National Party policy of group representation, paradoxically at the very moment when the old racist party has foresworn any reference to race or ethnicity in its constitutional blueprints.

Yet the pragmatic balancing of ethnicity in the parties and executives of a plural society is required by a political reality that is still largely perceived in ethnic terms, perhaps as much by the ruled as by the rulers. Mandela realistically senses this culture of ethnic perceptions, but he prescribes an unsuccessful remedy. In his noble attempt to avoid racial polarization and build a broad, ethnically diverse movement, he overlooks the fact that the non-African ANC members are not considered community representatives precisely because they have long disassociated themselves from their ethnicity by embracing ANC-style nonracialism.

Indeed, among the fifty elected members of the ANC's National Executive Committee are seven whites, seven Indians, and seven Coloureds. In terms of statistics, then, the latter two groups are over-represented in the ANC leadership, the Indians in particular. However, they do not represent "the Indian community"; they are not active in the ANC as Indians but as marginalized dissidents from the Indian community. They rejected the primacy of their Indianness long ago in favor of nonracial individualism. NEC and SACP member Mac Maharaj stated explicitly that he does not wish to be referred to as an Indian: he considers himself a third-generation South African, does not know any Indian language, and finds his only link to his Indian origin in a fondness for curry. Although most Indian South Africans share this political acculturation, they would nevertheless remain suspicious of Maharaj's rejection of his cultural background. In short, the "Indian" representatives among the ANC officeholders are the wrong Indians as far as attracting support from the Indian sector is concerned. Similar perceptions of Coloured and white NEC members are held by their respective communities.

The whites on the NEC are all self-confessed members of the SACP and longtime political activists who have fought bitterly against the predominant attitudes among their ethnic peers. While the sophisticated tolerance of an Albie Sachs attracts admiration among liberal whites, the actions of someone like Ronny Kasrils—his unconventional behavior, the manipulative games he plays—serve to deter other whites from supporting the ANC. In fact, the state television network seems deliberately to put characters like Kasrils on its programs in order to discredit the ANC.

Perhaps the most amazing feature of the 1991 NEC is the total absence of liberal whites who have fought the anti-apartheid struggle inside the country in sympathy with the ANC. The ANC made no effort to woo into its ranks some of its potential high-profile supporters, people like F. van Zyl Slabbert, Alex Boraine, or Wynand Malan, who enjoy great popularity among anti-apartheid whites. The SACP faction, which in the past exercised the power of vetoing which whites were allowed to join the ANC, does not wish to share its monopoly with strategists of a different ideological outlook. A few white Members of Parliament switched from the Democratic Party to the ANC in 1992, but their very move alienated them from their former constituency. They were not influential public figures in the first place; nor have they risen in the ANC hierarchy or determined the ANC's image for the non-African public.

As in many political organizations, longtime activism on behalf of the party as a foot soldier is ranked higher than expertise or appeal to voters. Candidates have to earn their mandate through long service, or suffering. However, as long as the ANC has no prominent liberal minority members among its officeholders, it is unlikely to make any inroads into skeptical (as opposed to hostile) minorities. Ironically, the previously racist National Party, particularly if it bills itself as a "Christian Democratic law-and-order, free-market alliance," may turn out to be the most nonracial grouping by attracting widespread support from security-conscious conservatives across the racial spectrum.

Public opinion polls show that the ANC-SACP has failed to attract supporters from the three minority ethnic groups (see Table 1). Although black support for the National Party increased between 1991 and 1992, it remains quite weak. The most dramatic change since 1990

TABLE 1.   ESTIMATED VOTING PREFERENCES
ACCORDING TO RACE, 1991 AND 1992

Racial Group	Percentage of Electorate	ANC-SACP			National Party		
		May 91 %	*Oct 91* %	*July 92* %	*May 91* %	*Oct 91* %	*July 92* %
Africans	72.3	46	68	56	3	6	7
Indians	2.8	8	8	4	27	52	59
Coloureds	8.8	3	7	11	47	53	62
Whites	16.1	1	3	1	56	49	53

Sources. Nationwide HSRC polls; Lawrence Schlemmer, *Indicator South Africa* 9, no. 4, Spring 1992, p. 13; Rory Riordan, *South Africa Foundation Review*, October 1992, p. 8.

has been the massive support for the National Party among Coloureds and Indians, which in July 1992 exceeded white support for the ruling party. The National Party being accepted as the political home for these two minorities is surprising for several reasons: during elections for the tricameral parliament, Indians and Coloureds overwhelmingly (80 percent) boycotted the event; besides declaring itself nonracial, the National Party has not changed its program, name, Afrikaner symbolism, or high-profile personnel in any way in order to appeal to Coloured or Indian voters. Therefore, it is clearly the fear of ANC domination and Africanization that drives minority voters into the orbit of the National Party. The party may even have additional potential appeal for African voters as the guarantor of law and order. In a survey of 3,500 Africans, 35 percent responded that they "feel close" to the National Party (Schlemmer, *Indicator South Africa*, Spring 1992, p. 13). Although Mandela, de Klerk and Buthelezi all lost support during the squabbling over negotiations, the lineup at the end of 1992 is approximately ANC, 45 percent; NP, 25 percent; PAC, 5 percent, Inkatha, 10 percent; CP, 5 percent; Democratic Party and others, 5 percent.

QUESTIONING THE ANC-SACP ALLIANCE

A strange discrepancy exists between the reaction of liberal, nonsocialist anti-apartheid activists in South Africa and their counterparts in the international anti-apartheid movement. Foreign supporters of the ANC hardly ever mention the ANC's alliance with the South African Communist Party, while South African liberal democrats are greatly concerned about the influence of the SACP in a future ANC government. Foreign activists, however, either ignore these anxieties or dismiss them as red-baiting or relics of the cold war. Yet Oxford political scientist R. W. Johnson has rightly called attention to the success of the SACP in setting the agenda for the anti-apartheid forces worldwide: "Bolstered by Eastern bloc financial and political support, the SACP became the paymasters and organisers of the ANC in exile, effortlessly colonising anti-apartheid 'support organisations' in many countries, and dictating terms to non-Communist sympathisers such as the World Council of Churches, trade unions, student organisations, U.N. agencies and so forth."[4] Johnson, who is considered to be on the British Left, would certainly be criticized for this view by those who do not feel that they were duped by the SACP and who supported the anti-apartheid cause without consulting mentors. However, he correctly stresses the influence of the growing and committed group, which has some twenty-five thousand members.

Inside South Africa, the ANC's alliance with the SACP constitutes probably the single most important reason why so few whites, Coloureds, and Indians have formally joined the ANC, even though their ideological sympathies and hopes for the future lie with that organization.[5] Peter Brown, a victim of state persecution, a sterling liberal of long standing, and a close associate of Alan Paton, has perhaps most clearly articulated these concerns in his journal *Reality*. The SACP is a separate party with separate policies within the ANC, and, as Brown observes, "it has not been SACP policy in the past for its members to leave their convictions and their practices outside the door when they join another organisation." Brown thus asks whether the "high proportion of what seem to be members of the SACP on the new ANC national executive committee" does not mean that the ANC as a whole is influenced in the SACP direction (*Reality*, July 1991). Indeed, the more the ANC becomes a normal political party, the hollower sounds the standard answer—that the Communists are only loyal members of a liberation movement from which they take orders. When the same personnel serve crucial roles in both parties, either their policies have merged or the one is using the other for its own ends. At issue is not only the economic vision of self-proclaimed Marxist-Leninists but also the commitment to multiparty democracy and the tolerance of political dissent.

As Idasa executive director Alex Boraine has pointed out, voters

have a right to know whom they voted for and the specifics of the
policies a candidate supports. However, this will not be possible if the
ANC and the SACP continue to fuse their images. "It is in the interest
of both the ANC and perhaps the SACP to have a very clear distinction between them because the current alliance will inevitably come
back to haunt them" (*Cape Times,* July 10, 1991).

The government, too, perceives problems with the SACP. As long
as the ANC-SACP alliance exists, a genuine NP-ANC coalition government of national unity will be resisted by sections of the National
Party, because of potential objections from the right wing. Simply put,
the government makes itself vulnerable to the accusation of having
allowed Communists into the halls of power. Such a perception gives
the right wing a major boost and could trigger more terrorist acts,
quite apart from the fact that it works to delegitimize the historic
compromise among whites more generally. Pretoria would therefore
want to see the ANC-SACP marriage end as soon as possible after the
first election. At the same time, in the first democratic election campaign, a nonracial coalition led by the National Party could also
greatly benefit from the ANC-SACP alliance. The association of the
ANC with the Communists would deter conservative black voters
from supporting the ANC, while permitting the National Party to
parade itself as the guardian of religion and free enterprise.

SACP strategists, who piggyback their socialist vision onto the
populist ANC, do not see the propagandistic benefits that this alliance
grants their mutual adversary. Instead, they elevate the alliance into
a great threat, of which the government is supposedly very afraid. In
the words of Jeremy Cronin, "What the regime most fears, and with
good reason, is the combination of a working-class political party
with a relatively large following (the SACP), and a massive national
liberation movement."[6] The West European model of a capital-
oriented conservative party ("Christian Democrats") and a labor-
oriented social-democratic ANC sharing the political center in
roughly equal measure would marginalize the Communists, relegating
them to the same status as fringe parties on the Right. Therefore,
Cronin quite logically insists on "a broad national democratic front,
and not a charade of a west European democracy." The need for such
a broad united front is justified by the task of overcoming three
centuries of underdevelopment, which can be accomplished only
through democratization in conjunction with "the socialist project."
In contrast to the feasible social-democratic vision of reformed capi-

talism stands the SACP vision of a historically discredited socialism which denies emphatically that such socialism would impede both economic development and democratic competition in the post-Marxist reality of South Africa in the 1990s.

In its own eyes, the ANC leadership made its peace with business long ago. However, it has in fact failed to communicate its social-democratic program convincingly, allowing the specter of Marxism and the fear of expropriation in a command economy to impede much-needed economic growth. Even sober liberal analysts abroad take the ambiguity of the ANC's economic stance and its alliance with the SACP as serious threats. For example, under the heading "South Africa Not for the Squeamish," an editorial in one British paper commented: "The biggest single question continues to be the attitude of the African National Congress to private ownership. Marxism may be a dying creed in Eastern Europe, but it is alive and well in the ANC, which remains formally committed to nationalisation of leading companies" (*The Independent,* September 4, 1991). Thus, the ANC is faced with a predicament. If it openly declared its accommodation with capitalism, it would lose major sections of its radical constituency; however, if it played the card of socialist rhetoric much longer, it would not attract the essential investment to enable it to deliver on even a minimum of the high economic expectations. Instead, the cultivated ideological ambiguity of the ANC, the contradictory signals it emitted, contributed to the further deterioration of an already weakened economy, in part by foreclosing on the option that the negotiations could be legitimized by material gains. At the same time, the lack of political education among black South Africans did nothing to alleviate the anxieties of much-needed investors with access to risk capital.

Mandela has repeatedly affirmed the ANC's close cooperation with its long-standing SACP ally. In an interview with Stanley Uys, Mandela declared: "We don't think that we have been persuaded to feel that there is something wrong in the alliance. I don't think that we could ever be persuaded to put an end to that alliance" (*The Star,* July 18, 1991). If the ANC were to push for a separation now, before the new constitution is accepted, the split would not only deprive the ANC of many leading activists but would divide the movement along ideological lines. This dilemma is largely responsible for the ANC's reluctance to transform itself from a broad liberation movement into a political party espousing precise economic policies.

Who or what, then, is the SACP? How serious a political and intellectual force is the group in the aftermath of the cold war? Is the party a band of unreformed Stalinists? Or a collection of reluctant social democrats? What does it mean to be a communist after the collapse of the communist metropole?

Few political groups are as misunderstood and misrepresented as the SACP. While in the past the South African government regularly painted the SACP as militant, KGB-led terrorists, the American press has characterized them as "not of the Gorbachev stripe but more along the lines of fire-breathing Trotsky of yesteryear" (*The Wall Street Journal*, February 5, 1990). If anything, however, the SACP has been influenced more by Trotsky's main opponent, Stalin. Until 1989 the party regularly endorsed Soviet policy and criticized its detractors as "childish Trotskyist ultra-leftists" or "ghetto-nationalists."

The alliance between the ANC and SACP makes the strategic logic of South African communists particularly important for the future of democracy. Joe Slovo, the former SACP general secretary, is Mandela's right-hand man in the negotiations. Most leading members of the ANC's National Executive Committee are self-declared communists. Only in the apartheid state does the hammer and sickle proudly fly at mass rallies. Francis Fukuyama may naively proclaim the end of history because the "principles of liberal capitalism have won" and "cannot be improved upon,"[7] but as long as gross inequality and the historical exclusion of the majority persist, all hopes that Eastern Europe's embrace of capitalism will prove infectious in South Africa will remain wishful thinking. The director of Anglo-American, Michael O'Dowd, may invoke the recent mass retreat from socialism or "the stifling of initiative and progress implicit in Slovo's hatred of profits,"[8] but the dream of greater equality and nonexploitation is fueled rather than stifled by Anglo-American monopolies. This reality gives the SACP's pronouncements a special importance, its quaint orthodoxy and discredited Stalinist past notwithstanding. The end of state socialism, many argue, heralds the future of democratic socialism in South Africa.

South African socialists, like their comrades elsewhere on the continent, face the problem that socialist decolonization has met only with failure; there are no successes to emulate. In Zimbabwe socialist forces were subjugated to the national struggle, the unions eventually becoming as emasculated as they had been under the Smith regime, despite the Marxist rhetoric of the state. After national liberation,

socialism in Angola and Mozambique became entrenched in an official Marxist state agenda, but it proved as disastrous an economic
failure as it was for their East European sponsors. Neither Zimbabwe
nor Angola nor Mozambique, let alone the "market Stalinism" of
China or the one-party dictatorship of Castro, can therefore serve
South Africa as a model for socialist transformation, quite apart from
the differing economic bases of the countries in question.

Slovo has made the first attempt to shed the ideological ballast of
a Stalinist past and to come to grips with his party's role in supporting
Stalinism.[9] But Slovo's rather partial description of Stalinism does not
go nearly far enough in criticizing a tyrannical system whose terrors
are akin to those of fascism as well as of apartheid. Moreover, he fails
to recognize the intrinsic causes of Stalinist tyranny, since he blames
human error rather than fundamental Leninist tenets. But the Leninist
notion of a "vanguard party" possessed of "moral superiority" remains incompatible with liberal equality. Even if the vanguard role
must be earned rather than assumed, as Slovo now realizes, commitment per se is no criterion of truth or higher morality.

The exclusivity of SACP membership is rationalized on the grounds
that the party wants only tested and committed activists, not opportu-
nists or deadwood on whom the leadership cannot rely. In practice,
this has given rise to a self-styled elite within the opposition movement. SACP members are credited with a higher consciousness and a
deeper insight into political reality. In Mac Maharaj's definition of the
vanguard, "Its selectivism is to ensure that those who say they want
to join the Party come to a higher level of consciousness at the level
of activism and at the level of understanding the political realities."[10]
It is, however, the party hierarchy, rather than adherence to any
particular theory, that determines what constitutes "correct consciousness." Maharaj despises the "ultra-Left," dismissing them as
"armchair theorists." He urges his leftist critics to "move to a constructive mode of thinking and acting" if they do not wish to disap-
pear as chaff "into the dustbins of history." In Maharaj's Leninist
vision, ultra-leftists will have to abandon their "puritanical forms of
principles in the furnace of struggle" and emerge, like the communists, as "steel." Not even the handpicked members of the Broederbond are expected automatically to display such "steeled" loyalty to
the cause of the *Volk*. Only after a six-month probation period of
supervised study and activism can a potential comrade be admitted to
the SACP.

Yet an elite group may be needed to discipline and educate a vast pool of undereducated and brutalized youth. Furthermore, for sheer self-protection the party may have to be selective about potential members, who might otherwise threaten the leadership, upset the cohesion, and discredit the party by questionable actions carried out in the name of communism. Those problems already constitute the negative side of the ANC's open membership policy, problems for which the organization has found no answer other than futile exhortations for better political education. Since the ANC has yet to develop an effective pragmatic strategy for politicization, almost by default it is the SACP that provides political guidance and organizational clout.

During the period when the ANC was illegal, its organizational vacuum was obscured by the emphasis on underground structures. The government's exaggeration of the clandestine ANC-SACP threat, on the one hand, and, on the other, the activists' wish to believe themselves a threat encouraged both antagonists in the same illusion. One of the most surprising revelations since the normalization of South African politics in February 1990 has been how little the opposition is in fact prepared to assume its self-proclaimed role. Mandela's virtual deification after his release, together with his undisputed role as leader, can rightly be explained only in the context of an organizational and ideological vacuum, hidden behind the myth of a mass democratic movement. As many critics have pointed out, neither its mass nor its democratic character should be accepted at face value.

STALINISM RECONSIDERED

During an interview in 1988 Slovo admitted that the SACP was part of a cult of personality worship. "I was defending the Stalinist trials of the thirties." To his credit, he does not plead ignorance, as so many other converts from tyrannical regimes often do. "It's not that we did not know what was going on, but we just rejected whatever evidence was produced and rationalised our way out of it. . . . It resulted in a defence in principle of everything Russia did both domestically and internationally."[11] Indeed, the party that in 1929 was told by the Kremlin to campaign for a black republic in South Africa subsequently supported the Soviet invasions of Hungary (1956), Czechoslovakia (1968), and Afghanistan. Long after Arthur Koestler's seminal account of the show trials in *Darkness at Noon* (1945), long after most European intellectuals on the left had grown disillusioned with the

Soviet Union, long after Eurocommunism and Solzhenitsyn, the SACP's solidarity with the Soviet Union remained unshaken.

Only a few months before the collapse of the East European client states in 1989, the SACP adopted a program that stated: "Socialist countries today represent a powerful international force. Some of them possess highly developed economies, a considerable scientific base, and a reliable military defence potential. . . . A new way of life is taking shape in which there are neither oppressors nor the oppressed, neither exploiters nor the exploited, in which power belongs to the people."[12] How can a people with such an acute sense of the injustice that prevails in their homeland become so blind to oppression elsewhere? The admirable early commitment of South African communists to the cause of liberation has fed on this self-definition of the SACP as the guardian of a universal political and economic rationality, of which the Soviet Union was considered the first realization.[13]

Although the SACP was never an offshoot of the Soviet Communist Party, its intention to root itself as an African communist party acquired momentum only with the collapse of the party in Moscow. The reaction of the South African communists to Gorbachev's abolition of the party bordered on the frivolous; it refused to draw historical lessons. In the opinion of the SACP's Essop Pahad: "If you lose your mother you cry and bury her, but you don't jump into the grave with her" (Financial Mail, August 30, 1991). Pahad argues that events in the Soviet Union merely confirmed what the SACP has believed all along: "You can't build socialism in an undemocratic society." As his critics point out, though, the SACP somehow managed to keep this belief very quiet. Pahad further maintains that "it is true that we were often in common agreement with the party in Moscow, but we didn't take our line from it." If past SACP policy was indeed based on independent judgment rather than on necessity, however, it makes the fault that much worse.

Concurrently, an editorial in the anti-apartheid, pro-ANC Weekly Mail offered a rare frank criticism: "It is deeply shaming to reflect that the South African liberation movement—not just the SACP but the ANC too—could uncritically support a system so dehumanising and so lacking in the qualities that the movement espouses in South Africa" (August 30–September 6, 1991). For fear of seeming to join the government's anticommunist hysteria, the independent alternative press and the democratic South African Left in general failed to elaborate the Weekly Mail's point and reprimand the movement about its dubious ideological baggage. Slovo now claims that he had his personal doubts since the mid-1950s. However, he remained silent on the subject, and the party continued to endorse subsequent Stalinist practices. When pressed as to why, Slovo can only answer in terms of expedience: "It became almost risky and counterproductive to battle this issue out in our Party. It would have caused an enormous split, and it had less and less bearing on our own work" (*Die Suid-Afrikaan,* February 19, 1989). That opportunism could shape policy, and on such a vital issue, disproves Slovo's current claim that internal democracy has always existed in the SACP. If the party could not take a principled position on Stalinist crimes for fear of a split (or, more likely, for fear of being denied Soviet assistance), then its internal debates on relatively peripheral issues are reduced to meaningless distractions.

Given the political goal of effectively opposing apartheid but the ethical necessity of denouncing Stalinism, the SACP was obviously in a predicament. The Soviet Union construed any criticism as disloyalty. Under these circumstances, had the SACP taken a public stance against its sole sponsor, it would have found itself cut off from financial and military assistance. In the absence of alternative sources of support, the SACP would have condemned itself to organizational ineffectiveness and political paralysis, which would in turn have jeopardized the very purpose for which the Party was formed: the liberation of South Africa. Faced with such a dilemma, the Party opted for organizational clout rather than morality—perhaps understandably, although the choice of expediency over ethics must be difficult to rationalize for a party that claims to possess moral superiority.

The issue, however, is not whether members of the SACP made the wrong choice in favoring politics over morality. The real question is whether the party overstepped the bounds of political necessity and in fact enthusiastically endorsed Stalinist practices. There is considerable evidence that this was indeed the case. The majority of party members identified with Soviet strategy as politically desirable and ethically justifiable. They glorified and romanticized the Soviet Union, defending it against all criticism. In so doing, they also discredited the anti-apartheid cause. For adopting this politically foolish, but above all morally reprehensible position, the party ought to be held responsible, just as former supporters of apartheid should not now be let off the hook with the lame excuse that the grand experiment has failed. Association with a criminal system characterizes both antagonists, although they had different motives.

To be sure, there was also some internal dissent. Some party members left with a troubled conscience; others were purged by the Stalinists themselves. As an individual, Slovo cannot be equated with the organization. Yet the record shows that, in all its public and official pronouncements, the party spoke with one Stalinist voice. Party publications did not reflect any debate—not even slight qualms—about taking a stance that had become, at the very least, greatly taboo.

There is now a new myth emerging that has whites joining the SACP for the noble cause of fighting apartheid rather than advancing socialism. As George Fredrickson put it: "Many of the whites who joined the Communist Party seem to have done so more because they hoped to prevent race war and to achieve a racially integrated and egalitarian South Africa than out of support for the Soviet Union or even for a proletarian revolution."[14] Fredrickson here chooses to overlook the fact that only a small percentage of party members are white. Nor does his statement sufficiently attend to the possibility that committed Communists might very well have a dual motive, seeing in the ascendancy of the Soviet Union and of socialism the most effective way to defeat South African racism. There is ample evidence, however, that whatever the initial motivation for joining the party, it was frequently soon overshadowed by the advocacy of Soviet policy—sometimes at the expense of the goal of an egalitarian South Africa, since the Soviet doctrine of "socialism in one country" subjected all local concerns to the overriding interests of Moscow. The SACP's submission to all Soviet foreign policy decisions is in fact clearly documented in the party's publications. Not only did the party invariably and uncritically accept this submission to its sponsor—even on such controversial issues as the Hitler-Stalin pact—but party publications and resolutions consistently endorsed and defended Soviet imperialism, while inveighing militantly against its Western counterpart.

The SACP's initial rejection of South Africa's entry into World War II offers a good example. The party denounced South Africa as exhibiting the worst kind of fascism, which should be fought at home rather than in Europe on the side of the Western imperialists; one editorialist for the party organ declared in June 1940 that he "would rather be a Jew in Hitler Berlin than a Native in Johannesburg."[15] It was only after Hitler attacked the Soviet Union in June 1941 that the Party changed its antiwar stance. "Accordingly," a party historian writes, "the Party launched a series of dynamic campaigns to transform South Africa's contribution to the Allied war effort in accordance with the potentialities."[16]

The question remains: Can the Communists' dedication to the anti-apartheid cause, the suffering they endured like no other group, and the bravery they showed obliterate their simultaneous political foolishness and moral culpability in supporting Stalinism? The tendency is now to forgive and forget, to excuse past failings in light of other achievements. Thus, in a review of Baruch Hirson's bitter Trotskyite critique of his Stalinist comrades, Jeremy Kridler concludes: "Whatever their involvement in expulsions of Party members and despite their subservience to the Moscow line, what they strove and bravely fought for threatened a racist and authoritarian state. And in the last analysis, this—not the shoddy, Moscow-induced politics in which they sometimes engaged—is their legacy" (*Weekly Mail,* June 22, 1990). However, assuming human rights are indeed universal, the anti-apartheid struggle, no matter how noble and dedicated, cannot turn a blind eye to violations of human rights elsewhere. Expedient silence destroys credibility. As long as the party does not come to terms intellectually with its errors, its support for one of the worst tyrannies will invalidate its egalitarian claims. The Stalinist past haunts the democratic future.

One striking feature of the renewed debate over socialism versus capitalism in the wake of Eastern European developments is the emphasis both protagonists place on performance. Slovo goes beyond a sterile comparison of output but still cannot resist praising the Soviet Union for its cultural and material achievements: "There are more graduate engineers than in the U.S., more graduate research scientists than in Japan and more medical doctors per head than in Western Europe. It also produces more steel, fuel, and energy than any other country. How many capitalist countries can match the achievements of most of the socialist world in the provision of social security, child care, the ending of cultural backwardness and so on? There is certainly no country in the world which can beat Cuba's record in the sphere of health care."[17]

Even if these statistics were taken at face value, one would have to ask what they mean in broader terms. The former Soviet Union is the only industrialized society in which life expectancy is declining. The country has to import food and, despite its large number of graduates or its level of steel production, it lacks basic consumer goods. Cuba may have the best health system, but it also quarantines anyone diagnosed with AIDS. Finally, what does "ending of cultural backwardness" really mean, when after seventy years of socialism a country like the Soviet Union is racked by ethnic riots, religious intolerance, and anti-Semitism? As Western Europe denationalizes, the socialist East renationalizes, and with the worst kind of nineteenth-century chauvinism. How is "cultural backwardness" to be measured?

All the same, while the rest of the world is celebrating with the oppressed Eastern European populations the downfall of corrupt regimes, the editor of *The African Communist,* Brian Bunting, regrets the new search for democratic socialism that the liberalization in Eastern Europe has made possible: "The disappearance of the communist governments of Eastern Europe has been an undeniable setback to the liberation movement" (*New Nation,* June 22, 1990). In true cold war fashion, he equates "the threat to the Soviet Union, Cuba and other communist governments" with "the domination of imperialism."

For other members of the SACP, the collapse of the communist movement merely represents a process of "cleansing." One editorial in *The African Communist* (no. 121, 1990) reiterated the SACP's goals: "to establish a socialist republic in South Africa based on the principles of Marxism-Leninism, to promote the ideas of proletarian internationalism and the unity of the workers of South Africa." As the same editorial makes clear, the party is quite capable of defiantly closing its eyes to Eastern Europe: "Nothing that has happened in Eastern Europe or elsewhere makes us believe that this perspective (Marxism-Leninism) needs to be altered." As if cocooned in a dream world, in 1989 the party's Congress declared that "the advances of the socialist countries inspire the working people throughout the world." Such dogmatic statements simply refuse to acknowledge that events in Eastern Europe have discredited the socialist idea generally.

A last example of the ANC-SACP's relationship with Honecker's German Democratic Republic (GDR) further illustrates the problematic attitude of the ANC toward dictatorships. Long after this embarrassing "socialist" model mercifully passed into history and long after its domestic oppression had been exposed in all its lurid details, the official ANC journal *Sechaba* in its last issue, published in December 1990, celebrated with a front-page picture of Honecker and an editorial about the cordial ANC-GDR relations. The ANC writer bemoans "the loss the liberation movement has suffered with the disappearance of the German Democratic Republic as we knew it, and the emergence of a new Germany." The ANC author in all earnestness asserts that "*Sechaba* was printed voluntarily by GDR workers" in what was the state-owned and Stasi-controlled "Erich Weinert" printing press. Without noticing the contradiction that for the first time the workers could really make a voluntary decision after the disappearance of their regime, *Sechaba* explains that "the new conditions under which our supporters have to operate do not allow direct assistance . . . , such as we have been receiving all along, to be given." The ANC blames "capitalist competition" because now the plant "must give all its available time to this competition." Any student press in a basement could have typeset and printed the thin "official organ of the ANC" during a few overtime hours, if they were really committed. But far more serious moral issues arise from this false lament.

The SACP and the ANC have yet to question the morality of accepting support from a dictatorship, be it the GDR, Libya, China, or Cuba. It could be argued that American foundation money is also tainted by slavery and imperialism, or that even pious Scandinavian or Canadian government grants are ultimately derived from workers' exploitation. But at least these donors do not impose their will on their subjects, who can get rid of them if they disagree strongly. In this respect, donations to the ANC indeed are based on consent of the people. The East German, Chinese, or Libyan citizen has no choice or say in who their executives are, how their taxes are spent, or how they are collected. This remains the essential difference between a democratic and a criminal autocracy. Even if no support is available from the right side, is it therefore justifiable to align oneself with the criminal camp? No church, charity, or other worthy cause, no matter how much in dire straits, could knowingly accept money from the Mafia without discrediting its own cause. Yet the ANC has for decades known about the undemocratic privileges of an East European nomenclatura in the midst of the misery of its people. ANC representatives themselves had the luxuries of a socialist elite showered on them and willingly participated in their prescribed role. The East German ANC representative even went hunting with Honecker, who cunningly subsidized *Sechaba* in return for praise by a universally acclaimed liberation movement. Yet it never occurred to the South African exiles that by accepting "fraternal solidarity" from such a dubious source they also ignored the plight of the oppressed in East Germany, let alone that they harmed their own goal of establishing democracy through association and praise for dictatorships. To this day, most ANC leaders would find such moral reasoning odd and mischievous. They instead argue pragmatically that they had no choice but to take money, regardless of the sponsor's record, if they wanted their organization to survive.

The concern for the democratic Left must now be what life is left of "Marxism" after being espoused for decades by the Honeckers, Castros, or Mugabes of this world. As indeed has been argued by many democratic socialists, if Marxism or any critical counterforce against an unfettered, triumphant capitalism is to be retrieved, it has everything to gain from being thus "discredited." By reappropriating the original Marxism from its Leninist and Stalinist detractors, the democratic Left faces a unique historic opportunity to develop alternatives free of the bureaucratic coercion of "really existing socialism." Instead, a pedestrian ANC-SACP mourns the breakdown of its own chains, because it lost a printing press in the process! The Eastern European transformations in 1989 constitute the most fundamental change in the world since the French revolution two hundred years earlier. What does it say about the state of mind of a liberation movement and an allied Communist Party that it laments the event, not to speak of comprehending it?

Slovo defines Stalinism as "socialism without democracy." When discussing its failings, he repeatedly refers to "distortions" from the top. In other words, it was pilot error, not the plane's structure, that was responsible for the crash. And even the pilot's faults are referred to euphemistically. Ruthless purges—such as the systematic killing, before the German invasion, of substantial sections of the Russian officer corps by a paranoid clique—are described as "damage wrought to the whole Soviet social fabric (including its army) by the authoritarian bureaucracy." There is no comprehension of Stalinism as "internal colonialism," akin to apartheid.

Slovo's use of the phrase "judicial distortions" is tantamount to a rationalization of the show trials: by merely deploring the excesses of Stalinism, it leaves the principle intact. Had Stalin killed a few million people less—even if he had killed only one comrade—it would still be a crime. Yet nowhere in Slovo's account does one find an adequate explanation for the Stalinist holocaust, let alone moral outrage. Instead, the SACP chairman attempts to distance himself from an embarrassing past and to deflect attention from his failure to examine the causes of the Stalinist tyranny onto one of the unfortunate consequences of that tyranny: the discrediting of socialism. Accurate nam-

ing, rather than metaphor and euphemism, remains crucial to understand and overcome a criminal past.[18] Stalinism's primary fault was
not that it ended up discrediting socialism. Slovo's laudatory attempt
to reflect critically on Stalinism ultimately fails, because he does not
draw the obvious connections.

Almost alone on the left, Frederick Johnstone insists that the Gulag
is about apartheid, that Auschwitz is about Cambodia. "It is certainly
no accident that even now, by the end of the twentieth century, the
horrendous fact that the human toll of Stalinism exceeded Nazi crimes
against humanity remains greatly unreflected upon in its deeper implications. Or that many on the Left would dismiss any attempt to think
about the Leninist state in terms of the apartheid state."[19] But, as
Johnstone rightly reminds us, the victims of Auschwitz, the Gulags,
and apartheid are not concerned in whose name they were killed or
maimed.

The apartheid labor system compares almost favorably with the
Leninist system that prohibits independent trade unions. Both combat
idleness. But forced labor cloaked in rhetoric about discipline for the
people's cause is worse, because of its pretenses. In the original Marx-
ian vision, alienated labor was to be abolished, Leninists glorifying
higher productivity as the patriotic duty of selfless brigades. The
apartheid laborer at least knows of his exploitation; he complies only
grudgingly, because there is no alternative. But in addition to exploiting them, the Leninists and Stalinists betrayed their victims. This
explains the magnitude of the fury for revenge when those victims
were set free. Blacks in South Africa, in contrast, have always known
that racial rule was for the benefit of the ruling race. That rule now
drawing to a close, they do not feel cheated as hardworking Communist Party members did when the luxurious corruption of the people's
representatives was finally revealed. Hence, rather than wanting to
turn the tables, most blacks merely desire their proper share.

Slovo reiterates the scientific nature of Marxism. It is a "revolutionary science" or a "social science whose fundamental postulates and
basic insights into the historical processes remain a powerful (because
accurate) theoretical weapon." The insistence on the scientific nature
of historical processes, which can only be established by positivistic
methods, has long been abandoned by most historians and critical
theorists, who instead stress the hermeneutic, interpretive task of
analysts. In this view, the very term social *science* is a misnomer,
inasmuch as it assumes that human behavior is predetermined by laws

similar to those in the natural sciences that can be verified or disproved by some objective method, whether Marxist or otherwise. But such a postulate denies human agency and the essential open-endedness of history. It usually results in a crude reductionism or an economistic approach that neglects the fact that people have not only material interests but ideals as well. The infinitely varied subjectivity through which people perceive, interpret, and act on their world cannot be reduced to an epiphenomenon, the powerful attraction of materialist rationality notwithstanding. Individuals are more than agents of interests.

Slovo restates the central tenets of "Marxist revolutionary science," namely, that the class struggle is the motor of human history, that "all morality is class-related," and that "working class internationalism" is the most liberating concept. Who, however, are "the people"? What is the "working class"? Who is the "society as a whole" that, according to Slovo, should assume control? In the context of the South African debate of democrats against Leninists, Mervyn Frost has rightly called attention to a point made at the turn of the century by Robert Michels and later documented by Max Weber. "In modern states control by society as a whole means in practice bureaucratic rule," Michels wrote. "Those who say organisation inevitably say oligarchy." As Frost argues, oligarchic tendencies can only be counteracted from below, by a democratic culture, not by Leninist "democratization from above."[20]

Like Marx, Slovo hypostatizes an abstract working class. But the real working class is comprised of blacks and whites, men and women, religious adherents and agnostics, homosexuals and heterosexuals, skilled and unskilled workers, all of whom live in urban or rural settings. Most important, there are the employed and the unemployed. By ignoring all these faultlines, the abstract concept of a working class misses the crucial social texture. Yet whether a group is or can become the leading force in a conflict depends as much on those differing social conditions as on common material interests.

To expect a group to feel solidarity because of shared exploitation is a long-standing illusion. Yet it is precisely on such a self-deception that the SACP bases its strategy. Working-class unity and solidarity have failed worldwide. Ever since the German social democrats voted for the Kaiser's war budget in 1914, the dream of internationalism has suffered repeated setbacks, although the idea has managed to retain an elusive attractiveness. In a crisis, organized labor will want to prove its patriotism, especially in the face of conservative accusations of disloyalty. Workers thus participate in nationalist euphorias in different political cultures as readily as their class antagonists—from the World Wars, to the Falkland conflict, to the Armenian-Azerbaijani clashes in the Soviet Union. External enemies defuse internal class conflicts (albeit only until the enemy is defeated). The split labor market that exists in most Western states—more expensive indigenous labor pitted against cheaper, more exploitable immigrant labor—proves an ideal situation in which to counteract union solidarity, let alone militancy. Ethnic divisions also undermine solidarity. Even so, working-class racism and chauvinism remain among the great taboos within the Left.

Given this record, it is all the more surprising that the dream of working-class unity lives on in the society whose white and black segments are politically and legally furthest apart. Because the economic recession also hurt the privileged white working class, the SACP argues, the prospect of a common struggle with black workers has arisen. "It is becoming clearer to sections of white workers, faced with growing impoverishment, that they have to stand up in the face of economic policies aimed at appeasing big business and strengthening the Apartheid regime." Despite the long tradition of evidence to the contrary, the South African Left continues to hope that resentment of big business by white workers will translate into common action with black unions. "This has opened up some possibilities for these workers to be drawn into struggle, and in action, to realise more clearly that their true interests lie with their fellow black workers and the democratic trade union movement."[21]

However, in the perennial conflict between common interests and nationalist-racist surrogates for class solidarity, it is futile to bank on the superior rationality of interests winning out. The symbolic satisfaction of belonging to an imagined community possessed of superior qualities easily defeats the potential real benefits of solidarity. The appeal to emotional rewards overpowers calculations based on material interests. Thus, rather than joining Cosatu or the ANC, the few remaining white workers flock to the neofascist AWB. Deep resentment over loss of status, especially in combination with immediate economic insecurity, drives its victims into the camp of those who long for the restoration of a lost past. That was one of the lessons of Nazi Germany, and also explains the resurgence of right-wing extremism.

By building its strategy on the prospect of a white-black working-class alliance, the SACP not only starts from a false assumption but also neglects to address an increasingly significant split in the labor movement: the competition between employed and unemployed. Neither the ANC nor Cosatu has devised a strategy to cope with the one-third to one-half of the national workforce that is permanently unemployed. Increasingly, unions represent only the employed. But mere employment in South Africa almost qualifies one for membership in a "labor aristocracy": having a job is already a mark of privilege. A whole range of opportunities, from access to housing and medical care to education and pensions, depends on employment. Those millions who live outside the formal economy—in the backyards of townships, in the shacks around the cities, in desolate huts in the barren countryside—form a permanent underclass. The liberation movements have yet to organize these permanently marginalized outsiders; unions have yet to address the relation between the employed and the totally deprived. With the ranks of the unemployed swelling, the state finds ready recruits for its various police forces; local warlords organize vigilante groups, drawing on a vast pool of resentment; puritan, fundamentalist church cults vie with drug peddlers and petty criminals for the souls and pockets of the downtrodden. Orthodox Marxism has traditionally written off this *Lumpenproletariat,* which constitutes a substantial section of the South African population.

WAVERING SOCIAL DEMOCRATS

The 1989 SACP program "The Path to Power" claims to be "guided by the theory of Marxism-Leninism" as well as its own and others' experiences of revolutionary struggle. Repeatedly invoking the "seizure of power" as its goal, it asserts: "We are not engaged in a struggle whose objective is merely to generate sufficient pressure to bring the other side to the negotiating table." Yet barely a year later the SACP was officially negotiating with "the enemy," and Chairman Slovo was assuring capital that only a mixed economy guarantees growth. He even declared that "the narrow issue of nationalisation is a bit of a red herring" (*Argus,* February 28, 1990). In Slovo's newly pragmatic assessment, the South African economy cannot be transformed "by edict without risking economic collapse." Instead of bureaucratic *state* control along Eastern European lines, Slovo now advocates *public* control through effective democratic participation by "producers at all levels." This amounts to a classic social-democratic program of codetermination, wherein large firms are held publicly accountable and union representatives sit on boards. Since such widely legitimate visions are also considered negotiable, little that resembles economic orthodoxy survives among former Leninists. The collapse of Eastern European state socialism has finally made an impact on some of its last, most fervent adherents.

Classical Leninism misled the SACP in its understanding of a totally changed constellation of interests. The SACP's orthodox world view prevented it from comprehending three crucial developments that did not conform to predetermined patterns. First, the ANC-SACP leadership was surprised by the active support that calls for sanctions received in the West, the reaction of Margaret Thatcher notwithstanding. In the SACP theory, Pretoria, as the outpost of imperialism, had been and always would be propped up by its international sponsors. Pressure on the apartheid regime would thus have to emanate primarily from progressive socialist and nonaligned countries. In fact, the opposite occurred. South African trade with African and various other Third World countries increased; diplomatic contacts between, for example, Pretoria and the former Soviet Union and East European states improved, while South Africa's relationship with the United States, Canada, Australia, and the EEC deteriorated—an eventuality that the SACP had not anticipated.

Second, these trends increased the need for Pretoria to seek a negotiated solution, particularly in the light of the loss of foreign investment capital, which now threatened to bypass South Africa in favor of Eastern Europe. Faced with benign neglect by its traditional allies as long as it failed to reach a political settlement, South Africa had to change course if it aspired to remain part of the global economy and avoid becoming another Albania. By its own admission, the SACP was caught off guard when it was legalized on February 2, 1990. After preparing thirty years for liberation, the ANC also found itself unprepared. Believing the ANC's propaganda about a fascist, racist enemy, most exiles never took seriously the warnings that their opponents might have the potential to adapt, to relinquish racism and modernize.[22] Lacking an adequate theory of the antagonist, the opposition wasted precious years pursuing ineffective strategies.

Finally, its slavish support for the Soviet Union made the SACP one of the last foreign parties to understand Eastern Europe. A worker's party that backed the Polish government against Solidarity, the SACP proved unable to sense the people's growing anger that would finally sweep East European rulers out of power. Deprived of Honecker's support, the SACP exiles suddenly found themselves searching for new international allies almost against their will. Despite its newly professed anti-Stalinism, the SACP held its 7th Congress in 1989 in one of the last Stalinist redoubts: Havana. Observers have interpreted this choice as "perhaps indicative of the schism between the SACP and CPSU" that perestroika and the flagging Soviet interest in regional confrontations with U.S. allies had brought about.[23]

Because SACP members are the major force in the theoretical debates within the broader apartheid opposition, the party's own practice of internal democracy influences the style of the entire movement. Whether the SACP's declarations of its support for democracy should be taken at face value or treated with skepticism is best tested by the behavior of the party itself. Will the SACP nevertheless continue placing its members in strategic political and union positions in the same way the secret Afrikaner Broederbond has infiltrated influential Afrikaner and government institutions? As long as the Party has to "authorize" its chairman to circulate a discussion paper, it resembles more an authoritarian Jesuit order for the organic intelligentsia than an open, broad-based vehicle for the self-critical exploration of feasible socialism. Pallo Jordan, one of the few unorthodox socialist thinkers in the ANC's top hierarchy and himself a onetime victim of paranoia within the movement, has harshly pointed out that "the political culture nurtured by the SACP's leadership over the years has produced a spirit of intolerance, petty intellectual thuggery and political dissembling among its membership."[24] Such a culture of authoritarianism does not augur well for the chances of democracy in the postapartheid era—despite the SACP's new lip service to democratic values. However, the pressure for democracy from below, particularly from the unions, may well force the SACP to abandon the relics of Stalinism.

The way in which the ANC leadership has dealt with two other moral crises within the movement provides signs of encouragement. The Winnie Mandela episode and the revelations about widespread systematic torture and human rights abuses in ANC camps were not suppressed. Both incidents were fully aired, despite internal pressures to close ranks around the guilty. By accepting collective responsibility and letting the internal democracy take its course, the movement has been morally strengthened and set a noteworthy example for handling aberrations on the other side. It can only be hoped that the ANC-SACP leadership also grapples eventually with its problematic ideological past in exile.

Finally, there remains the problem of the lifestyles some ANC leaders have adopted. Critics point to this embourgeoisement as the visible betrayal of a dream. In contrast, in his inimitably reflective, generous manner, Albie Sachs comments, "We must reject the kind of revolutionary asceticism that equates purity with poverty." He continues: "It is not inappropriate that our leaders should move into well-appointed houses and be supported by secretaries, drivers and security staff. It is only the psychology of underdevelopment on the one hand, and the habits of arrogance on the other, that say they must forever live in the back yards of cities and ride around on mopeds in old suits with battered briefcases."[25] This touches a sensitive chord that preoccupies the fantasies of many ANC supporters and opponents alike.

There seems nothing wrong with political leaders living in comfortable conditions, particularly after being deprived of luxuries for decades. However, the ostentatious display of affluence in the midst of poverty becomes even more problematic when wealthy business interests "donate" million-rand houses, cars, and free vacations. These perks create expectations and potentially compromise leaders. It is difficult to imagine how one can be an advocate for squatters and enjoy the company of a hotel tycoon. A three-day wedding for Mandela's daughter, with a glittering reception for five hundred well-groomed guests in the most expensive Johannesburg hotel, may fit Hollywood tastes but hardly honors Soweto. Yet, the intriguing aspect is the clamor of the poor for their own "royalty" to live in style. The workers of the Mercedes plant, unpaid and on overtime, built the most expensive model as their gift for Mandela.

In this respect, the conspicuous consumption of some ANC leaders contrasts sharply with India's postcolonial liberators, who shed their British suits in favor of homespun cotton clothing. But Gandhi's ideal of cultural liberation from the values of one's oppressors has never been part of the African value system. Even as the ANC celebrates its victory, it lays the basis of common consumerism.

What white South Africa has not yet fully understood is the recent development that turned rhetorical Stalinist ideologues into the ANC's more pragmatic force. With a disintegrating Soviet bloc seeking peace and investments instead of world revolution, South African communists have nowhere else to go but home. The SACP now considers reconciliation and trust useful methods for bridging differences. As a result, they have become the allies of Pretoria's negotiation project, and "without a hidden agenda," as Slovo assured the government during the first Groote Schuur talks. Contrary to all tenets of Marxist orthodoxy, an editorial in the party journal asserted that "recent events have proved abundantly that long-standing prejudice can be dispelled by personal contact," as if antagonistic interests could be wiped out by pleasant small talk at cocktail parties and conferences.[26] Furthermore, according to Slovo, the SACP's attitude toward socialism once democracy has been achieved will depend on the "class forces in play" at the time. In practical terms, this puts socialism on ice. Once nonracial capitalism delivers the goods, Marxist socialist parties shrink or turn into social-democratic parties, as has been demonstrated the world over.

Because of its past radical image, moreover, the SACP leadership can entice skeptical youths into the negotiation process. From this perspective, the government should welcome the red flags. If anyone can prevent a counterracist backlash and make a rational, colorblind attitude prevail, it is the traditional Marxists with their ideological indoctrination in internationalist universalism. That is the historical merit of South African communists, their undemocratic Stalinist baggage notwithstanding. Whatever its flaws, Slovo's self-critical account of the failure of socialism constitutes the first indication of a democratic renewal, one that may lay to rest van den Berghe's pessimistic comment that "South Africa, which has already spawned the world's last official racists, may also see its last Stalinists."[27]

The question remains: To what extent does the SACP's residual Stalinism color the ANC? Especially given that many members of the ANC hierarchy are also SACP members and that the close alliance between the two groups is likely to continue for a while, the prospects of compromise and democracy are directly affected. With the apartheid enemy officially gone, the amorphous ANC alliance is in danger of ideological disintegration. The only group with sufficient discipline and cohesion to come out of this internecine strife relatively intact is the SACP, based as it is in the unions. Redefined as a social-democratic party that advocates redistribution alongside economic growth, the SACP would be well placed to survive the discrediting of socialism elsewhere. In view of the long-standing mass poverty of a black proletariat in South Africa, no fictional consumer nationalism or yearning for a market is likely to pacify the quest for socialism for some time. The initial radical advocates of change in South Africa, therefore, are likely to remain a formidable force. However, whether their socialism will have a human or an authoritarian face is unclear. Mandela's moderation is not necessarily an indicator of the things to come when political competition starts in earnest. The real problem, in short, is the lack of a democratic culture in black politics, and the rejection of social democracy. For example, Cyril Ramaphosa's first public act as ANC secretary general was to forbid ANC members to publicize their membership in the SACP: "We felt that the press had no business to subject members of the ANC to such an inquisition" (*Vrye Weekblad*, August 9–16, 1991). Quite apart from encouraging rumors and red-baiting by this interdict, Ramaphosa denied legitimate inquiries into the political beliefs and loyalties of public figures.

At the SACP's 70th Anniversary Congress in December 1991, the overwhelming majority of the 413 delegates reaffirmed the Marxist-Leninist nature of the party and rejected a proposal by the leadership to define its future goal as "democratic socialism," voting instead to drop the word *democratic*. The 330-strong majority argued that the adjective was tautological, since the SACP's vision of socialism was inherently democratic, in contrast to the "distortions" of socialism in Eastern Europe. At the same time, however, the congress praised Castro's Cuba as a socialist model, and Slovo criticized Gorbachev for having abolished the Soviet Communist Party after the failed 1991 coup.

The Congress was generally interpreted as an assertion of greater organizational independence of the SACP from the ANC. But it also demonstrated how strong the overlapping membership between the party, the ANC, and Cosatu still is. Both the president and vice president of Cosatu were elected to the central committee of the SACP, and eleven of thirty members of that committee are also on the ANC's National Executive Committee. Adherence to a multiparty system remains half-hearted and contingent. In March 1990 a meeting of the SACP and Cosatu in Harare resolved that "in general" the multiparty system "provides one of the favourable conditions for democratic participation" but also stated that "a one-party-system cannot be ruled out in principle—particular conditions may make it necessary."[28] It would, of course, be the SACP that decides when formal democracy has to give way to a more suitable "people's democracy."

The constant invocation of "the will of the people" sounds almost totalitarian, as if the people were monolithic and had a single will. Speeches by ANC leaders and articles in ANC or SACP journals hardly ever refer to competitors such as the PAC, Azapo, or Inkatha by name; they merely denigrate them. To be sure, the ANC no longer makes hegemonic claims to power. It now recognizes that Afrikaner nationalism has to be accommodated and that a simple transfer of power is an unrealistic demand. But the SACP still claims ideological hegemony in representing the interests of "the masses," an ironic assertion given its history as an elitist personality cult.

One of the most astonishing features of the Stalinist show trials was the humble plea by most of the convicted that they be duly punished or even executed for their crimes. In the end, the brainwashed defendants—previously all strong, self-confident, highly placed and committed communists—themselves believed in their "unintended crime," because the party's collective wisdom had decreed it to be so. As an analyst of the Slansky affair put it succinctly, "The main point of the trials was the violation of reason, of logic, of common sense. They proved that lies can be impossible or outrageous, and still be taken as truth; they are protected not by logic but by state power."[29] When one reads the rationalizations of Stalinism by some South African communists today, it seems as if common sense and hard evidence can be violated all too readily, without any particular psychological torture. A theme articulated by Harry Gwala—that "the excesses committed under Stalin, while not justified," must be seen in the light "that spies and saboteurs were being infiltrated into the Soviet Union"—finds constant repetition.[30] Gwala, an influential local leader in Natal and member of the SACP Interim Leadership Group, goes on to explicitly reject "the denunciation of Stalin" by Slovo: "This sort of nihilism only clouds the issue and does not deal with the problems of socialism scientifically." In Gwala's view, the talk of giving socialism a "human face" is incorrect because "to us Marx's socialism has only one face, the scientific face." Against all evidence, there is an unyielding dogmatism. According to Gwala, "The saying that the term 'dictatorship of the proletariat' has been abused and therefore we must shy away from it sends shivers down our spine." The cold war and the siege of the communist bloc by the forces of Western imperialism are said to justify, or at least explain, the need for "extreme measures." While Soviet domination "protected" Eastern Europe from such machinations, in Western Europe "the American troops saw to it that the working class was stifled." These are the views of a leading South

African communist who, together with his comrades, proved powerful enough initially to veto the planned meeting between Mandela and
Buthelezi.

After the military coup against Gorbachev in August 1991, the
SACP presented another picture of confusion, despite Slovo's previous
support for democratic socialism. While the attempted takeover had
already been condemned by the world as "unconstitutional" and
"disturbing," the first SACP statement asserted that "information on
developments in the Soviet Union is still sketchy. Without adequate
information and a proper study of it, we are unwilling to comment on
these events." The Natal Midlands branch of the SACP even issued
what Slovo later described as an unauthorized statement welcoming
the downfall of Gorbachev: "His government could have become
destructive to the socialist objective." The October 1991 issue of the
ANC journal *Mayibuye* gave a prominent place to Gwala's denunciation of Gorbachev and the defense of the military coup against him:
"Those who employ bourgeois morality and imperialist norms in
dismembering a socialist union and suppressing the Communist Party
can expect any method to be employed in defending socialism."

Gwala and his Natal supporters are not alone in arguing for a
stricter adherence to Marxist-Leninist principles. Dave Kitson deplores the departures from orthodoxy and "ill-informed denigration
of the doctrines" by an SACP that in his view has descended into a
social-democratic "Kautskyist-Luxemburgist" position.[31] Insurrectionists on the Left would like "to arm the masses in the townships."
Rather than democratize the SADF and integrate MK into it (as
current SACP chief and former MK commander Hani advocates) they
dream of seeing the state displaced and its security apparatus dismantled. Because of this ideological disarray in the ranks, the party is
careful not to tamper with its unifying symbols, particularly its name.
The party journal scoffed at the suggestion to adopt a social-democratic label and suggested that its ill-informed critics "should consider
changing their prejudices instead."[32]

Yet the fate of the future South African democracy may not hinge
on the past alliances of the most committed component of the apartheid opposition but on how democratic culture will be practiced in the
new internal constellation. The recognition of union independence by
the SACP, together with the conditional endorsement of a multiparty
system and traditional liberal freedoms, bodes well for South African
democracy, despite the Leninist relics and the repressed legacies of a

Stalinist past. More significant than any ideological posturing remains the SACP practice of active cooperation in the negotiated compromise. The calamity of Eastern Europe seemed to have finally dawned on at least some of the SACP leadership because they now accept full responsibility for the "task of confronting the reality of the crimes committed in the name of the cause for which we stand."[33]

THE FALLACY OF THE LEIPZIG OPTION

What would be the worst scenario for successful negotiations in South Africa?[34] If a compromising ANC leadership were rejected as sellouts, the eventual historic accord would not be worth the paper on which it is written. Were Mandela to be perceived as a co-opted stooge, he would share the fate of the sidelined Muzorewa.

The deadlock of Codesa II has prevented this nightmare. An elitist ANC leadership, which was out on a limb in its pace and scope of accommodation, aligned itself anew with its skeptical constituency and power base. Inasmuch as the Nationalists could not be sure of their mandate before the March referendum, so the ANC had to renew its legitimacy by walking out of Codesa. In the absence of the franchise, the ANC is left with the street to gauge support, to mobilize and to discipline an increasingly undisciplined grass-roots. The heterogeneous ANC alliance had never reached an enthusiastic consensus about abandoning confrontation in favor of negotiation. The unconvinced insurrectionists among the youth—always distrustful of the "new site of struggle"—found a golden opportunity to make up for lost ground during the two-year demobilization. The secret deals had not brought any tangible benefits to the townships.

Therefore, neither unsolvable disagreement over constitutional percentages nor the much-exploited tragic Boipatong massacre stalled negotiations. Codesa developed into a pre-election campaign where both sides needed time to consolidate support. Tragically, they also squandered a historic moment of unprecedented possibilities.

The ANC leadership's newly reaffirmed credibility among its constituency has been acquired at a high price: the risk of discrediting violence and further economic decline. If the "Leipzig option" of massive street demonstrations, the occupation of factories and city centers could "topple the regime," it would have been replaced long ago. But de Klerk is hardly in the position of Honecker, their similar domestic illegitimacy notwithstanding. The ANC expects world applause for its street theater, the kind of support the West offered the pro-democracy movement in Eastern Europe. However, the capitalist West backed an anticommunist upsurge in East Germany. In South Africa, on the other hand, a communist-aligned opposition aims at transforming an arch-capitalist order. Why would Bonn, Washington, or London empathize with "left" experiments of redistribution in South Africa? A like-minded, "reasonable" de Klerk strikes a far more amenable chord.

The denunciation of de Klerk as a Nazi by Mandela, the mock trials and murder charges, not only poison the climate for negotiations but discredit the ANC among informed observers. The demonization of the opponent is also shortsighted because it will backfire: if the ANC leadership continues to peddle the Nazi label, Mandela will be perceived as a sellout for even talking to fascists, let alone compromising with them. The ANC plays into the hands of its purist competitors, who, quite logically, argue that Nazis ought not be talked to but only defeated in battle. Thus, a negotiating ANC leadership digs its own grave by encouraging blind militancy.

In this predicament a new factor was introduced: the ANC initiated, and the government accepted, a plan for international collaboration with local peace commissions. As long as the sovereign South African state does not allow international control over its wilder security operatives, however, foreign missions are reduced to monitoring, facilitating, and pleading. The new feature of this outside involvement is its balanced, impartial exhortation—compared with peace activists' former automatic endorsement of apartheid's victims. Given this experience, the legalized ANC overestimates its current international standing and clout. Indeed, the ANC has frequently misinterpreted international solidarity. Apart from a declining Left, anti-apartheid movements in the West were always more motivated by embarrassment about and disgust with an intransigent racist regime than support for the ANC's goals. But the ANC confused the two and miscalculated that it would receive as much foreign endorsement during the era of a liberalizing de Klerk as in the period of a stubborn P. W. Botha. Instead, foreigners of all political hues are more likely to lean on the ANC to be "reasonable" than to propose that the government abdicate.

It is also doubtful that any foreign monitoring can diminish the township violence. Only a political accord that includes acceptable provisions for the hostel migrants and, regrettably, perhaps a general amnesty for the killers among all factions can achieve a lasting peace. The sensible recommendations of the Goldstone Commission on how to handle demonstrations civilly and professionally can lead the way toward curbing the violence. Nonetheless, as long as every policeman is considered to be an enemy of the community, as long as the president of the ANC Youth League approves of the harassment of policemen's families, impartial policing would seem beyond the human capacity of equally brutalized uniformed youngsters.

The National Party has stalled a possible constitutional compromise about a minor percentage difference, which it has conceded in the meantime. Pretoria also wanted time to build up its African support beyond the estimated 10 percent at present. Ironically, the Leipzig option of turmoil and inevitable intimidation may well play into the hands of the government by discrediting the ANC among the mass of apolitical, law-and-order–oriented voters. Instead of retaining the moral high ground, a remarkably moderate liberation movement will be associated with anarchy and economic decline. Only the advocates of violence without victors can hope to benefit from such a course of events.

CHAPTER FIVE

Psychological Liberation

Black Consciousness and Africanism

Although the activities of the ANC continue to dominate press coverage of events in South Africa, the ideals of Black Consciousness and Africanism, represented by the PAC and Azapo, respectively, may well develop into the prevailing black outlook in postapartheid South Africa, as they had been in the early 1960s and again during the Soweto upheavals in 1976. At present the PAC and Azapo have only minority support, but their noncompromising stance may force the ANC into policy positions which it might not take in the absence of a serious challenge from a left Africanist flank.

INTERNALIZED COLONIALISM
AND THE PSYCHOLOGY OF LIBERATION

In the late 1960s the idea of Black Consciousness heralded an era of alternative political awareness in South Africa. A self-empowering, vibrant, reconstructionist world view emphasized the potential role of black initiative and responsibility in articulating the power of the powerless. Between 1968 and 1976 the Black Consciousness Movement (BCM) was one of the most significant developments in South Africa, not only because of the self-confident protest and rebellion that it unleashed but also "because of the questions it posed about the nature of oppositional politics in South Africa and its relation to the nature of South African society."[1]

Indeed, blacks in South Africa in the 1960s were ready for an ideology of liberation. The oppression of apartheid society was overt and blatant; all opposition had been silenced, and institutionalized racism flourished triumphant. Centuries of exclusionary practices led to what might be described as the "inferiorization" of blacks: Blacks were portrayed as innately inferior, accustomed to dehumanized living, sexually promiscuous, intellectually limited, and prone to violence; blackness symbolized evil, demise, chaos, corruption, and uncleanliness, in contrast to whiteness, which equaled order, wealth, purity, goodness, cleanliness, and the epitome of beauty.

Inevitably, these racist stereotypes were at least partially internalized by South African blacks, although their self-doubt never matched that prevalent among blacks in the United States, where the official proclamations of equality misled many blacks into blaming themselves, rather than discrimination, for any miseries they experienced.

But undoubtedly, apartheid society also produced self-hatred. The limited range of opportunities open to blacks gave rise to rationalizations in favor of the status quo, and self-doubts and self-accusations led some blacks to accept their oppression as legitimate. In short, blacks blamed themselves. In addition, the fragmentation of the three black groups through differential privileges and incorporation led to a reinforcement of an intrablack hierarchy.

Thus, Black Consciousness emanated from the differential material and political circumstances in which blacks were situated. Its prime movers in the early phase were relatively privileged medical students, not workers, who served as educated articulators of the plight of the underprivileged and politically excluded. Yet, unlike most medical students elsewhere, many of them came from working-class backgrounds and were not insulated from the harsh conditions of apartheid society. They were joined by other students on the newly created segregated black campuses, where they operated under severe restrictions, and had to depend on the white-dominated National Union of South African Students (NUSAS) to speak and act on their behalf—though blacks were prohibited from joining this organization.

Yet even as some blacks at the open universities worked with NUSAS, they experienced the bifurcating effects of academic integration coupled with social separation. Much of their alienation was due to the vast gap between the life circumstances of black and white students. At the University Christian Movement, too, the initial promise of a liberal alternative soon evaporated when black students once more saw themselves reduced to the role of followers. The banning of the ANC in 1960 and the arrests of its leaders meant that blacks had to rely on liberal whites to articulate the case for black rights. Steve Biko, the best-known proponent of Black Consciousness, described how such enforced passivity dulled one's originality and imagination: "it takes a supreme effort to act logically even in order to follow one's beliefs and convictions."[2]

In the editorial introduction to the 1972 annual *Black Viewpoint,* Biko referred to the absence of black writers in the media: "So many things are said so often to us, about us and for us but very seldom by us."[3] He deplored the images of dependency created for blacks by the white press and expressed the need to deconstruct the implicit interpretive connotations, underlying values, attitudes, and interests of both the financial supporters and the readership of those newspapers. Biko articulated a general insight into conquest: that defeat for the losers has always meant more than physical subjugation. It means, as two historians of the Soviet Union have described in other circumstances, "that the conquerors write the history of the wars; the victors take possession of the past, establish their control over the collective memory."[4] In short, the victors' definition of reality becomes the dominant explanation.

The difficulty of working bilaterally with even the most sincere whites posed a moral dilemma for black students, who were the last to want themselves labeled racist. Yet for Biko and others the need for exclusive black organizations was very clear, something Ben Khoapa referred to as the need for "regroupment."[5] Blacks were considered to be an interest group, like workers in a trade union or teachers fighting their own battles. The collective segregation and oppression based on skin color therefore provided an eminently logical basis for self-assertion and independent organization. No longer would blacks allow themselves to be objectified in the negative image of "nonwhites"— instead they would reconstruct themselves as blacks, as self-defining initiators. Gone were the days when they appealed to whites by seeking to convince them that blacks too had civilized standards. Black Consciousness was about pressuring whites through contesting the self-definitions of their opponents.[6] Accusations that this was a racist act were dismissed on the grounds that "one cannot be a racist unless he has the power to subjugate."[7]

Later, when Black Consciousness developed a socialist tinge, cooperation with white liberals was rejected not because of race or privilege, but because these would-be compatriots were seen as representing a bourgeois class enemy. Collaboration with representatives of racial capitalism would amount to betrayal. "Black Consciousness," writes George Frederickson, an American historian, "had evolved from an effort to overcome a black sense of inferiority through independent, nonviolent action into an explosive combination of race and class revolutionism."[8] Whatever the meaning of the latter phrase, Black Consciousness remained above all an awareness-raising movement, rather than an organization that practiced revolutionary violence.

The origins of blacks' disillusionment with nonracial opposition organizations go back to the adoption of the Freedom Charter in 1955 by the Congress of the People, which gave rise to a split between the Charterists (ANC) and those who formed the PAC. The latter's racial definition of *African* later evolved into a broadly inclusive subjective one, in that it included people of any group who considered themselves African and who identified with Africa and its people (as opposed to the exploiting settlers). By contrast, Black Consciousness utilized an objective definition of *black* to describe all those denied privileges by whites, as well as a subjective definition of those who consciously rejected white domination in all its forms. Even Bantustan leaders fell into the former category and were recognized as such for a while by the South African Students' Organisation (SASO).

What was distinctive about the BCM was "its originality in elaborating an ideology of hope rooted in a theology of liberation which emphasized the solidarity of the oppressed regardless of race."[9] Unlike the PAC, which, despite its stated goal of including all "Africans," is perceived as narrowly Africanist, Black Consciousness as an ideology was genuinely inclusive. From its inception the new movement sought to incorporate Indians and Coloureds. However, while it had its appeal for this "middle group" in expressing political identification, as G. J. Gerwel points out, it failed to provide the psychological identity they needed.[10] In general, the BCM enjoyed greater support from activist Coloureds than Indians, not least because some students and clergy identified with its rejection of the label "coloured" in favor of an inclusive black category that focused on political oppression. Many Indians, on the other hand, while prominent in the early leadership of SASO, came to feel rejected as insufficiently black enough, and they felt pressured to replace their cultural heritage with African symbols. Indeed, a few gave their children African names as a way of identifying with the movement. However, they were the exceptions—

often alienated community members—rather than the precursors of a groundswell of Indian sentiments toward identification as blacks.

The fragile unity among the oppressed groups was frequently exposed. The ease with which Indians could be condemned for not identifying sufficiently with the black cause, and even for considering themselves a minority, is evident in a not untypical SASO newsletter article published in 1972, "Ugandan Asians and the Lesson for Us." In addition to exonerating Idi Amin for his treatment of Asian Ugandans, the latter were portrayed stereotypically as "refusing to see themselves as part of the soil of Africa": "middlemen who continually saw themselves as a minority and by their practice of exploitation of the Africans through money lending at inflated interest rates, through the practice of bargaining . . . they contributed to the growth of animosity between themselves and the Africans who saw them as a hostile exploitative minority."[11] Here the East African model was uncritically transposed to the South African situation, with no attention to the crucial fact that most Indians in South Africa were descendants of indentured laborers. Unlike the trading minorities and the colonial civil servants in East Africa, the majority of Indian South Africans are members of the working class. But class analysis was not a tool of the movement at this initial stage.

The categorization of Indians as exploiting traders also ignored the fact that even the minority shopkeepers had to compete with white-owned monopolies in order to corner some of the increasing African consumer market. But because the owners of family stores came into direct contact with African shoppers, unlike the white owners of larger supermarkets and department stores, Indians' and Africans' perceptions of each other frequently focused on unequal exchange relationships. The mutual ambivalence was reinforced by the widespread practice in Natal industries for African workers to be supervised by Indians who, in turn, had to justify to their white employers their preferential treatment. Here, then, the message of black solidarity came up against a formidable institutionalized racial hierarchy in employment.

BCM transformed negative attitudes about subordinate "non-whites" into a positive discourse of resistance. It offered psychological support to oppressed groups by providing a model for positive identification, and sought to alleviate the self-contempt often felt by the oppressed. Despite their efforts to provide an alternative to past descriptions, however, movements such as Black Consciousness have been criticized for implicitly accepting the legitimacy of color as a marker. In doing so, it is argued, they also reinforce the accuracy of the dominant discourse of race, by which they have been signified and exteriorized as the other.[12] In rebuttal, Sam Nolutshungu argues that "the character of the state conditions not only the terms of domination and submission but also the ideologies and political behaviour that challenge and reject it." The very role that the state gives to national and racial oppression, Nolutshungu explains, calls forth "alignments among the subject population that are focussed primarily on the terms of political domination rather than those of exploitation."[13]

Notably lacking in the initial stages of the formulation of Black Consciousness was an economic perspective on the nature of exploitation. Conceptualizations of South Africa in class terms remained peripheral and there was no systematic analysis of what was later termed racial capitalism. In part, this disinterest represented the rejection of Marxism as a white ideology and as the tool of the South African Communist Party. However, this indifference also reflected the censorship of Marxist literature at the tribal universities, as well as the students' exposure to existentialism, phenomenology, and philosophical psychology—subjects that were popular among some of the European-oriented faculty. Hence the movement's focus on values and essences, while its rejection of capitalism was couched in terms of dehumanization and materialism, not commodity fetishism.[14]

Although there was little of the "black is beautiful" sloganeering that characterized American black protest, the BCM was influenced by trends in the United States. The movement worked to raise consciousness about the extent to which blacks, at great costs, were trying to copy white images of beauty, and the BCM helped to restore blacks' sense of self-appreciation and self-acceptance. Indeed, in the early stages of the movement in Natal, there were reports that some African men had beaten African women who had straightened their hair or lightened the color of their skin. One indicator of the success of Black Consciousness on this issue was the vastly reduced advertising and sale of bleaching creams in South Africa.

Barney Pityana describes the inspiration for the BCM as originating in African religious movements and prophets, in attempts by Africans to regain their land, in the history of the Industrial and Commercial Workers Union of Africa (ICU). Pityana also stresses the significance of both the Africanist and nationalist strands within the traditions of struggle. Philosophically, Black Consciousness was broadly influenced by the writings of Léopold Sédar Senghor, Aimé Césaire, Albert Memmi, Frantz Fanon, Eldridge Cleaver, Stokely Carmichael, and Paulo Freire—each of whom expressed the humiliation as well as the dignity of the colonized and also the power of the powerless. Though the BCM turned to these works on the psychology of oppression and the exorcizing of colonial humiliation, there is little evidence in the Black Consciousness literature that, for example, Fanon's central notion of the cleansing power of anticolonial violence found resonance among South African activists. At the early stage Black Consciousness also maintained a rather skeptical silence about the ANC's "armed struggle."

Unlike Black Power groups in the United States, the BCM had no need to become a revivalist movement, reconstructing a distant past and golden heritage, since African linguistic and cultural traditions had persisted despite apartheid. In the absence of the American trauma of slavery, young black Africans felt no need to search for putative roots. Leaders made a clear distinction between Black Consciousness and Black Power in the United States, where already enfranchised blacks wished to constitute themselves as a pressure group in a white majority society. In South Africa, the BCM was seen as a way of preparing people for equal participation in a transformed society that would reflect the outlook of the black majority.[15] Psychological liberation was sought through a return to African values of communalism, shared decision making, and more personal communication styles, in contrast to the individualism of white consumer society.

Despite the BCM's designation of the black community as communalistic, the division of labor within the BCM followed traditional sexist lines. All five officeholders in the 1972 executive were men. Women for the most part were relegated to taking responsibility for child care, moral education, and socialization in black cultural heritage, for health, nutrition, and the making of clothing. This view permeated the women's own self-definition, as is evident in the preamble to the constitution of the allied Black Women's Federation:

>   1. Black women are basically responsible for the survival and maintenance of their families and largely the socialisation of the youth for the transmission of the Black cultural heritage;
>   2. They need to present a united front and to redirect the status of motherhood towards the fulfillment of the Black people's social, cultural, economic and political aspirations.[16]

In contrast, the Institute of Black Studies, formed in 1975, was "to provide a forum where the Black *man* can express himself. . . . a platform where issues facing the country can be analysed and interpreted."[17]

The repetition of masculine pronouns, which prevailed in the SASO Policy Manifesto of 1971, may well have reflected and reproduced standard English usage of "he" and "man" in what was viewed as their generic sense. But despite the black cultural ideal of an inclusive communalism, the male is constructed as the empowered speaker, and women—even when included as "sisters"—are presented as the other, powerless and voiceless.[18] The ancillary role of women in the leadership of SASO further corroborates this gender-based disparity. Few women were prominent in student representative councils or in campus activities. But structural factors may also have kept women from participating on a more equal basis—one cannot automatically attribute their underrepresentation in the movement solely to exclusionary practices.

FORMS OF PROTEST

In its earlier phases, the BCM was characterized by spontaneity and an easy evolution, without any rigid plan or agenda. The style was informal, free of organizational trappings, as exemplified by Biko's "I Write What I Like." Politics were consensually based, until the rude awakening caused by Temba Sono's public criticism of the BCM's directions in July 1972. After that, the membership was more carefully screened and the style of speeches became more prescribed.

Consciousness-raising often took the form of light-hearted, satirical, humorous utterances. College campuses during the late 1960s were the base for frequently staged political theater. For a while, it amused even Nationalist-oriented staff members, who seemed to rejoice at the way in which "the natives" entertained themselves, in images derived from "their own lingo." The style of acting and diction was a refreshing change from the previous stilted, imitative, colonial models of the speech and drama genre. Afrikaner faculty at the tribal colleges loved this rejection of the British yoke, and there was a self-congratulatory air about how well these colleges allowed students to express themselves. The National government, however, was not amused at these developments on campuses it had established in order to ethnicize, depoliticize, fragment, and control the opposition. The theatrical performances were among the subversive activities charged by the state at trials of BCM leaders in the 1970s.

From the late 1960s until the arrest of its most articulate proponents in 1977, Black Consciousness filled the political and cultural
vacuum created by the silencing of the ANC and PAC leadership. The
main tenets of the BCM permeated the thinking of a generation of
students, regardless of political persuasion. The movement's initial
analytical focus on culture, identity, and value systems gradually
shifted, and the struggle was defined in terms of racism and capitalism. In 1971 the preferred focus was to radicalize the population
through direct political criticism of the regime; through infiltration of
ruling organizations, including collaborating institutions, and conversion from within; and through "orientation politics" that addressed a
range of educational, cultural, religious, and economic needs. Under
the influence of Julius Nyerere's ideas about self-reliance, various
community projects explored ways in which blacks could become
more self-supporting.

Black Review 1972 cited black community projects—literacy campaigns, health projects, and home education programs—throughout
the country, mainly in rural and semirural areas in the Transvaal,
Natal, and Eastern Cape.[19] Popular short-term notions of an immi-
nent revolution were replaced by patient, disciplined preparation. The
editor of *Black Review,* B. A. Khoapa, proposed that the philosophy
of liberation required a frank appraisal of white institutions and
policies and "an advanced programme of economic democracy" in
order to expand black interests to universal interests.[20] He called for
a broadening of the movement beyond sheltered student politics toward a mobilization of the work force. If Black Consciousness was to
effect a major transformation in society, the intellectuals would have
to reach workers.

This goal implied not only a modification of language, but also a
fundamental shift of concerns: establishing positive self-images
seemed peripheral, at best, to people whose lives were heavily burdened by the daily drudgery of earning a living. The new projects,
however, were severely hampered by the constraints of student life.
Distances between campuses and townships, inadequate financial resources for travel and free time, and the need to work with Bantustan
authorities inhibited outreach efforts. So, too, did the marginal status
of young students, who could hardly hold themselves out as leaders
to the workers. All these factors served to identify the need for an
adult branch of the growing student movement.[21]

What was distinctive about the BCM at this time was its pragmatic willingness to forgo the rhetoric-laden, sterile, noncompromise party lines adopted by other opposition organizations. For a while the BCM even had contacts with adversaries like Gatsha Buthelezi. Indeed, Steve Biko and Buthelezi shared a platform when the BCM brought together an alliance of diverse black groups. Another sign of the BCM's openness was its effort to establish a socialist dispensation, while striving for nationalist liberation.

This unconventional mix of tendencies hampered fundraising. Prospective financial supporters were few, and those willing to fund the nationalist cause balked at supporting a movement marked by socialist sympathies. On the other hand, those who might have supported radical political initiatives would not back an organization that emphasized the significance of color. Faced with the choice between compromising its principles in order to attract funds or being independent, principled, locally based, and underfinanced, the BCM characteristically settled for the latter.[22]

Up through the early 1970s the BCM's relatively modest means and low-key profile provoked little reaction from Pretoria. During this period of tolerance the regime even praised BCM students for their "apartheid-like" thinking, their enthusiasm for the state's program of separatist black education. On the surface the BCM appeared to be using the same symbols as the state, even as it refashioned black identity into a more inclusive category by raising awareness about the structure of oppression. SASO emphasized black content in education and attempted to subvert the authority structure by divulging the relations of power and Eurocentric bias in institutional life. At the SASO banquet of June 1973, for example, Ernest Baartman gave an eloquent address, "Education as an Instrument for Liberation," that demystified the relationship between knowledge, control, and hegemony.[23] Such analyses only highlighted the dialectic of apartheid education for the colonized, as had been predicted.[24] The ruling regime now came to understand that the BCM was appropriating the state's idioms in order to challenge its motives and subvert its power.

After a series of industrial strikes throughout Durban during 1973, for which the BCM was blamed but neither claimed nor disclaimed responsibility, the government retaliated by arresting eight SASO organizers, although there was little connection between SASO and the strikes. The last straw, from the government's point of view, was a Durban rally that SASO organized in 1974 to celebrate Mozambique's independence. The "Viva Frelimo" cries of the crowd at the banned meeting were only intended to express black solidarity and strengthen the BCM, but the police violently overreacted. A series of arrests and bannings followed, culminating in a number of deaths in detention.

In response to massive arrests and police intimidation, some students saw armed struggle as the only alternative. In 1976 the rebellion of Soweto students was primarily headed by members of the South African Students' Movement (SASM), infused with the spirit of Black Consciousness in their rejection of Afrikaans-language instruction as a tool of their subjugation. Large numbers of these students subsequently escaped the country. Many were absorbed into ANC camps, although a Black Consciousness Movement in exile was also set up as a third South African liberation group.

The BCM's platform of education *for* liberation was in danger of devolving into what some viewed as calls from abroad for liberation *before* education. The deteriorating conditions in black schools and the unbridgeable rift between children and school authorities under the Department of Education and Training led a group of concerned parents to found the National Education Crisis Committee (NECC). Hoping to get the children to return to schools, the NECC promoted the idea of people's education as an alternative. The detention of most of NECC's active members prevented this initiative from gaining any momentum. Meanwhile, individuals and institutions sympathetic to Black Consciousness continued to conduct research and develop curriculum materials and policy perspectives for an alternative South Africa.

In the 1970s the BCM was said to have been cocooned as an intellectual crusade with little grass-roots support, lacking a solid base in organized labor. Some critics said the movement was heavy on moral purity and faced the danger of stagnating at the level of black solidarity, unable to translate its ideas into the "politically possible" for "political action."[25] Others expressed concern about whether the movement was forward-looking enough to prepare itself for a post-apartheid society.[26]

While Black Consciousness has always been weak at best among organized workers, it did spawn its own union during the 1970s. The Black and Allied Workers' Union (Bawu) criticized its stronger Fosatu rival for employing white intellectuals. This practical nonracialism in a fledgling independent union movement contrasted with BCM's "antiracism" under "black leadership." Successor organizations like the Council of Unions of South Africa (CUSA) and the Azanian Confederation of Trade Unions (Azactu) later formed the National Council of Trade Unions (Nactu), which has kept its organizational and ideological distance from Cosatu to this day, although both federations increasingly cooperate on tactical issues.

In 1978, after the banning of all constituent components of the BCM the previous year, the Azanian People's Organisation (Azapo) was formed. Its leaders incorporated a class analysis into their policy and directed attention toward the political involvement of the black working class. A focus on psychological liberation and blackness gradually gave way to more talk of socialist, anticapitalist alternatives. Those speaking on behalf of Azapo refuted charges that theirs was merely an intellectual movement, and they insisted that Azapo enjoyed wide support.

While initially favoring the Black Consciousness tendency, the state as well as liberal institutions in the 1980s began to look more favorably at the ANC supporters' nonracial promise. In 1991 Azapo students at Witwatersrand University, for example, complained about the university's nonrecognition of the BCM on the grounds that the organization was exclusively black and, therefore, violated the university's nonracial charter. The students argued that exclusively Jewish or Islamic student societies were always recognized, and that student fees were used to subsidize Charterist organizations through the local student representative councils. The vice-president of Azapo, Gomolemo Mokae, listed a series of incidents to argue that "'liberal' universities like Wits and Natal are guilty of complicity in Stalinistic censorship against non-Charterists" (*Frontline*, May 1991). His grievance reflects Azapo's practice of not distinguishing between legitimate ethnicity (cultural and religious groups) and illegitimate racial categories. In black and white nationalist thinking, ethnicity and race are identical.

Black Consciousness continues to rely on the development of a fictive kinship between all three "nonwhite groups" who have experienced the shared indignity of oppression and material deprivation. The psychological appeal of this kinship arouses many in all groups, and the effectiveness of Black Consciousness relies on the moral feelings it evokes. But can these feelings be channeled into a sustained movement? One of the major obstacles to a broad coalition is to be found in the differential experience of apartheid. Material rewards co-opt and "whiten," as does feared loss of cultural terrain.

AFRICANISM IN THE POSTAPARTHEID ERA

Analysts of black politics are currently puzzled by the dispute between the two main black groups that oppose negotiations and seem ideologically so close together, Azapo and the PAC. At the beginning of the 1990s, both groups have been marginalized by their opposition to the Charterist power-sharing project, and they appear to have escalated their bickering. According to Patrick Lawrence, a journalist: "Given the convergence between their ideological positions, including their insistence on black leadership and their commitment to socialism, Azapo and PAC were strongly hostile to one another. Azapo accused the PAC of intolerance, of forcing Azapo members to wear their T-shirts inside out at a Sharpeville Day commemorative service instead of welcoming them as brothers-in-the-struggle, and of belatedly pressing for a constituent assembly, an idea first promoted by Azapo in 1984."[27] Behind the quarreling, however, lies a class difference that often is overlooked.

The PAC speaks on behalf of some of the least-privileged and least-educated members of the oppressed majority. With a reservoir of Africanist sentiment in some rural areas and among recent migrants, the social base of the PAC resembles that of Inkatha rather than the more professionally led, urban-oriented ANC. On the other hand, Azapo has always attracted a better-educated elite, being particularly popular among university staff, clergy, journalists, and other professionals. Owing in part to its sprinkling of Indians in prominent leadership positions, Azapo continues to be resented by some Africanists—just as the PAC initially objected to the perceived inordinate influence of Indians and white communists in the ANC. Azapo leader Gomolemo Mokae seems to have succumbed to this anti-Indianism in 1992, when he accused BC of having "molly-coddled the Indian component of the black community": "Given that this component has yet to show, across the ideological spectrum of the liberation movements, much passion and willingness to engage in the struggle at grassroots level, is it not incongruous that they command such considerable power within all sections of the liberation movement?" he asks in an apartheid-like mode (*Work in Prog-*

ress 85, October 1992). Although the PAC also has a few prominent non-African members, it offers essentially a very down-to-earth articulation of diverse grass-roots sentiments. To oversimplify: Azapo constitutes a sophisticated intellectual elite in search of a constituency, while the PAC's potentially powerful army has been poorly served by its disorganized, quarreling generals.

The PAC's repeated internecine conflicts and petty ideological disputes stand out especially in comparison with the united ANC. The ANC has also had the advantage of much wider international recognition, diplomatic support, and a sympathetic international press (which has virtually ignored the PAC). Moreover, the ANC has benefited from a wider pool of experience and expertise in resistance politics. The popular symbols of resistance—the toyi-toyi dance, songs, and colors—are all associated with the ANC tradition, and they are also used by Inkatha. Contrary to expectations that an Africanist cultural revival would engender strong political emotions, these emotions originated from the internationalist-oriented ANC.

In terms of external support, the Soviet bloc's preference for the ANC far outweighed China's initial support for the PAC in the intersocialist rivalry. Only in a few China-aligned Frontline States, such as Zimbabwe and Tanzania, did the PAC receive some external support. But this rapidly evaporated after Mandela's release. The PAC's ambiguous stance toward negotiations and the joining of a short-lived "patriotic front" with the ANC in 1991 further illustrates the lack of cohesiveness among its constituency.[28]

In defining who is an African, PAC General Secretary Benny Alexander distinguishes "two strains." The first consists of indigenous people "who historically cannot be traced out of Africa." Whites and Asians whose only home and sole allegiance is to Africa constitute the second strain.[29] For the PAC this formula amounts to a nonracial concept that defines the nation. It accepts self-declarations of allegiance, so that those who define themselves as non-African do so by choice. "Settlers" applies only to those whites who oppress indigenous people.[30]

Oscar Dhlomo has rightly stressed that the PAC's position that anyone can be an African by choice, regardless of color, "will only become meaningful the moment the movement begins to admit non-black members" (*Sunday Times,* September 1, 1991). At present, the absence of whites in the PAC implies that this group does not identify with its own commendable nonracial postulate about Africans.

Another contradiction lies in the PAC's insistence on armed struggle even as it enters negotiations with the government. The PAC's policy is to attack security forces only, and it has not renounced armed struggle as the principal method to bring about liberation. The Azanian People's Liberation Army (Apla), the armed wing of the PAC, has generally concentrated on the assassinations of policemen. The few Apla guerrillas convicted in South African courts, even after the suspension of armed struggle by the ANC, had mostly received training in Tanzania and Libya. According to estimates by the International Institute for Strategic Studies, the PAC commands about 350 trained operatives. The ANC and PAC ridicule each other's claims of military confrontations with the enemy as fantasies, with the PAC pointing to the "random terror" of the ANC. The PAC does not disclose any information about incidents involving its combatants unless it loses people.

Benny Alexander also claims that at the end of 1990 "our membership was bigger than theirs [ANC's]" and that the PAC has "the support of most of the oppressed intelligentsia." Few would view these claims as accurate in the light of attendance figures at rallies and surveys that generally indicate three to four times greater support for the ANC. However, if negotiations fail or turn out to be too compromising, the PAC and Azapo could potentially regain mass support and again eclipse the ANC. Yet by beginning to negotiate with the government in 1992, the PAC has lost its radical image and adopted a posture closer to that of the ANC. This leaves Azapo as the sole proponent of the purist stance.

Azapo now portrays itself as the vanguard for the struggle for socialism in "occupied Azania." The SACP is viewed as having betrayed the struggle for socialism "by riding the ANC towards a negotiated settlement of compromise with the de Klerk regime, which has the potential to set back socialist transformation by many decades" (*Work in Progress* 73, March–April 1991). Both Azapo and the PAC are vague when pressed to describe their vision of "scientific socialism" more concretely. A forty-one-page official booklet published by the PAC, "Towards a Democratic Economic Order," concludes that the "political and economic mission shall be: redistributive, development, reproductive, accumulative, restorative, entrepreneurial-supportive, human needs' oriented and equi-beneficial." If the ANC needs to strengthen and update its economic research capacities, the other anti-apartheid movements are in even weaker positions.

In 1991 Azapo made a tactical error that undermined its influence and public profile. It withdrew from the Patriotic Front that it initially convened together with the ANC and PAC. The contentious issue was the participation of fourteen homeland parties in the tricameral parliament that, together with seventy other organizations, was invited to form a united front for the forthcoming constitutional negotiations. Two weeks before the conference, Azapo General Secretary Don Nkadimeng unilaterally wrote to the homeland parties demanding that they resign from "system-oriented structures" before they "sit with patriots." With the ANC eager to have the widest possible representation, including particularly the Democratic Party, it could hardly give in to the unrealistic Azapo demand. Azapo thereby missed the chance to present itself with twenty delegates as equal to the ANC and PAC at the founding conference. ANC-oriented observers commented that "it was a suicidal move by an organisation which has been steadily losing influence for the past 15 years" (*South Scan*, October 25, 1991). However, Azapo can claim that it had never engaged in false compromises in the interests of controversial negotiations.

In conclusion, in the 1990s the BCM and the PAC-aligned Africanists, though outmaneuvered by the ANC, continue to spread their message through community development programs, health awareness projects, and women's organizations. These groups have left an indelible mark on the discourse in black politics, although they have been overshadowed by the publicity, diplomatic success, and organizational clout of the ANC. Compared to the ANC, Azapo remains primarily an intellectual force. Supported by a number of influential opinion-makers in the universities, as well as by some clerics and trade union leaders, Black Consciousness endures, though more as an alternative vision than an active political movement. Its success and failure lie in the extent to which its ideas have shaped the attitudes of political actors and some of the organizational rivalries—physical clashes between ANC and Azapo supporters notwithstanding.

The historic highpoint of the BCM, the 1976 Soweto uprising, and that of the PAC in 1960 were eclipsed by the subsequent rise of the Charterist hegemony, in which many of the exiled Africanists and Black Consciousness supporters were absorbed. Although the BCM continued as a third exiled liberation movement, separate from the ANC and PAC and without the sponsorship of a major world power, many of its members found their home abroad in the ANC, which in turn benefited from the influx of committed students. Without this infusion of a new generation of young radicals, the subsequent rise and renewal of the Charterist tradition would have been inconceivable. In shedding both the internalized colonial mentality and liberal tutelage, Black Consciousness laid the ground for a self-confident challenge of the apartheid state, whether through negotiations or refusals of co-optation.

A number of observers have stressed the transitional character of the movement; David Hirschmann concludes that the BCM was "ultimately a victim of its own success."[31] To be sure, many of its promoters found their home in the ANC and the current numerical support for Azapo's strategies remains small, according to all surveys. However, the situation might change if the ANC is perceived as too moderate and accommodating. The continued significance of Black Consciousness as well as Africanism lies in their potential. That the ANC leadership feels obliged to use strident language and ultimatums in the negotiations testifies to the latent impact of the more radical alternative.

CHAPTER SIX

Political Violence, "Tribalism," and Inkatha

I have never once had any discussion with any National
Party leader in which we talked about Zulus and
Afrikaners ganging up against a black majority
government.

M. G. Buthelezi, *Sunday Times,*
September 29, 1991

Probably no other aspect of the South African conflict has elicited
more divergent explanations and misinterpretations than the ongoing
political violence. It is variously attributed to (1) de Klerk's double
agenda and unreformed police; (2) a "third force" of right-wing elements in the security establishment, bent on derailing the government's negotiation agenda; (3) the Inkatha/ANC rivalry, engineered
by an ambitious Buthelezi who fears being sidelined rather than
treated as an equal third party; (4) the ANC's campaign of armed
struggle, ungovernability, and revolutionary intolerance; (5) ingrained
tribalism, unleashed by the lessening of white repression that resulted
in "black-on-black" violence; (6) the legacy of apartheid in general,
migrantcy, hostel conditions, and high unemployment among a generation of "lost youth." Helen Suzman, for example, singled out sanctions for at least "part of the blame" in her 1991 presidential address
to the Institute of Race Relations, while John Kane-Berman, the
institute's director, stated that all parties had "bloody hands."[1]

Our analysis refutes any single-cause explanation. Rather than
focus on the policies of various leaders, we find it more useful to
examine predisposing social conditions, such as the rural-urban divide, the intergenerational cleavages, and the differential living conditions, social status, and heightened competition of long-time urban
residents, shack dwellers, and migrants in single-men hostels. Regardless of peace accords signed at the top, antagonistic groups at the

bottom often act violently, independent of leadership control. Such behavior has, in particular, been undertaken by elements of the official security establishment, linked to right-wing agendas of destabilizing the negotiation process.

A credible comprehensive account of the violence has yet to be produced, despite dozens of articles and books on the topic.[2] Indeed, most academic analysts either adopt a single conceptualization—clientelism or vigilantism (Charney, 1991)—or blame "lumpen elements" (Saul 1991). The focus on the state's use of vigilantes, while highlighting important auxiliary forces, fails to explain the underlying causes of vigilante success in attacking a vastly more popular liberation movement.

Obviously, youthful activists are challenging traditional African patrimonialism, the role of petty bourgeois powerbrokers in the townships and chiefs in the countryside. Traditional authority clashed with the newly autonomous, better-educated segments of the urbanized working class. Analysts of political violence are aware of this larger context, but they list, label, and categorize a variety of contributory factors without explaining their origin or relationship. Here is a particularly comprehensive example by Cape Town political scientist Peter Collins (1990, 96): "Gangsterism, vendettas, banditry, protection rackets, individual and group psychosis, competition for turf and treasure, a spreading mood of anarchy in which everyone thinks they possess a license to kill, the resurgence of antique hatreds, desperation born of unendurable poverty or fear—all these factors have variously contributed to outbreaks of violence." At the least, one would want to weigh these causes against each other and denote the historical conditions under which they express themselves simultaneously.

Other South African academics readily point fingers at the system of apartheid as the cause of the township conflict. In the words of Rupert Taylor (1991), "Apartheid has succeeded in engineering group divisions among the oppressed." While one can agree with Taylor that the conflict "is not of some essential ethnic forces," to blame it only on the manipulations of apartheid is an oversimplification. Ethnic antagonisms exist in societies that do not have apartheid. Above all, in demystifying ethnicity, the analyst needs to show why the manipulators are so successful in constructing and exploiting ethnic cleavages. Apartheid did not invent all ethnic divisions; it skillfully utilized collective memories and distinct histories. Analysts who deny this historical reality invoke magic formulas to wish away deep-rooted perceptions that can be mobilized for progressive as well as retrogressive ends.

A much more promising and sociological approach to township conflict has been adopted by Lawrence Schlemmer (1991), who distinguishes between general background conditions, predisposing factors, and triggering events. Background conditions include the dislocation brought about by urbanization, the high levels of unemployment and dependency, the breakdown of the traditional family structure, and the erosion of normative restraints on murder. Short-term measures cannot easily address these conditions. On the other hand, predisposing factors and, in particular, triggering effects, Schlemmer points out, can be reduced or directly counteracted. Among these predisposing conditions are the social alienation of rural migrants in an urban youth subculture and the heightened competition for limited opportunities in a social climate of politicized mass action. Once set in motion, the violence becomes self-perpetuating. Distrust increases and is reinforced by partisan reporting. Clearly, interventions aimed at apportioning blame or taking sides are doomed to failure. Instead, bringing the feuding groups together, supporting independent monitoring committees, ensuring impartial policing, taking grievances seriously, and balancing the press reporting through a better understanding of both sides are more likely to reduce violence.

Schlemmer has rightly pointed out that the South African violence is not of the type of an internal war with "massive revolutionary motivation at both the elite and popular levels."[3] Most striking is the constant talk of peace by the leadership but escalating clashes on the ground, despite an overwhelming popular sentiment for negotiations. Therefore, the violence is better classified as conspiratorial and turmoil-producing in nature, originating from politically active networks of people in several camps (the government, Inkatha, and the ANC) who act according to their own agendas. They view the leaderships' overtures cynically. In the words of the ANC Natal Midlands leader Harry Gwala, "No amount of talk between them will bring an end to the violence" (*Cape Times*, October 29, 1992). Similar sentiments can be heard from extremists on the right wing and in Inkatha. Localized acts of aggression against leaders and supporters of the various factions provoke immediate retaliation or else the many grievances are exploited to teach the other side a lesson. Even the long-standing factional fights between local communities in certain areas of Natal are now carried out under the banner of political labels, though these

disputes do not necessarily have an ideological content. The mediators and peace commissioners originate mostly from outside these
semirural communities and, as ethnic outsiders, carry little weight.
When local strongmen are literally dragged into these peace-making
sessions, they consider the occasion at best another forum to assail the
enemy or achieve a propaganda victory.

Many English-language South African journalists, as well as most
foreign correspondents writing for a liberal opinion abroad, are more
favorably inclined toward the ANC's interpretations than "tribal"
Inkatha or Africanist visions. In South Africa, liberation politics is
largely conducted in English, which paradoxically makes it more
accessible to outsiders than to the two-thirds of the locals who have
only Standard 6 education and a minimal understanding of English.
Few journalists or liberal academics bother to explore the views of
rural people, migrants, and squatters, who are thought to be ably
represented by a popular sophisticated elite. This constellation of an
unspoken understanding between technocratic opinion-makers and
progressive leadership may well mislead election forecasts by vastly
underestimating the strength of the less-accessible PAC and Inkatha
constituencies. The PAC, in particular, hardly receives any exposure
in the South African and international media. Political violence has
been generally attributed exclusively to the state and Inkatha—an
assumption that only the liberal Institute of Race Relations has que-
ried. In a letter to the institute's members, dated October 16, 1992,
President Helen Suzman wrote: "It was shown that while the state and
the Inkatha Freedom Party are responsible for much of the violence,
so too are the African National Congress and its allies, a fact which
has been covered up or excused in many instances."

Anthea Jeffery has provided thorough documentation for the
charge that the 1992 reports by Amnesty International, the International Commission of Jurists, and the South African–based Human
Rights Commission engage in disinformation about violence in South
Africa.[4] Jeffery asserts that these reports ignore ANC-inspired violence and instead focus only on the collusion between Inkatha and the
South African security forces in perpetrating violence. She points to
the ANC's strategy of fostering "ungovernability," which has led to
widespread intimidation, and notes that the refusal to disband Umkhonto or ANC "self-defence units" is often ignored in reports about
township anarchy. Through such biased reporting, Jeffery argues,
these human rights organizations not only distort the causes of vio-

lence, but also set the stage for increased confrontation and undermine attempts to generate lasting solutions to the conflict. In the
politicized atmosphere of South Africa, however, it can hardly be
expected that the members of the South African Human Rights Commission, who are also ANC members, would criticize their own party.
Even the reporting and monitoring of the political violence is inevitably politicized.

THE STATE, INKATHA, AND THE "THIRD FORCE"

At the height of the sanctions campaign and the civil war with the
ANC, the South African government viewed the antisanctions Inkatha
movement as a valuable ally. It courted the free-enterprise advocate
Buthelezi as a useful counterforce against the "socialist" ANC-SACP
alliance. Initially, Pretoria was concerned that Inkatha might be
eclipsed by the ANC. To prop up the only credible black moderate
who was assumed to have a large following, the government provided
propagandistic educational and military training assistance, delivered
by front organizations of military intelligence, which a besieged Inkatha readily accepted. However, there is no evidence that the relatively
small amount of money ($100,000) transferred for an Inkatha rally—
the revelation of which triggered an uproar—or the more substantial
contributions for a semi-defunct in-house union were given to foment
violence. John Saul's (1991, 14) assertion that the de Klerk regime
"directly sponsored the resulting mayhem to the tune of several million rand" assumes a Machiavellian conspiracy that would have run
counter to Pretoria's desire to forge a working relationship with the
ANC and regain international legitimacy and foreign investment. To
achieve these ends, the South African state needed to project an image
of stability. Black violence would frighten white voters into support
of right-wing parties, and a decimated ANC would either be unwilling
to make an alliance or incapable of enforcing a compromise against
an enraged constituency. The entire project of a negotiated transition
and renewed legitimacy would have been jeopardized by state-sponsored violence.

The instigators of the violence can be found in the same circles of
semi-independent military intelligence operatives who, disagreeing
with de Klerk's policy change, wanted to see negotiation fail and the
right-wing agenda succeed. P. W. Botha had accorded these securocrats unprecedented autonomy. De Klerk had cautiously begun to

dismantle their institutions and allowed their illegal activities to be publicly exposed by the Harms and Goldstone commissions. Nonetheless, de Klerk appointed the head of the Special Forces Command, General A. J. (Kat) Liebenberg, as chief of the South African Defence Force in November 1990 and kept other implicated officers in order to bind them to the reform course and isolate more inflexible opponents in the lower ranks. "In return," observers conclude, "an SADF political education programme won back much middle-rank support for the de Klerk line" (O'Meara 1992, 22). Yet some of the generals were the same decorated forces that had trained Renamo and Unita and had proceeded with covert funding to ready Inkatha and the KwaZulu police for paramilitary action. Once part of a state-sponsored de-stabilization campaign to make the surrounding region economically dependent, the hardline ideologues had acquired a life of their own, long after the state ideology had fundamentally changed.

There is evidence that some of the leading *verligtes* themselves, particularly Pik Botha's Foreign Affairs Department, had to take precautionary measures against the bizarre machinations of this "third force," operating under its own rules and out to defeat the negotiation course. Dan O'Meara (1992, 22) aptly comments: "As de Klerk sidelined the generals . . . he had to move with great caution. Plots against him were commonplace in the SADF Special Forces and other dirty trick units after February 1990 and support for the CP in SADF middle ranks mushroomed." The securocrats' dealings with blacks merely reflected the much more vital struggle among whites. In the conflict over strategies for Afrikaner survival, even the faction in control of the state could not afford to suppress its opponents directly. While de Klerk certainly prevaricated, it is illogical that he would have been personally implicated in fomenting violence, as his critics charge.

The same political realignments are played out at the level of daily police behavior toward opponents. There is no question that the South African police, especially its black members, and particularly in KwaZulu, do not behave in an impartial manner; police have frequently colluded with Inkatha demonstrators at the expense of ANC supporters. However, the right wing's obvious sympathy for Zulu warriors does not mean that Buthelezi is a mere paid stooge of the government. On the contrary, Buthelezi's refusal to participate in an ANC-NP pact has become more vociferous, the more the government's initial, clumsy attempts to support Inkatha have isolated and discredited the movement. Various surveys report that among urban blacks Inkatha is more unpopular than the AWB.[5] More than 50 percent of ANC, NP/DP, and Azapo/PAC supporters blame Inkatha for instigating the violence. In Schlemmer's survey of 905 black respondents in the Witwatersrand townships in early 1991, only 5 percent said they would vote for Inkatha in a hypothetical free election, although 71 percent of hostel dwellers in the sample said they would do so.

How have the revelations in August 1991 about Inkatha having received funding from the state affected the standing of the main players since these surveys were conducted? Two immediate implications favoring the ANC flowed from the scandal. First, Buthelezi's claim to being an independent, equal third player in the negotiations could no longer be maintained. What both Inkatha and the government had hoped for—a creditable conservative counterbalance to the ANC-SACP alliance—they themselves had destroyed and, in the process, they undermined the chances of third parties in a multiparty democracy. Second, the ANC's demand for a neutral interim government of national unity to oversee the transition received a major boost. Pretoria itself conceded its lack of neutrality. Inkatha, too, endorsed the ANC's accusations of Pretoria's partiality by now rejecting the money it had earlier accepted, allegedly without the knowledge of Buthelezi. Above all, Buthelezi's credibility was diminished by his plea of ignorance. While Inkatha's internal support, particularly among the illiterate rural population in Natal and the migrant workers, remained unaffected, Inkatha's international reputation and its support among South African business suffered. In short, the exposure somewhat leveled the uneven playing field between the government and the ANC, locking both sides more tightly into negotiations by discrediting third-party claims. These were the unintended side effects of the episode, which, although overblown abroad, produced only a muted and restrained response from the ANC.

Earlier relations between the government and Inkatha have been widely misinterpreted. For example, the noted historian George Fredrickson writes: "One might also question the appropriateness of his [Buthelezi's] negotiating with the government on behalf of the African majority when he strongly opposed the economic sanctions that, more than anything else, brought the government to the bargaining table in the first place" (1991, 38). Leaving aside the controversial issue of whether sanctions were the main reason for Pretoria's shift in 1990, one must realize that Buthelezi has never negotiated with the government on behalf of the African majority. He successfully resisted "independence" for his Bantustan and the consequent denationalization of its inhabitants. He opposed the 1984 tricameral constitution, as did most liberals—with the exception of South African business. Above all, throughout the 1980s, Buthelezi consistently argued that the release of Mandela and free political activity were the preconditions for his entering into negotiations about a national settlement with Pretoria. For this and other reasons P. W. Botha and Buthelezi never saw eye to eye and had scarcely any contact. Indeed, the National Party always considered Buthelezi "very much his own man," as Botha put it.[6] He was viewed as being in a different league from the other more opportunistic Bantustan leaders and "system politicians" in the Coloured and Indian community. It was precisely this higher credibility that made Buthelezi an attractive ally for government and business.

Why then did Inkatha's influence decline? Why did Inkatha and the ANC fail to resolve their deadly feud? Premature predictions of Inkatha's "terminal decline" (*SouthScan*, January 17, 1992) rest, above all, on the autocratic behavior of Buthelezi, who turned the organization into a tightly controlled one-man show. It was this isolation of an idiosyncratic person that allowed apartheid apologists of his own antisanctions stance to sponsor him.[7] His opposition to sanctions did not harm him since it was also shared by a wide variety of respectable anti-apartheid liberals, including Helen Suzman and F. van Zyl Slabbert. Moreover, sanctions evoked considerable ambivalence within the black community, despite rhetorical majority support for tough international action against Pretoria. Buthelezi primarily articulated the fears of his less-privileged constituency of migrant workers and rural traditionalists who had the most to lose from higher unemployment and economic decline.

After hailing Inkatha as a nonviolent, free-enterprise, responsible black counterforce, the North American mainstream press has now for the most part uncritically adopted the ANC's version of Buthelezi as the instigator of violence. Typical of this perspective is a lengthy piece by Peter Tygesen, a Danish correspondent for the American magazine *Africa Report*. Tygesen calls Buthelezi a "radical warmonger" and assigns him personal responsibility for all the atrocities: "Nowhere else in South Africa has bloodshed taken place on such a scale as in Buthelezi's Natal, and by exporting this conflict to the Witwatersrand, he has plunged South Africa's most popular area into horrifying carnage."[8] The predictably opposite conservative view has it that all of Buthelezi's speeches at dozens of rallies are genuine pleas to his followers to bury the hatchet and ensure peace. These speeches often invoke the rich imagery and language of the rural audiences: "When a tree falls across your path, you remove it so that you can walk. When you have a thorn in your foot, you remove it. When there is a fire you put it out. And when there is violence and when there is Black brother killing Black brother, you put an end to it."[9]

Hardly any ANC supporter believes such exhortations, and most academic analysts echo this incredulity. Typical is a judgment by Robert Price (1990, 294): "With his mass support dwindling to insignificance, and with the domestic and international political spotlight firmly focused on Mandela, Buthelezi apparently decided to guarantee himself a central role in negotiations over South Africa's future by demonstrating that unless he is taken into account, there will be no peace." John Saul (1991, 16) calls Buthelezi simply "a hired tool of the security services." To assess such strong accusations requires a detailed understanding of the predisposing conditions and of the motivations of the antagonists, an analysis of the unrecognized fault lines and collective psychology that allows "mass endorsement of violence." Before we turn to these issues, we want to take another look at the role of the security forces, their relationship to the state reformers, and the reformers' own shortcomings.

As stated earlier, ample evidence exists that right-wing forces within the police and military intelligence either actively foment black violence and exploit cleavages or do not care much to suppress black violence and charge perpetrators. Court evidence on the activities of the now disbanded Civil Cooperation Bureau, as well as testimony by defectors and survivors, reveals a story of unimaginable atrocities.[10] There are poorly trained policemen and security officials in various government agencies who resent both the negotiation course and the ascendency of blacks. On the other hand, a well-disciplined police force can be successfully mobilized to defend the state, regardless of officers' personal sympathies, as the Ventersdorp clashes in 1991 showed.[11] While there has been a slow shift toward a professionalization of the South African police, up through 1991, during Malan's and Vlok's command of the military and police, the de Klerk government was either unwilling or, more likely, unable to control the vestiges of the death squads, special forces, and Recce commandos. Only in the wake of the Inkatha funding scandal were new security ministers installed. However, Pretoria has yet to come clean on the unreformed elements within its security machinery, despite progressive changes at the top.

Jonathan Gluckman, a respected pathologist, charged that in 90 percent of the two hundred postmortems he had conducted in recent years, the police were responsible for the killings (*Sunday Times,* July 26, 1992). Yet, occasional prisoners in police custody are still found hanging from cell ceilings or are reported to have jumped to their deaths out of eighth-floor windows. It is this routine brutality of a militarized, poorly trained, and unprofessional police force—rather than grand designs of destabilization—that accounts for the massive state violence in South Africa. Both the Goldstone Commission and independent outside investigators, among them British criminologist Peter Waddington, found no evidence of state complicity in the widely reported Boipatong massacre in June 1992. Rather, they blamed the local police for incompetence and indifference.[12]

Widespread acts of omission, rather than rarer acts of commissioned violence, therefore, characterize the South African conflict. With the deeply ingrained stereotype that blacks are by nature violent people, police fail to protect ordinary township residents from the fallouts of battles for political turf. Until August 1992 the state allowed "traditional weapons" to be carried for likely confrontations and generally failed to secure prosecutions once clashes had taken place. The resulting distrust of the police among black activists does not facilitate collecting evidence for convictions. Witnesses are often intimidated. Police work for prosecutions is carried out so casually that only determined attorneys are able to pass the stringent hurdles necessary to obtain convictions in independent courts.

Since the police themselves have become frequent victims of counterattacks by misguided political activists and criminal gangsters alike, frightened middle-class members of all groups sympathize with the few remaining "agents of law and order" rather than demand their drastic reform. Since the de Klerk government cannot afford to alienate its only guarantor in case negotiations fail, the securocrats even get away in instances where hard evidence of atrocities exists. For example, General C. P. van der Westhuizen remained head of Military Intelligence despite his message that four Eastern Cape activists should be "permanently removed from society," which was dutifully carried out in 1985.

However, because the ANC has portrayed itself as the sole victim of state-Inkatha violence, even though some of its self-defense units are also involved in perpetrating less-publicized massacres, the ANC's claims have also become discredited. Indeed, only in August 1992 did Hani and Mandela finally admit that some self-defense units were out of community control, had fought among themselves, flogged and necklaced opponents on spurious charges, imposed taxes on black businessmen, and even fired indiscriminately on vehicles traveling on the Golden Highway.[13] When the secretary of the ANC Youth League, Peter Mokabe, declares even the families of black policemen legitimate targets of harassment, the equally brutalized men in uniform feel justified in fighting rather than protecting their community.

To attribute all violence to a state-directed "third force" does not explain the attacks against Inkatha officeholders and the police. Among the fatalities are equal numbers of ANC and Inkatha members or sympathizers. There is also evidence that both movements have their own "third forces" that are not under the direct control of the national leadership. When MK units "take out" specific Inkatha targets in Natal and local Inkatha warlords organize attacks against ANC leaders and sympathizers, it is difficult to ascertain which side has started the violence and which exercises revenge. Generally it can be said that the MK violence is carried out more professionally and with the use of sophisticated firearms. In comparison, the more primitive ("cultural") weaponry of Inkatha members lends itself more to random violence by excited mobs against anyone who is not part of the crowd. For example, unable to find those who have attacked them, some hostel dwellers take revenge on those whom they believe are sheltering their enemies. In turn, this incenses the surrounding communities against all hostel dwellers—whether or not they were involved in the violence or are Inkatha supporters—and their children often cannot attend schools in the townships for fear of attack. Bus drivers are sometimes told by commuters "not to stop for that hostel dog," and the mere identification as a Zulu-speaker carries the risk of death. Hostel dwellers compare the proposed fencing of the hostels to the caging of animals in a zoo. The carrying of shields, spears, axes, and knobkieries ("cultural weapons") has become elevated to a question of asserting Zulu identity after a sensible government decision to ban the display of all weapons in public demonstrations.

The two camps have become so polarized that in some areas even nurses in hospitals refuse to treat patients who belong to the other side. ANC supporters are unwelcome in Ulundi's civil service, and several homes in the area were burnt down by unknown assailants after a particularly mobilizing speech by Buthelezi in September 1992.

While Inkatha accuses Mandela of using "inflammatory language" at the United Nations when he suggested that the party was a "surrogate" of the government, Buthelezi responds in kind by urging his youth brigade to "bugger up" the ANC, unless they and their future would be "buggered" by a reckless ANC strategy (*Cape Times*, September 7, 1992, p. 5). On the other side, the call by SACP Chief Chris Hani "to clear townships of puppets," means exactly the same for black councillors and policemen. As John Kane-Berman, the executive director of the Institute of Race Relations, has pointed out, South African liberals have generally failed to speak about the right black policemen have to a fair trial, instead of instant assassination.

John Argyle has argued that much of the Natal conflict is now motivated principally by the desire for revenge and therefore resembles century-old blood feuds. In the past, such feuds originated not only over land but also over insults to honor or violations of women. Both sides cite provocation as a defense. As Kentridge (1990, 19) notes, "In a war there are no aggressors; ostensibly no side ever initiates an attack. . . . if an attack is made, it is always retaliatory." Yet, while it is wise "to believe neither side" until independent conclusive evidence is available, as Argyle cautions, one cannot simply blame the conflict on long-standing cultural traditions of habitual feuding. The waxing and waning of the feuds can be traced in the changing conditions that precipitate or repress intergroup and interpersonal violence.

The continued violence by current and former state agents was unwittingly nurtured by the failure of the de Klerk government to make a moral break with apartheid. By not offering any apology, let alone compensation to the victims, the government reinforced the impression that previously a just war had been fought, though now, for tactical reasons, it had come to an end. Pik Botha, for example, in defending the Inkatha funding, reiterated defiantly that he would repeat it under the then-prevailing circumstances. During the undeclared war, the state's killers had been celebrated as heroes. Their bravery in a war the government never refuted could not now suddenly be redefined as an atrocity, particularly since the perpetrators disagreed with the government's new tactical policy of reconciliation with "terrorists." By treating apartheid as a mere mistake and costly error, not a crime or a moral aberration, by failing to officially condemn the murders it had once sponsored, the government forfeited its opportunity to pressure unreformed state agents to now conform to the rules, rules that everyone knew had been ignored in the unofficial war.

Of course, de Klerk's cabinet could not announce a moral rebuff of apartheid because they had been involved in its conception and execution. They broke with the system not because it was wrong but because it did not work. Just as the former Stalinists in the new Soviet republics now pose as democrats, so the former apartheid rulers now behave as reformers. In the absence of any program for the moral rehabilitation of a society, the depth of social transformation remains unsure. When unrepenting incumbents remain in office, the past literally haunts the future and reveals itself in the continuation of the same practices, regardless of the new era.

In the delicate climate of generalized anxiety and confused transition, even small third forces thrive and with little effort trigger major confrontations. Moreover, the state, Inkatha, and the ANC have each lost full control of some of the ground forces acting in their names. The new element of the 1990s is the indiscriminate attacks on train commuters as well as the professional random shooting of both ANC and Inkatha supporters. The failure of the security police to identify the culprits suggests indifference, if not collusion. There is little doubt that collusion between the police and Inkatha takes place, yet for the time being one has to accept R. W. Johnson's (1991) judgment: "How far up the hierarchy of either the security forces or Inkatha such collusion goes is impossible to know."

The accord signed in September 1991 between the government, the ANC, and Inkatha lays down useful rules for the behavior of the police and politicians, yet no document can regulate the death squads and freelance hit-men. While these renegades ought to be suppressed by all means possible, one would not want to see any crackdown on organizations that have a genuine constituency. Nor can civil war be averted through negotiations as long as relatively autonomous agents are free to scuttle a fragile accord. Unless the leaders exercise effective control over their followers and the leaders themselves strive to make peace through negotiations that include all substantial forces, regardless of their ideological position or record, an end to the violence is unlikely.

"TRIBALISM" IN PERSPECTIVE

In a truly divided society it is almost impossible for an individual to assume any identity other than one of those prescribed by the communal division. In Northern Ireland, people see only Protestants and Catholics; in Israel, only Jews and Arabs. Within such frameworks, as many social scientists have suggested, people define and interpret social existence. In divided societies the everyday social reasoning based on familiar labels and expectations has little to do with doctrinal issues of religion. Rather, it signifies likely power and status differentials, based on a long history of communal conflict that encompasses every member of the community.

South Africa differs from those communal conflicts in that apartheid labels have engendered so much opposition and comprise such a variety of crossracial common characteristics that many whites and blacks can afford to act as if they live outside their communally imposed category. In fact, the democratic nonracialism espoused by most major actors in South Africa is quite distinct from the entrenched, exclusivist communalism elsewhere. The state construction of official ethnicity in South Africa has no precedent in any other divided society, although the post-apartheid ethnic strife may in the end come to resemble communal divisions elsewhere.

One of the great surprises of 1990, therefore, was the sudden emergence of the "tribal" factor. Hitherto, it had been taboo for the disenfranchised to talk publicly about Zulu and Xhosa forces. Only apartheid's ideologues used such labels. Why then has simmering ideological conflict suddenly been recast by participants as a tribal clash? While both leaderships proudly display their nontribal stance, some of their followers, nevertheless, kill each other as Zulus and Xhosas.

Despite historical competitions and conflicts between the two Nguni-speaking people, the ANC, the premier organization to combat tribalism politically, has always had a fair succession of leaders from both ethnic groups and had managed to overcome tribal consciousness to a large extent—at least as far as the political activists were concerned. The ANC's last president before its banning, the Nobel Peace Prize–winner Albert Luthuli, was a respected Zulu chief, and the ANC's National Executive Committee in exile always included some, though disproportionately few, Zulus. NEC members assert that the ethnic background of candidates was never an issue; in some cases, they say, they were not even aware of the origin of comrades in exile, although this is flatly contradicted by other insider accounts (see Ellis and Sechaba, 1992). Similarly, the SACP's ideology had always embraced cosmopolitan internationalism, at least in theory.

Attitudes gradually changed, however, after 1979, when Buthelezi's Inkatha movement began to pursue an independent policy.

That the ANC initially approved of Inkatha is nowadays often unmentioned. Oliver Tambo in particular encouraged Buthelezi to assume his Bantustan role. The ANC served as the midwife of Inkatha, which was envisaged as an ANC internal wing, a Trojan horse, under the protective umbrella of a Bantustan, led by Buthelezi. A shrewd former member of the ANC youth league, Buthelezi knew his aristocratic descent from a family of the king's advisers would aid his popularity.

The ANC offspring quickly outgrew its parent, and Inkatha began to pursue an independent line. Buthelezi refused to recruit for the MK camps; to have complied would have been to risk direct clashes with Pretoria. Among the ANC's cadres Zulus became underrepresented, although surveys indicate that about half of all Zulus support the ANC. The much higher support for the ANC in the Xhosa heartland of the Eastern Cape and the ANC's invisibility in rural Natal are also reflected in the composition of the organization's leadership.

Tribal separateness was reinforced not so much by Buthelezi's style or cultural symbolism as by his divergent policies. After all, the Xhosa Transkei was the first Bantustan to accept tribal independence, while the allegedly tribalist Buthelezi harbored national ambitions and refused to steer a secessionist course. But his rejection of the armed struggle and support of foreign investment deepened the rift between Inkatha and the ANC, and drew Inkatha closer to the South African establishment than to the anti-apartheid exiles abroad—despite Buthelezi's consistent anti-apartheid stance.

The turn of events traumatized the ANC, whose former ally had now become a potential partner in a dialogue that could further marginalize the exiles. The ensuing war of words culminated in the South African Youth Congress (Sayco) declaring Buthelezi "an enemy of the people" in 1990. For the ANC, Buthelezi's name had become anathema. During the various meetings between ANC executives and South African academics that preceded the legalization of the resistance, one could talk rationally about any controversial subject, but not about Buthelezi.[14] Similarly, many overseas South Africa watchers have informally adopted the ANC line that Buthelezi is "a pathological case" and that Inkatha consists of "a bunch of murderers" akin to the Khmer Rouge.

While Buthelezi's Bantustan regime is singled out for vilification, other ANC-aligned Bantustans have been exonerated. The ANC's habit of uncritical silence reinforces double standards and counterproductive developments, as in the case of the ANC-Transkei relationship. Instead of attacking all Bantustan structures, the anti-apartheid movement has exempted the Transkei and others whose leaders have aligned themselves squarely with the ANC. This strategy allows Buthelezi to dismiss the ANC's demand for the dismantling of KwaZulu as a Xhosa-led plot against Zulus, thereby legitimating the ethnic suspicions of beleaguered Zulus. The collaboration between the ANC and the Transkei military ruler General Bantu Holomisa—who defends the integrity of the Transkei, its use of detention without trial, and its repressive security legislation—runs counter to the very core of the democratic movement. Securing civil service positions for returning exiles in the Bantustan administrations now functions as a justification for their continued existence in the new South Africa, although ANC-aligned Bantustans have all agreed to be reincorporated.

As a consequence of the ANC-engineered boost to the legitimacy of Transkei, other Bantustan-based pocket dictators now seek to strengthen their fragile bases through relations with the new emerging powers, while others seek closer alliances with Pretoria. Instead of the desired unity of the disenfranchised in one patriotic front, the ANC's various flirtations with Bantustan leaders have created new animosities and potential fragmentation.[15] The two sizeable Bantustans, KwaZulu and Bophutatswana, now resist being drawn into an ANC-led alliance for a centralized state, instead insisting on federal solutions or even potential secession.

The violent struggle for territorial control of townships, squatter camps, and hostels has also entered the even more vulnerable factory floor. Owing mainly to the explicit political stance Cosatu adopted, the formerly integrated union movement became fragmented and labor relations heavily politicized. Conflicts on the shopfloor emerged as the consequence of Inkatha's founding of the new union Uwusa, which was applauded and endorsed by shortsighted employers in retaliation for Cosatu's backing of sanctions. Elijah Barayi, the president of Cosatu, promised at a mass rally in Durban in November 1985 "to bury" Buthelezi. In retrospect, even Cosatu activists consider this declaration of war a serious political error. Jeremy Baskin (1991), a former national coordinator of Cosatu, now deplores Barayi's speech: "It gave the impression that Cosatu's major aim was to oppose Buthelezi and the homeland system. His speech ignored the lesson learnt by Natal unionists over the years: winning workers in the region to progressive positions was achieved by hard organizational work and not by attacks on Buthelezi."

In July 1990 Inkatha's perception of being under siege was heightened by the ANC-Cosatu decision to elevate the Natal regional violence into a national issue. National marches and strikes were supposed to demonstrate that Inkatha was not a national force, that it could be sidelined in the forthcoming negotiations and Buthelezi could be buried politically. Inkatha now felt compelled to demonstrate its clout on the Rand as well. The migrants in the hostels became the obvious force to be mobilized. If the ANC was going to demonstrate the irrelevance of a rival, Inkatha was going to prove its relevance through ferocious impis. Isolated hostel dwellers who were looked down upon by the ANC youths in the townships were ready to teach them a lesson, although both segments of the urban proletariat had coexisted side by side for decades. With the exception of clashes between residents and migrants during the Soweto upheaval in 1976—disputes largely instigated by the police—tribal cleavages had never played a role in the multiethnic townships. In fact many township residents, including the majority in Soweto, are of Zulu origin. Migrants and permanent residents of Zulu, Xhosa, and mixed origin lived side by side in shabby hostels and backyards. Aggressors would be unable to distinguish township residents according to ethnicity. But with the hostels labeled "Zulu" and the townships "Xhosa and ANC," an ideological conflict and socioeconomic cleavage became transformed into a tribal war. The transformation was triggered by the ill-advised ANC strategy to isolate Inkatha rather than include it in the broad anti-apartheid alliance. Former Inkatha General Secretary Oscar Dhlomo rightly concluded from his independent insider's perspective: "Buthelezi has skillfully utilized ANC blunders to his advantage. He is now able to claim, thanks to the ANC, that anyone who demands the dismantling of the KwaZulu government is challenging not only the Zulu nation but also the Zulu King" (*Sunday Tribune*, August 26, 1990).

In contrast to the paramount chiefs of the Tembus and other Xhosa clans, where the royal house plays a largely titular role, the Zulu king is a higher-profile figure for his people. The king is supposed to stand above politics and act as a unifying symbol to whom all Zulus, regardless of ideology, owe allegiance. For Zulu speakers, there is only one king. That the current king, Goodwill Zwelithini, a nephew

of Buthelezi, is strongly aligned with the Inkatha position bestows
legitimacy on Inkatha but also undermines the authority of the king
and contributes to Zulu disunity. Although the violence in Natal is
between Zulus, any conflict acquires a tribal connotation as soon as
the chiefs, indunas, sangomas, and shacklords present it to their large
followings as a matter of defending the traditional order against
"outsiders." And by labeling hostilities in tribal terms, the leaders
reinforce this perception and broaden their own constituencies. "I
want to make it quite clear that ANC attacks are not only attacks
against Inkatha," said Buthelezi at a rally in Bakkersdal. "They are
attacks against Zulu people just because they are Zulu" (*Guardian
Weekly*, May 12, 1991). Similarly, KwaZulu minister Ben Ngubane
charges, "We are in a critical situation. The police are stretched to the
limit and cannot protect us. Our options are stark: either we run for
cover or we defend ourselves. Obviously we are opting for the latter"
(interview, October 25, 1992).

Thus, as in most ethnic conflicts, each faction views itself as the
victim of the others' aggression, against which self-defense is only
natural. Inkatha, which is generally viewed as the main perpetrator of
violence by the media, is no exception. In Ngubane's view, "Our
information is that highly mobile, highly efficient MK members,
dressed in SADF uniforms, are bussed in from the Transkei. They
move quickly, digging up hidden arms caches, killing community
leaders and whoever else is in the way, bury their guns again and then
flee back across the border." Ngubane's sources are probably correct,
but the MK members would justify their actions by claiming that they
were revenging ANC victims and protecting ANC leaders.

INTERGENERATIONAL
AND URBAN-RURAL CLEAVAGES

Traditional Zulus who have a reconstructed memory of a precolonial
independent kingdom are deeply offended by the young comrades'
rejection and denial of this identity. In the view of traditional Zulu
leaders, the younger generation's attitudes threaten the established
cultural hierarchy. Thus King Goodwill Zwelithini complained: "Everything Zulu is being ridiculed. Our cultures are now being torn
apart . . . the Hlobane violence was triggered off by Cosatu members
who stated that when Dr. Nelson Mandela was released, my uncle the
Chief Minister [Buthelezi] and I would be his cook and waiter respec-

tively" (*Front File,* September 1990). Perceiving his traditional constituency to be withering away, the aristocratic leader invokes resistance in the name of history: at a meeting in Ulundi he told Zulu chiefs that their ancestors would turn in their graves if they saw how the strapping Amakhosi (elite corps) and their warriors were fleeing before ANC children. "The Amakhosi of Kwa Zulu must now stand firm because any retreat is the first step towards a rout" (*Front File,* September 1990).

The call for cultural revival is heeded by the most deprived among the Zulu people in search of responses to their humiliation. The invocation of a mythical past and images of pride and success in battle offers a source of dignity and identity to the rural poor, the hostel dwellers, and unemployed migrants. In their predicament, tribal identification carries with it a badge of honor.

In this context, citing the power struggle between the ANC and Inkatha supplies only a superficial explanation of the political violence. To be sure, the threat of isolation by the emerging NP-ANC alliance triggered Inkatha to play the tribal card. But similar frustrations exist on the other side, and the conflicts between youthful ANC supporters and traditionalists among Xhosa squatters follow a similar pattern.

In Cape Town, for example, a vicious war between two black taxi organizations reflected the conflict between two patronage groups, each claiming allegiance to the ANC. The heightened competition for scarce ranks and an outdated permit system that favored newcomers over old-timers represented a local variation of clientelism among a deprived Xhosa group, a situation that had been played out among Zulu speakers in Natal many times before. Members of the older taxi association, Lagunya, who were confined to intratownship routes, wanted their share of the more lucrative city traffic, which the newer Webta association had pirated and monopolized. But longtime residents and their civic organizations resent the more recently arrived "outsiders" and the competing patronage system of "town councilors" in the expanding Khayelitsha shack settlements. Police partiality toward Webta drivers further inflamed the conflict, resulting in a level of mutual distrust that even Cape Town city council–sponsored mediation and peace efforts could not break. The long-simmering conflict has cost several dozen lives, including that of the widely respected civic leader Michael Mapongwana, who was assassinated, as well as two million rand in damage.

In Cape Town it is neither tribal animosity nor political ideology that has caused such deep rifts and violence among the deprived. As Tony Karon has rightly stressed: "The legacy of Apartheid has created an urban context in which hundreds of thousands of desperately poor people compete for the allocation of scarce resources." Another example in a somewhat different arena illustrates a similar outcome.

In April 1991 residents of Katlehong squatter camps clashed when people from Holomisa Park attacked inhabitants of Mandela Park, both strongholds of the ANC. At the center of the dispute were stolen portable toilets that the Mandela Park squatters had tried to reclaim from the other side. Mandela Park is a long-established community, with running water and roads. Its ethnically mixed residents were accused by the homogeneous Pondo settlement of harboring hostile Zulus. While all squatters had lived in peace before, competition over the toilets quickly escalated into tribal suspicions. Rival political strategies heightened intracommunal frustrations, and Chris Hani barely succeeded in calming the residents by reminding the crowd that the ANC was a home for all ethnic groups.

Strikes and mass protests enforced through intimidation by overzealous youth constitute another trigger for violence. In December 1990, at the Mandelaville squatter camp near Bekkersdal, youth belonging to the ANC-aligned Bekkersdal youth congress wanted to stop pupils in the area from writing end-of-year examinations. The Azapo-aligned Azanian Students' Movement and the Azanian Youth Organisation rejected the move, and the ensuing fighting left a trail of death and destruction (*Star*, December 20, 1990).

The leadership on all sides has lost control over some local segments that act in their name, and gangs exploit the insecurity and political confusion. The killing of thirty-seven mourners at the wake of a murdered ANC leader in Sebokeng in January 1991 had its origins in a dispute between the ANC and a local gang whose activities included rape, theft, and murder. When local ANC chairman Christoffel Nangalembe called for an end to gang terror and reported to the police that the gang had AK-47 rifles, he was kidnapped and strangled to death by local gang members. The organizers of the wake for Nangalembe requested police protection for the mourners, but the police failed to provide it. Accusations of police connivance with the gang in the massacre of ANC activists are widely believed in the township.

Urban-rural tensions in the townships are marked by generational, cultural, and political differences. The predominant urban black identity emerged from a mixture of traditional elements and rural customs, the street wisdom of survival in the townships and in the modern workplace, and the consumerist aspirations of secular Western society. This politicized, individualistic urban culture defines itself in sharp contrast to the ethos of the rural inhabitants and migrants, who are considered illiterate, unsophisticated country bumpkins. In the status hierarchy of the townships, the people with rural ties are often scorned as ignorant ancestor-worshippers who don't speak English and practice a social life of tribalism and witchcraft. The denial of ethnicity and rejection of most cultural traditions by urban blacks reflect not only the government's attempts to manipulate ethnic differences but also an arrogant predilection to associate rural customs with false consciousness.

The ANC leadership embodies the urban views of those who have left tribalism behind and now wear suits and ties. At most they may stage tribal traditions as ceremonial events, which they attend with amused smugness in much the same way as some urbane Westerners enjoy folk dances. The ANC's internationalism and cosmopolitan universalism jars with the attitudes of the traditional African rural population. For many of them, the ANC appears as an elitist urban group whose leadership speaks English and looks down upon the ethnic customs of the peasants.

Many people in the rural communities and the migrant hostels deeply resent the political activism of the urban-based youth as a subversion of the traditional order in which children obey and politics is left to the elders. For the older generation, youthful activism is an ungrateful waste of the educational opportunities for which the parents sacrificed so much. On the other hand, youth accuse their parents of having compromised themselves with the system. This generational conflict has torn apart many families and pitted communities against each other, particularly in the semiurban settlements surrounding Pietermaritzburg, where rural and urban values clash directly under conditions of dire poverty.

In some parts of Natal, in the Durban townships of Lamontville and Chesterville, for example, youthful activism also has greater space because the area has traditionally been one of freehold settlements not under the jurisdiction of the KwaZulu Bantustan authorities. Their potential incorporation into KwaZulu was particularly resented by the residents in the 1980s. In Durban, in contrast to black life in

Johannesburg or Cape Town, KwaZulu reaches right into the suburbs, and the rural and urban exist side by side throughout much of Natal. Since KwaZulu never applied influx-control measures, unplanned squatting on the outskirts of cities was common, while the rural newcomers found a much more regulated and planned environment in Cape Town or Johannesburg.

The late conquest of Natal compared with other parts of South Africa meant that the traditional economy remains more intact there than elsewhere. The failure of employers to hire Africans as supervisors and middle managers also impeded African upward mobility in Natal. Although the majority of homesteaders in rural Zululand are dependent on remittances from migrants in Johannesburg, fewer families have moved out permanently, and the majority of migrants consider the rural area their home, to which they periodically return and plan to retire. Together with the reconstructed and revitalized memory of more successfully organized resistance against colonial conquest under powerful kings, a more traditional way of life has survived among segments of Zulu speakers. Both their self-definition as proud warriors as well as their objective differentiation in attitudes and geographical movements form the background to the clashes in the cities.

There is some empirical evidence that political and historical views among Xhosa and Zulu-speaking students in Soweto differ significantly. M. Roth found that Xhosa speakers tended to view apartheid more frequently as a result of capitalism but also agreed with the statement that "the country belongs to all the people equally."[16] Zulu speakers disagreed more frequently with the statement "People who came to our country three hundred years ago cannot be called settlers"; they thought that it did matter whether whites or blacks came to South Africa first. In short, the ANC's vision of nonracial sharing is more firmly held among Xhosa speakers, while Zulu-speaking students in Soweto, the majority of whom are by no means Inkatha supporters, tend to view South Africa more in nationalist terms. That the Zulu-speaking students' vision resembles the Africanist PAC outlook more than the liberal inclusive ANC view makes the white conservative support for Zulu cultural revival particularly ironic.

ISOLATED MIGRANTS IN SINGLE-MEN HOSTELS

The single-men migrant hostels on the Rand, the majority of whose inhabitants are Zulus, provided a flashpoint of resentment for both hostel dwellers and local residents. In Alexandra in March 1991 close to a hundred people died in riots that erupted after an unprecedented accord was signed between the Transvaal Provincial Administration and the ANC-controlled Alexandra Civic Organisation. The agreement amounted to a local model of what had yet to be negotiated at the national level: phasing out of the black council, which was widely considered to consist of corrupt collaborators, and the placing of township land on the Far East Rand under the joint control of ANC-aligned civic organizations and the surrounding white areas. To all intents and purposes, the accord represented an ANC victory over the traditionalists who, under Alex "Mayor" Prince Mokoena, had controlled Alexandra. Mokoena's office had been occupied for several weeks by community activists who put up posters declaring "Away with Mokoena—out of our hostels." Many councillors had been killed or driven from office during the ANC campaign to render the townships ungovernable. Many remaining councillors, therefore, aligned themselves with Inkatha for protection.

Like the councillors, the hostel dwellers expected they too would be driven out of Alexandra, although the civic organization denied such intentions. However, the accord provided for the "upgrading and possible conversion" of the hostels, and the perception easily spread that the hostels were to be demolished. The political power struggle acquired an ethnic dimension when the besieged Mokoena mobilized the hostel dwellers by appealing to Zulu pride with the slogan that the other residents were "undermining the Zulus."

The migrants, at the bottom of the social hierarchy, had always felt humiliated by the better-off township residents, and sexual rivalries were not uncommon. Now the single men felt their homes and very existence were threatened. Although the civic organization claimed it had consulted the hostels in all negotiations, such consultation clearly did not forge any bond or political loyalty.[17] On the contrary, the promise of better housing for families was perceived as abolishing the last foothold of the illiterate migrants in the city, many of whom did not want their rural wives and children to stay with them in the ramshackle hostels. Yet they had attached meaning to their own deprivation. The Weekly Mail observed: "The stench-ridden 'single-mens' ' hostel, built decades ago for migrants labouring in the factories and homes of Johannesburg but with no legal right to bring their families to the city, resembles a prison. Yet it is home to these men and their loyalty to such a place is surprising" (March 22–27, 1991).

Intent on inflaming animosities, a third force distributed leaflets, written in Zulu and carrying the ANC logo, demanding that Zulu people be evicted from Johannesburg.[18] Instead of issuing counter-statements or sending Zulu emissaries into the hostels to explain the ANC's position, the ANC simply ignored the leaflets—another missed attempt to communicate with poor blacks whose fragile foothold in a hostile environment was being threatened.

The sense of social isolation and marginalization felt by the migrants was reinforced by trends in union politics. As Eddie Webster, professor of sociology at the University of the Witwatersrand, has pointed out, union leaders are increasingly drawn from the better-educated and more skilled urban-based stratum. At the same time, he notes, union leaders have also become involved more in national politics, and the sectional interests of rank-and-file members have been sacrificed to the overall demands of a national agenda. Among those most hurt by these trends are the shopfloor representatives of the migrant underclass. Webster concludes: "Indeed, the failure of unions to address hostel-dwellers' grievances has contributed to the feeling of alienation among many and made them an ethnic constituency more easily mobilised by Inkatha's labour wing, Uwusa" (*Business Day*, August 2, 1991).

As the political violence in the Transvaal continued, the Inkatha leadership also felt besieged by a prospective ANC-National Party deal. In response to the labeling of Inkatha as a "minor party"—while both the government and the ANC referred to themselves as "senior players"—Buthelezi bluntly warned de Klerk at the opening of the KwaZulu Legislative Assembly that Inkatha would "tear down piece by piece and trample on" any plan that the NP and the ANC designed in a private arrangement. In this respect, the political violence in the Transvaal benefited Inkatha by demonstrating the national scope of the party. The defensive aggression need not have been orchestrated from above, as the ANC asserts, given the enmity on the ground. However, the clashes weakened the ANC and gave Inkatha the profile it could not expect from elections.

The fury and irrationality with which gangs of hostel dwellers have lashed out indiscriminately against township residents can only be understood in this context of isolation and anxiety. The magic rituals among the combatants in Natal, the fact that many could not even identify the cause or the name of the leader for whom they were fighting, points to their search for symbolic compensations to counter depths of powerlessness. Such despair can readily be exploited by the strongmen on each side.

During the battles in Natal both sides "press-ganged" youth into the fighting. In some areas, each household was required to pay ten rand for "equipment," a euphemism for weapons and *muti* (traditional medicine). "People's courts" implement the "call-ups" and war taxes with a hundred lashes for offenders. On both sides elements of traditional superstition motivate the combatants:

> Before we go into the fighting, some people at the houses near the battlefield stand outside with buckets of water and *muti*. They dip a broom into the mixture and sprinkle it over us as we run past. If you want extra protection, you can also go to an *inyanga,* but that costs more. Comrades believe the *muti* will stop the bullets from hitting them and will give them courage.
> (Carmel Rickard, "When you see the enemy's shacks blaze, you can't help feeling good," *Weekly Mail,* February 23, 1990, p.3).

The same "comrade" describes an enemy who was shot and tried to run away but fell and was stabbed. Then someone cut off his genitals and took them away.

Mutilations are reported in many communal conflicts. People are not just killed in Yugoslavia or Azerbaijan but in addition are often grossly disfigured. This unexplained practice points perhaps to deep-seated feelings of emasculation. It has yet to be satisfactorily explained by psychological insights, which are usually neglected in favor of the focus on national competition. Such mutilation robs the enemy not only of his life but of valued qualities that the victor symbolically appropriates: potency or eyesight or brains. To possess the vital organs of the enemy is to possess power, invincibility, and immortality. The more powerless people are, the more they become obsessed with the symbols of power. The rituals of protest and the preoccupation with an imagined armed struggle reveals other dimensions of the same phenomena.

Chris Hani, the former chief of staff of MK, observes that the suspension of armed activities "has not been really appreciated by most of our people," despite its having gained the ANC more international support and the moral high ground. Hani concludes: "Today we can't cope with the interest that young people are showing in Umkhonto we Sizwe." Some attribute such attitudes to political militancy. But, like the foot-stamping toyi-toyi and strident war songs ("Kill the Boers") ritually performed at rallies and the repetitious shouts of "Amandla!" (power), militant attitudes and militaristic gestures express something deeper than mere militancy. For the powerless, images and symbols of power must substitute for real clout.

Deep humiliation results in fantasies of power. The more the ill-fated armed struggle fades into the background, the more some of the township youth want to resurrect it. At rallies they sport a new folk art: imaginatively designed and carefully assembled imitations of homemade guns, MK47s, and bazookas, often grotesquely oversized. Their grim-looking bearers shout martial slogans and brandish their war toys, hoping from them to borrow the strength needed to conquer their own anxieties, like the children who pose on the tanks at war memorials in other societies.

CLIENTELISM AS SECESSIONISM

Among the majority of Zulu supporters of Inkatha, relationships between leaders and followers are based not only on ideological iden-tifications but also on reciprocal instrumental advantages and ethnic symbolic gratifications. Inkatha's poor and illiterate constituency de-pends on patronage, handed out by strong leaders and local power-brokers in return for loyalty, regardless of a leader's ideological out-look or ethical behavior. Political powerlessness reinforced the importance of African auxiliaries to whom the impoverished could turn for protection and favors. When the South African state decen-tralized control by letting trusted African clients police themselves and administer their own poverty, the leaders' status and importance were further strengthened. Thus emerged a classical system of clientelism and patrimony. Clientelism flourishes in conditions of inequality, where marginalized groups depend on patronage networks for sur-vival, or at least for small improvements. It is the exclusive control of scarce goods (permits, houses, civil service positions) that give patrons their power. This clientelism thrives with rightlessness.

Once equal citizenship, however, gives formal access to basic goods to all, and all are entitled to equal treatment, the monopoly of patrons is undermined. If the police, for example, act impartially, there is no need to be protected by a warlord. If people acquire confidence in the law, they need not rely on vigilantes. If justice is administered by impartial courts, it need not be sought through private vendettas. Thus a democratic equality that allows claims to be made through formal channels preempts local dependence on informal patronage.

However, as long as comrades attack the police as agents of a hostile system, the police will hardly act impartially. If town council-lors are forcefully driven from office, they will seek protection from whomever they can find. When the homes of "collaborators" are destroyed in the name of the people's anger, violent confrontations will persist. If a coalition for reconstruction is the goal, then civic organizations, at both the local and national level, would be much wiser to engage and co-opt the local notables instead of denouncing them as enemies to be replaced. In addition, had the ANC opposition appropriated Zulu cultural symbolism and heritage maintenance as its own goal, or incorporated Zulu history in its own mobilizing drive instead of ridiculing all ethnicity as tribalism, it might have had a much greater appeal among the more traditional segments of Zulu society.

There are two common objections to a policy of reconciliation with regard to Inkatha: that support for Inkatha is so weak that the movement can be ignored, preempted, or even eliminated, and that the price demanded for incorporation by Buthelezi is too high. Against the first argument Lawrence Schlemmer (1991) has pointed out that conflict resolution has to take into account not only the size and scope but also the intensity of interests: "The intensity of the IFP's interaction in the political process has clearly signalled the potential costs of excluding it, or reducing its leverage in negotiations." From a moral point, this position can be interpreted as yielding to violence. From a pragmatic perspective, however, there is little choice if greater damage is to be avoided. Weighing the costs of continued confrontation against the potential benefit of peaceful competition through compromise amounts to a political calculation that separates ideologues from pragmatists.

It remains to be seen whether equality before the law and new life chances for the formerly disenfranchised will preempt clientelism and the quest for ethnic separateness. The defeat of ethnonationalism may be easier to achieve with regard to Inkatha's constituency than with regard to the separatism of the white right wing. Observers remain skeptical. *Sunday Times* editor Ken Owen notes that a relatively autonomous Natal in a federal structure might be a cooperative partner in a greater South Africa, "while a KwaZulu forcibly incorporated in a structure controlled by its bitterest enemies, might become as indigestible as the IRA in Britain, or the Turks in Cyprus, or the Basques" (*Sunday Times*, September 8, 1991). Buthelezi too has threatened that the civil wars in Angola and Mozambique could pale in comparison with the future destructive upheavals in South Africa. The ANC, on the other hand, is not inclined to heed such predictions and would rather risk a repetition of Biafra than compromise on the relative centralization of political power or bend toward recognition of Zulu claims. This approach sets the new South Africa on a collision course not only with Inkatha but with the Boerestaat advocates as well.

In order to avoid civil war, the architects of the new constitution might do well to consider a suggestion by the American moral philosopher Allen Buchanan (1991), who has argued that any group in any state has the moral right to secede. Such a right to secede could be constitutionally recognized and specified (referendum, qualified majority support, treatment of minorities). A constitutionally guaranteed right to secede under regulated conditions and international arbitration might spare any country from civil disorder in the wake of a political divorce or the forceful retention of an unwilling partner. Buchanan considers even a discussion of the constitutional right to secede too divisive in the present South African climate. Nonetheless, he concludes: "If non-Zulus are unwilling to adopt constitutional measures that would add further power to the numerical superiority that Zulus already enjoy, the only possibility for a peaceful solution may be Zulu secession" (p. 161). However, Buchanan overlooks the fact that secession would elicit strong opposition from a large section of the Zulu speakers themselves—a key difference between the repressed independence movements in Eastern Europe and the apartheid-encouraged Bantustan sovereignties. In light of the recent events in Eastern Europe, however, it may be timely to consider a secession clause in the new South African constitution. A serious discussion of the right to secede would also provide the necessary incentive to bring the potential secessionist parties into the constitutional negotiations.

CHAPTER SEVEN

The Right Wing

The Option of Secession,
Civil War, and Social Disintegration

Ideologically, the black and white ethnic fundamentalists mirror each other in their intransigence to compromise, their advocacy of confrontation, and their single-mindedness. The difference between them lies in their relative strength and military capacity. While only a small portion of blacks currently support counterracist views, a third of the white electorate would vote for parties to the right of the ruling Nationalists. Moreover, the white right wing is overrepresented in the police and security establishment. Well-trained and armed, this faction has resorted to bombings and shootings to disrupt the ongoing accommodation. Individuals on the white right wing have also used "representative violence," the random targeting of outgroup members, which has been rare among black political activists.

The white ultra-right, however, is unlikely to provoke a military takeover under present conditions. Even if such a seizure of power were to take place during a future civil war, the right wing alone could not govern the country. Unlike military juntas in Latin American states, who can count on domestic financial endorsement and influential international support, a military coup in South Africa would meet with determined opposition. The hope of the ultra-right, despite its military rhetoric, lies not in a takeover but in secession from an increasingly integrated nonracial state.

A minority of conservatives are drawn to the vision of an independent Boerestaat out of ideological commitment to Afrikaner self-determination, but the majority of whites who have joined the right wing did so out of anxiety about an uncertain future. The economic recession has swelled this segment. The tangible rewards of a booming nonracial state, if only it could be allowed to boom, would substantially reduce this fear. It is generally recognized that the right wing represents the downwardly mobile sectors of the white population: white mine workers, farmers deprived of previous state subsidies, and the lower echelons of the Afrikaner civil service, who are very concerned about Africanization. Although political attitudes and identities cannot be crudely reduced to material considerations, a strong correlation between socioeconomic conditions and political outlook remains most striking in South Africa.

The white population is internally more stratified than is commonly realized. Although the white working class has consistently shrunk, due to state patronage, about 20 percent of urban adult whites still have a net worth of under 10,000 rand ($4,000). Over half the white population owns net assets of under 100,000 rand ($40,000); 6 percent over 500,000 rand ($200,000); and 1.7 percent are considered rand millionaires.[1]

There are different versions of a white homeland on which their respective supporters cannot agree. This disagreement has not only split the right wing but paralyzed the concept politically.

In the late 1970s the son of Hendrik Verwoerd set up the Orange Werkersunie in search of a nucleus for a white homeland. His choice of Morgenzon, a nondescript hamlet in the Eastern Transvaal, proved unattractive to all but twenty families who moved and bought land in the town. These odd inhabitants, surrounded by six thousand blacks, insist that they will not employ black labor and become dependent on "outsiders."

The Boerestaat Party of Robert van Tonder strives to revive the traditional Boerrepublics in the Transvaal and Orange Free State, but rejects the notion of a white homeland as racist. Just as Zionists asked for the ancient Jewish state to be reinstated without excluding all Arab inhabitants, so the Boerestaat will coexist with a black majority in its midst, according to van Tonder. But by dividing these blacks into different nations, the Afrikaners will become the majority. In this definition of the ruling group, even Cape Afrikaners who did not go on the Great Trek are excluded, as are of course English-speaking whites. According to Piet "Skiet" Rudolph, the Free State, Transvaal, and Northern Natal are still part and parcel of the Boerevolk. He equates the Boere claim for land with the dispossessed black community's demands for land restitution. The Boere homelands would then form a loose federation for economic cooperation with the rest of South Africa.[2]

Carel Boshoff, the head of the Afrikanervolkswag, presents the more sophisticated and pragmatic version of the nationalist territorial dream. He considers it unrealistic to move or dominate millions of people against their will. Instead, he seeks an area with low population density and great economic potential, "where a new settlement can be developed, and where new high technology can be placed, and where a country, a republic, a state can develop in time" (interview, 1990). Boshoff's most recent map identifies an area along the Orange River in the northwestern Cape bordering southern Namibia as the future Boerestaat, and Boshoff's Afrikaner Vryheidstigting (Avstig), which grew out of the Volkswag movement, has officially entered into discussion with the ANC about the proposed boundaries for an Afrikaner homeland. The Volksstaaters no longer insist on independence but consider regional autonomy of an Afrikaner heartland as an interim measure toward sovereignty, if necessary. The semidesert area, which has no major mines or industries, would welcome "anderskleuriges" (people of color) as equal citizens because it would define itself in cultural, not racial, terms. Therefore, the region's Coloured population, which is four times larger than its white Afrikaner population, would be considered equal Afrikaners. The distinction between a nonracial Afrikanerdom, comprising brown and black Afrikaners, as opposed to the Conservative Party's emphasis on white identity, now forms the most decisive split within the right wing. Afrikaner ethnicity stripped of its racial history could well become acceptable to the ANC, which has always recognized depoliticized culture, divorced from apartheid domination. However, the recognition of an Afrikaner heartland is widely resented by the ANC at present, not for ideological reasons, but because the precedent would certainly encourage similar claims by Zulu and other black nationalists.

The Conservative Party has also begun drawing up boundaries for a white state. It has informally dropped its earlier position that the whole of apartheid South Africa should be restored to white rule. For the Conservative Party, a minimal homeland would include the Western Transvaal, including Pretoria, the Orange Free State Province, and the northern Cape Province. Since this conservative heartland is interspersed with "black spots," influential white conservatives are seeking an alliance with the black conservative Mangope of the Bophuthat-swana Bantustan, who is equally opposed to ANC hegemony. This secessionist coalition in the name of national self-determination may well include Buthelezi's KwaZulu territory.

A tribal Afrikaner-Zulu alliance strikes a deep chord among local and international conservatives alike. British editor Peregrine Worst-horne sees the "only stable multiracial future" for South Africa "under a condominium of the two militarily strongest tribes—the Boers and the Zulus. . . . If there were to be a civil war, those tribes would certainly win it" (*Business Day*, October 12, 1992). A war they may win indeed, but legitimacy they have lost long ago. Such fantasies of repressive stability would simply ignore the perceptions of the two-thirds who do not belong to either group. But even among white Afrikaners (7 percent of the population) as well as Zulu speakers (25 percent, excluding TBVC states), the majority rejects a tribal alliance at the expense of the rest.

The Conservative Party is deeply split on whether such a plan should be negotiated with other parties and whether the conservatives should, therefore, participate in the ongoing all-party talks. In August 1992 five members of parliament broke away from the Conservative Party to form the Afrikaner Volksunie Party, which aims at securing negotiated Afrikaner self-determination in a smaller, not necessarily sovereign, Boerestaat in parts of the Transvaal and Orange Free State. The Conservative Party is in danger of being marginalized by its boycott politics. Its hope to gain power through another white-only election is increasingly exposed as a fiction despite a string of victories in by-elections. In the meantime, the militarization on its fringes continues.

The decisive defeat of the conservatives in the referendum of March 17, 1992, and the preceding wavering of whether to boycott or partici-pate in the referendum, has further exacerbated cleavages between conservative moderates and hardliners. On the one hand, the referen-dum alliance of the respectable "party conservatives" with the neofas-cists has discredited all conservative politics in the eyes of the majority of Afrikaners. Even on the right, political and legal strategies to achieve Boere self-determination are more popular than the violent antics of the AWB-affiliated associations. The street theater of these groups has been vastly overrated in the media reporting.[3] On the other hand, the marginalized, violence-prone ideologues could cause even more disruption through economic and industrial action than through direct violence. Even a powerful ANC-NP government would be powerless against the sabotage of those gold mines where the majority of the white miners show AWB sympathies. It is already established that "white miners are playing a significant role in supplying explosives to the far right" (*Africa Confidential,* March 20, 1992); targets have thus far included a few newly integrated white schools. A new government is likely to be saddled with the difficult task of controlling high-publicity terrorism unless these elements can be pacified.

The militants of neofascist groups like the AWB accuse the Conservative Party of "giving our country away" for a parliamentary salary. The CP members of parliament rejected calls to resign, knowing that countrywide by-elections would have demonstrated the decline of white support for the conservatives. In Terre'Blanche's view the by-elections would have been "the last chance" before "Tambo's communists start the black revolution." Others in this group openly announced: "The time for voting politics is over—it is now time for bullet politics" (*Cape Times,* March 1, 1990).

The Conservative Party deplores the violence associated with the AWB and likes to project an image of respectability. However it also emphasizes its ideological affinity. CP leader Andries Treurnicht declared: "What we have in common with the AWB is that we belong to the same people, speak the same language, have the same opponents and enemies and the same ideals to have our own fatherland governed by our own people" (*Cape Times,* August 1, 1991). Despite the contempt that the leaders of each faction express for the other's style, the AWB can be considered the armed wing of the CP. What the one party tries to achieve through legal and institutional means, the other complements through extraparliamentary threats and military mobilization for the coming "volks war."

Martial rhetoric by the ultra-right usually receives the loudest applause and foot-stamping at rallies where many wear khaki uniforms with the red-black-and-white swastika-like insignia. Referring to the Conservative Party's bid to gather one million signatures in support of its campaign against reforms, Terre'Blanche says: "The AWB does not want one million signatures, it wants one million guns." Other speakers emphasize that cherished symbols—such as Pretoria, the city of Boer republic leader Paul Kruger—would be taken only "over our dead bodies" while defending itself against its "third siege."

Ironically, the right wing now demands the abolition of the very security legislation that it once advocated, particularly Section 29 of the Internal Security Act. This act, argues Eugene Terre'Blanche, had been introduced by former Prime Minister Vorster for the purpose of destroying communism. "However, since the government has now made friends with the communists . . . the Act is now being used in the most cruel fashion to lock up, without any access to law, Boer freedom fighters" (*BBC Monitoring Report,* December 18, 1990).

In sum, the uniform demonization of all political activity to the right of the National Party in the South African English-language press and foreign media needs to be corrected with a much more nuanced view of conservative motivations and behavior. The swastika-waving fascists are but a vociferous minority outnumbered by many more honorable ideologues and plainly fearful voters in feudal rural settings or declining mining towns. Liberal editor Denis Beckett has dramatically illuminated the conservative spectrum: "Yet for every rightist who breaks up a black picnic, ten anguish over their role in Africa. For every barfly telling Kaffir-jokes, there's a pious householder praying for guidance. For every Terre'Blanche rattling sabers, there's a Boshoff seeking good neighbours through good fences. For every CP farmer who donders his labourers, twenty deliver their babies."[4] Neither South African liberals nor the Left, let alone Western policymakers, have yet engaged these anxiety-ridden ideologues, as unpalatable as accommodation will be for antiracists.

But, looking ahead, a future ANC-NP government faces difficult choices: it could accommodate the right-wing separatists, at least symbolically in some more or less autonomous territory; it could decide to repress a substantial section of the hostile group and thereby itself become undemocratic; or it could risk being destabilized by an uncooperative civil service and being sabotaged in the strategically crucial productive sectors of agriculture and mining. The wisest present course would be to make all efforts to draw at least some sectors of conservatives into the ongoing negotiations, although the ANC will have great difficulty in accepting the legitimacy of secessionist claims.

As the moderate middle sectors—the ANC and the National Party—explore their common interests and draw closer together, the extremes on the white right and black left have stepped up their rhetoric and even their physical attacks. In an intriguing analysis Donald Horowitz (1991) views this dynamic of pressure from the flanks as the best guarantee for the fragile center to hold. Yet the possibility of a low-level civil war cannot be ruled out: The right wing would not win a war but could certainly start one. Even if the ultraconservatives are unsuccessful in preventing a settlement between the ANC and the NP, they can prolong the uncertainty and mutual recrimination. Already the government is using the existence of MK as an excuse that it cannot ban private armies and disarm the right wing. By pointing to the threat from the right, the government strengthens its negotiating position. Even if it did not instigate the third-force violence among blacks, as many critics charge, Pretoria has benefited from the weakening of the ANC's forces. Thus the right wing can also succeed by causing friction at the center and undermining accommodation, just as negotiations have been prevented in Northern Ireland or in Israel.

At various times de Klerk has been faced with the danger of a "soft coup"—a threat by the security establishment not to take over Pretoria, but, on the contrary, to withdraw cooperation. If certain policies were pursued, he was advised, security could no longer be guaranteed (personal interviews, various dates 1990–92). One of his planned overseas visits was almost canceled because of this looming rebellion. A reputed judge, commissioned to evaluate the attitudes of leading military figures, reported after extensive interviews that most expressed intense resentment of the government's course and displayed varying degrees of cynicism.

The government responded in 1992 by offering generous retirement packages to those senior civil servants and generals willing to resign. At the behest of the security establishment, it also introduced at the special October 1992 parliamentary session an ill-fated "Further Indemnity Bill" that provided for the pardoning of politically motivated crimes. Secret hearings would be held before a judge, presiding over a national council of indemnity, appointed by the president. Only the names of those pardoned would be made public; their victims and their crimes would remain secret. The recommendations of this council would be granted or denied at the discretion of the president. The opposition, including white liberals and the majority Solidarity Party in the House of Delegates, blocked the bill by arguing that criminals cannot pardon themselves and that an ANC-led government would repeal the indemnity, as happened in Argentina. But the bill was finally rammed through the National Party–dominated President's Council in October 1992.

The debate, together with Buthelezi's pullout from the negotiations, revealed renewed deep cleavages in the white camp and governing party. When de Klerk and Mandela signed a memorandum of understanding on September 26, 1992, the government was increasingly perceived as "having joined the ANC" by white and black conservatives alike. The doves in the cabinet (Dawie de Villiers, Leon Wessel, Sam de Beer, Roelf Meyer, Pik Botha) succeeded in pushing for a working arrangement with the ANC at the expense of hardliners (Kobie Coetsee, Hernus Kriel, George Bartlett, Adriaan Vlok, Magnus Malan), who together with the security establishment always favored an NP-Inkatha homeland coalition against the ANC. The memorandum and the deterioration of the personal relationship between de Klerk and Buthelezi, who openly flirted with right-wingers, evidenced a fundamental realignment of political forces. For the first time, the National Party leadership seemed willing to shed its ideological allies, who were electorally weak, in favor of a more stable coalition of the center. Bilateral agreements between the ANC and the NP were seen as a precondition for multilateral negotiations. However, due to Inkatha's residual support in the establishment camp, Buthelezi still exercises considerable political clout beyond the disruptive potential of the movement. Inkatha has the capacity to exacerbate the rifts between liberal and conservative whites by aligning itself with the secessionist forces. Although KwaZulu's unilateral federalism has been rebuffed by Pretoria and the ANC alike, Inkatha's blueprints for regional autonomy encounter sympathy among the local business community, which views these plans as a last resort against an ANC-dominated central administration. Buthelezi's intransigent resistance to a National Party-ANC alliance has not only shed his image as a surrogate but put him back on the political stage as a proponent of extreme federalism. The Zulu-Natal confederal option at the same time allowed de Klerk to occupy the political center as defender of national unity and mediator between extremes. In reality, the KwaZulu administration headed by Buthelezi remains largely dependent on Pretoria, which pays 75 percent of the KwaZulu budget from central revenue. The Bantustans also continue to operate because they increase the government's maneuverability vis-à-vis their far more powerful right-wing opponents.

Some three years into the de Klerk presidency, the usually well-informed *Africa Confidential* (July 31, 1992) concluded, "De Klerk is an almost immobilised captive of a powerful clique of securocrats, aided by upper echelons of the DMI [Department of Military Intelligence], which is determined to obstruct his political initiative for a phased transition to shared power." While this assessment may have overstated the securocrats' influence in government decision making, there can be no doubt that this "third force"—a loose network of highly trained and motivated officers from the special forces of the military, the police, and previous intelligence operatives under P. W. Botha—had found a new base in the threatened regional power centers. The small Ciskei alone employed 288 reassigned officials in 1992, several in leading positions of the homeland police and military. It was a white commander who gave the order to shoot ANC demonstrators at the Bisho massacre in August 1992. The "soft coup" had thus succeeded in basically leaving township violence to itself, if not instigating it in some instances; in physically eliminating troublesome individuals at the local and middle-leadership level; and in politically impeding a settlement *at the center* by insisting on regional autonomy. In short, the more these ultraconservative forces were being phased out of power at the national level, the more the specter of an alliance of separate regional power centers in opposition to a national settlement emerged. It found its strongest advocate in Inkatha, which felt sidelined by the ANC-NP accord and by the ANC's continued hostility to third-party inclusion.

It was not only the fear of strong opposition from certain security circles that kept the government from acting forcefully against its third column. After all, the government could not afford to alienate the only remaining guarantor of law and order should negotiations fail. As a reliable fallback in such a case, the police seemed indispensable, quite apart from the personal bonds linking the Afrikaner political establishment. Moreover, the NP leadership also had to tread cautiously because several cabinet ministers were implicated in various scandals so far kept under wraps. Some securocrats held the exposure of embarrassing secrets as a potent weapon should their position be threatened. What is referred to as "dirt" in informed circles would have discredited some of de Klerk's leading allies.

In practical terms, the white right wing can be controlled only by the white center, and ultraconservative Afrikaners by more reformist Afrikaners. If this is to be a relatively nonviolent process, the center's legitimacy is crucial for carrying the right wing along. If the transition garners white majority electoral support and constitutional legality is maintained, the right-wing insurrectionists would have to choose between their fetish for "law and order" and their racist ideology. Therefore, the ANC has to allow the NP forces to maintain a posture of legal respectability, rather than push the party into what the ultra-right would perceive as surrender. Indeed, as many commentators have pointed out, if an NP-ANC solution were to be foisted on a defiant white majority, the ground would be laid for a costly long-term IRA-type destabilization. The paradox of the South African power equation is that each side can prevent the other from exercising power. Therefore, neither side can rule alone peacefully without taking the vital interests of its antagonists seriously. The alternative is violence without victory, which only the most rigid ideologues prefer over accommodation.

Against the optimistic scenario of a social-democratic compact with renewed high economic growth stand many well-documented pessimistic predictions of likely social disintegration. The pessimists do not doubt the goodwill of the leadership on all sides to reach an accord but question their ability to enforce it against overwhelming odds. In addition, some distrust the democratic motives of the major parties, who are said to be interested in a nonracial oligarchy at best. Newspaper editors like Ken Owen dwell on the theme of Africa reverting to the bush in the "heart of darkness," while Simon Barber warns of the white establishment "sliding into functional cahoots with the ANC and its totalitarian project" (*Cape Times*, April 24, 1990). The National Party is inclined to adopt this route, it is argued, because it strives for external recognition and that can be won only with ANC connivance. Both the National Party and ANC want order above the law. A future division of control—with the National Party holding the right wing in check, and the ANC disciplining the town-ships under an authoritarian leadership—is widely thought to be looming. Negotiations would mainly be about zones of influence and hegemony. The National Party must only ensure that the relinquished share of power does not threaten its own privileges. Barber's nightmare is "a one-party state condoned by a specially protected white nomenclature." If right-wing anxiety about "a sellout to blacks" represents one side of white consciousness, the vision of an authoritarian unholy alliance constitutes the liberal side of the same coin. Both sides deplore the moral decay of the ruling group. In Barber's phrase, "the establishment lacks either the guts or the basic humanity." The scenarios waver between de Klerk as the South African Gorbachev who loses control over the process he initiated, or de Klerk and Mandela as joint dictators.

In this vein, academics Pierre du Toit and Willie Esterhuyse argue that both the National Party and the ANC employ hegemonic models of bargaining.[5] In this view, democratic, inclusive rhetoric only masks the desire for total control. Negotiations aim at co-optation or defeat of the adversary by other means, as well as exclusion of those on the right or left who reject the new alignment. It is a despairing assessment.

There is little evidence at present that either side would abandon a negotiated democratic contest, although they both lack a democratic tradition and have illiberal hardliners in their midst. Even on the assumption that the pessimists are correct and the "regime models" of both camps—"technocratic liberation" versus "people's power"—allow at best a nonracial oligarchy, the question remains whether the objective constellation of power would not constrain the antidemocratic interests. South African social forces are so diverse and multifaceted that political legitimacy and economic stability simply cannot be reached by a new coercive alignment, even one acceptable to a numerical majority. The resulting unrest and instability would defeat the main purpose of the new pact. Sooner or later a more inclusive and pluralist order would have to establish wider legitimacy of a polity in which all disruptive forces are accommodated.

All such efforts at democratic recovery, however, depend on the fate of the South African economy. It has become a well-worn cliché to stress that South Africa sits on a time bomb of economic frustrations that could impel uncontrollable social disintegration. Fewer than one hundred of the estimated one thousand people who come on to the job market daily can be accommodated in the formal economy. The capacity of the South African economy to absorb new job seekers declined from 73.6 percent of the new entrants in 1970 to 12.5 percent in 1989. The time-bomb analogy, however, falsely suggests an impending explosion. The real consequences of the rejected underclass lie more in the nation's slow societal disintegration, as indicated by rising crime rates, political violence, family dissolution, and a breakdown of the social fabric and value system under the weight of general misery. An ANC government is likely to suffer the consequences of its advocacy of sanctions and ungovernability even more than the sheltered white sector, which has many more options.

A comparison with Lebanon during its fifteen-year-long civil war (1975–1990), as masterfully analyzed by Theo Hanf, illustrates the unique South African dilemmas.[6] For South Africans, an understanding of the Lebanese example is both encouraging and frightening.

Lebanon was primarily destroyed by outside forces; the Palestinians, the Israelis, the Syrians, the Iraqis, and even the Americans—all tried to impose their solution at one time or another on a weak central state. Unlike Lebanon, South Africa is relatively free from direct outside interference and sponsorship of competing factions. What has kept Lebanon together, on the other hand, is the persistence, throughout the war, of a surprising popular consensus on the unity of the nation, despite the progressive disintegration of the institutions of the state. "It is not fanatical masses that prevent a new consensus," Hanf concludes, "but shortsighted and power-hungry elites." In South Africa, the opposite holds true. Compromising leaders on all sides are constrained by militant and alienated constituencies.

Hanf demonstrates perceptively that during the war Lebanese society disintegrated at the top while life below continued with remarkable normality. Children continued to go to school; water and electricity were available; and the courts and the police, hospitals and fire brigades, banks and garbage trucks provided their usual services as best as they could under the most unusual conditions. Within their groups even the political gangs were relatively safe from attacks by opponents. The militia on the payrolls of feuding warlords behaved like private armies everywhere: ruthless against enemies from other communities, keen to enrich themselves through extortion, theft, and drug smuggling but also protective of their own communities. The civilian population on all sides of the barricades suffered from intermittent shellings and devastating car bombs, but they were not massively debilitated. People across the communal divisions hated and feared the disruptions of routine—as they demonstrated in several mass protests—but kept up a pretense of normality. Despair expressed itself mainly through emigration.

Everyday life in South Africa's black townships is qualitatively different. Although far more substantial weapons are available in Beirut than in Soweto or Khayelitsha, lives are much more at risk in South Africa than in Lebanon. Not only do crime and simmering political feuds make life more dangerous, but the psychological impoverishment, the hopelessness, and alienation seem almost worse. If the well-worn sociological concept of anomie can be applied anywhere, it is in Sebokeng or Edendale. Evidence of a brutal normlessness abounds: people dread to go to sleep in their own homes for fear of unprovoked attacks; thirty-nine mourners are blown apart at a funeral by a revenge-seeking gang; passengers in commuter trains scramble out of the windows at the cry "the Zulus are coming"; groups of girls are abducted from a Salvation Army home and raped.

Not only are murder rates rising, but criminologists note that previously nonviolent house-breaking and theft have become increasingly violent. The numbers of rapes and serious assaults climb every year. The violence and general lack of regard for human life indicate new levels of aggression and frustration, a reaction to disappointed expectations. For the long-awaited breakdown of apartheid has not improved material living conditions. Indeed, with the political insecurity and factional violence among competing black parties increasing, the lives of many township residents and squatters have become worse. Symbolic gratification, provided for a while by the legalization of political parties and the release of Mandela, turned into real bitterness when leaders could not deliver on their promises.

The political liberalization also gave common criminal activity greater freedom. Weapons from sources in Renamo and Umkhonto entered South Africa, facilitated by the influx of refugees from Mozambique and other strife-torn areas who thus began to destabilize the initial destabilizers. For the increasing number of school dropouts and unemployed youth, there opened a new field of making a living by trafficking in mandrax tablets, just as some members of the underclass in North American cities survive on the sale of drugs. Car hijacking and bank robberies increased, and when the banks tightened their security, armed robbers shifted to softer targets such as retail outlets and private homes. Breeders of bull terriers and Rottweilers cannot cope with the demand. The booming private-security industry has been no more effective in deterring the spread of crime than the overpoliticized police force. Not only do communities distrust the police, the alienated communities also make self-administered community policing a source of strife.

In 1990 the annual survey conducted by the Institute of Race Relations observed that the per capita murder rate was four times higher in South Africa than in the United States and that 8,000 people had been killed in political violence between September 1984 and 1990, about 850 of whom were "necklaced." Despite the ANC's disavowal of necklacing, after first having condoned it under the rubric of "people's resistance," this barbaric method of murdering political opponents continues to be practiced, though less frequently. The incidence of political violence attributable to extremist right-wing organizations has also increased, complementing the legalized police brutality re-

ferred to in township jargon as "system terror." The minister of law
and order has called his country "a nation of gangsters"—without
mentioning that it was chiefly his party's apartheid policies that brutalized the impoverished young. The illegitimacy of apartheid institutions tainted the legitimacy of all other social institutions.

In the matter of social decay and the life chances of the majority,
South Africa resembles the former Soviet republics more than Lebanon. The powerful Afrikaner institutions of the center still hold the
society together, but conceal the rot at the bottom. Like the leadership
during the repressive era in the Soviet Union, South African state
officials think that they can best combat crime through more police
deterrence without seriously addressing the underlying causes of
alienation.

The most telling indicators of decay are the schools. Black schools
hold classes, but often no teaching or learning take place there, as
pupils or teachers are engaged with other priorities. The ANC, like
the state, has failed to control teachers' organizations that recklessly
use school boycotts to further their own sectional interests at the
expense of students. On the rigid and outdated centrally administered
matriculation tests administered in 1991, the pass rates of non-African
students were unprecedentedly high, while the rate for black pupils
dropped to an all-time low. Only 39 percent of black candidates
passed, as compared to approximately 95 percent in other communities. The differences have nothing to do with the students' intelligence;
nor does the low pass rate primarily result from differences in expenditures, facilities, or teacher qualifications. Several equally poor black
homeland and mission schools achieved or exceeded the rate of the
more privileged minorities. As the ANC-aligned National Education
Crisis Committee self-critically stated, "Schools have been allowed to
become battlefields and students were compelled to find themselves in
the forefront of this political violence." The *Sunday Times* commented: "The implications of a massive black failure rate are un-
relievedly grim. It will aggravate youthful rage, incite racial envy, clog
educational facilities and, ultimately, worsen South Africa's real
Achilles heel: our desperate shortage of skills" (January 6, 1991).

Educational disparities also give rise to claims to entitlement that
run contrary to the meritocratic route to equality. Inasmuch as Afrikaner state patronage has secured advances for privileged groups in
the past, so African collective claims understandably advocate restitution and redistribution in the future. In such an ethnic division of

spoils, with differential access to scarce occupational opportunities, two unequal contenders are inextricably locked into different justifications of claims. The insistence on individual ability and achievement on the basis of existing privilege is countered by the hope that the new political system will deliver the valued goods and services. This disagreement over the legitimacy of claims bodes ill for accommodation.

Already a praxis of free entitlement to state services has spread widely, and normal administration has broken down. Rents are boycotted, electricity is cut, taxes remain uncollected, emergency calls go unheeded. Because apartheid laws and regulations were primarily designed to suppress and control, they have lost all legitimacy even when they potentially benefit the people. In a state of anomie, paralyzed by the daily struggle to survive, the majority of the population waits to be saved. A new black law-and-order party, not connected to apartheid institutions, could make substantial inroads in the townships at the expense of the ANC. It may be only a matter of time before a black Terre'Blanche emerges.

Even the ANC's leadership is increasingly viewed with suspicion and skepticism. The more it presses on with negotiations and confidential understandings, the louder the whispers about sellouts and the shouts about opportunistic behavior. At best, many activists view negotiations as war by other means, designed to culminate in a transfer of power. The ANC's leadership and returning exiles make heroic efforts to coax the grass-roots into line, but even the credibility of the SACP is strained by its advocacy of "guarantees for the bourgeoisie."

The thirty-year ban on liberation movements, between 1960 and 1990, reduced the complexities of "the struggle" to ill-understood slogans. Opposition to collaboration was interpreted as "making the country ungovernable." Resistance to the government's "Bantu Education" was intended to promote education for liberation, but was subverted into liberation before education, and ended in the slogan "pass one, pass all." Schools were proclaimed as "sites of struggles," although efforts are now underway to restore proper schooling. Where the resistance created counterinstitutions to replace the discredited apartheid authorities, it often merely compounded the anomie. The unelected "people's courts" and street committees of the "young lions" often exceeded the terror of the apartheid courts. Detention in Pretoria is preferable to being necklaced in Soweto.

Petty criminals continue to terrorize, traditionalist warlords attempt to extend their turf, and brutalized comrades retaliate. The political leadership preaches discipline and unity, but few heed the calls for reconciliation. South Africa needs to build legitimacy at the top by means of a constitutional accord, but is in danger of reaching a settlement by elites on a hollow base. In Lebanon an accord by the feuding elites on foreign military presence was sufficient to end the strife. In South Africa an agreement of this kind is crucial, but it won't remedy the underlying social decay. Unlike Lebanon, South Africa needs to experience a collective moral revival and recovery that cannot be decreed from above. Even if more houses and jobs will create an expanding postapartheid economy, economic growth must be accompanied by some sort of moral renewal.

In the absence of strong religious communities, and given the disruption of traditional family life by apartheid, the core of moral renewal should lie in the notion of a pluralist democracy. Rather than stressing the need for unity or submitting to the will of the people—as if the people had only one will—the opposition movements should speak up more loudly about respect for political opponents. Intimidation of antagonists—and worse—has a long history on a continent where the practice of loyal opposition hardly exists, and society easily fragments into warring factions with little hope for realizing such fledgling notions as individual autonomy, freedom of choice, and pluralistic empowerment.

To survive, a democracy requires autonomous citizens, civic organizations, and a host of disciplining grass-roots institutions, from apolitical sports clubs to associations of dedicated parents and committed teachers. The democratic state cannot create these foundations: it can only facilitate their emergence. The greater the variety within civil society, the better the chances for democracy. The emerging NP-ANC accord could well be built on shifting sand. Neither side has sufficiently prepared its constituency for the remarkable speed of the accommodations that its leaders have been prepared to make. The militant rhetoric is meant to camouflage all this moderation, but the talk raises expectations that may prove counterproductive when it comes to selling the inevitably disappointing compromise.

Should the South African economy decline further, an impoverished township society could conceivably produce a Peruvian scenario. There, Sendero Luminoso (Shining Path, or known simply by the faithful as the Communist Party), some five thousand guerrillas under a shadowy leader Abimael Guzman, captured in 1992, directed a violent campaign not only against the country's establishment but against foreign-aid workers, the clergy, and even the urban poor who engage in self-help relief efforts and cooperative industrial activity. The Maoist movement's followers view any improvement in the lot of the poor as counterproductive to the revolution. Organized relief is not to be tolerated since it pacifies the masses and thereby prolongs the war to overthrow capitalism and turn Peru into a peasant-worker state.

Sendero Luminoso's tactics are opposed by the rival Tupac Amaru Revolutionary Movement (MRTA), a group of Cuban-style Marxists who condemn the massacres of civilians (though not the use of violence per se to bring about a redistribution of resources)—much as the SACP prevented indiscriminate violence in South Africa. In both Peru and South Africa, an alienated and unemployed youth accounts for the appeal of radical movements. The difference in South Africa is that this frustration was successfully channeled into a national resistance organization that could legitimately claim to have the support of the entire world. By actively championing the cause of the excluded, foreign governments have preempted the rise of ultraradical, irrational protest. With Western states belatedly becoming sponsors of the ANC, even if that has meant turning a blind eye to the ideological antics of the SACP, foreign intervention has so far prevented the isolated irrational protest that has terrorized Peru. Given the interpenetration of reformist and revolutionary political cultures in contemporary South Africa, it seems unlikely at present that South Africa will turn into another Peru. However, unless substantial improvements occur in the life chances of the half of the South African population that is younger than twenty, even an ANC government could not rest for good on its record, particularly if the radical SACP ally were to lose its appeal to the PAC.

The proscription of racial domination does not necessarily ensure the achievement of democracy. How the process of dismantling domination is conducted will strongly influence the character of the post-apartheid order. Will South Africa create a culture of violence or will it lay the moral foundation for a lasting consensus about legitimate rules? A constitutional settlement in and of itself will not mark the end of the conflict. As F. van Zyl Slabbert has frequently stressed, "there is not an event that can be seized upon by the outside world to symbolize how and when South Africa moves from an apartheid to a post-apartheid era" (1992, 19).

CHAPTER EIGHT

International Intervention

From Anti-Apartheid to Development

The response of the international community needs to be
finely tuned to this complex and delicate process of
negotiations . . . encouragement, pressure and assistance
would need to be suitably applied as the process unfolds.

U.N. Secretary-General Butros Ghali, September
4, 1991

A POST–COLD WAR FOREIGN POLICY
ON SOUTHERN AFRICA

For almost half a century the policies of all Western powers regarding
Africa were to a greater or lesser extent influenced by the cold war
competition for hegemony and strategic parity in the remotest regions
of the globe. Now, these policies can be formulated without the
constraints of the cold war. The significance of this historical break
cannot be overstressed.[1]

For the United States in particular, less so for Canada and Western
Europe, sub-Saharan Africa had assumed primary, strategic significance as a battleground "to contain" the advances of the Soviet
Union, to check perceived Soviet proxies with Western clients, and to
bar access of the Soviet Union to what were declared vital mineral
resources and strategic routes for the survival of the Western economies. These alarmist assumptions were largely incorrect because Soviet policy in Africa was frequently more reactive in exploiting opportunities than in planning aggressive advances into Western orbits of
interest. For example, the Soviet-supported Cuban intervention in
Angola occurred only after the American-backed South African invasion of Angola in 1975. Moreover, Washington often exaggerated
Moscow's interest in Africa. On some occasions the Soviet Union
turned its back on willing clients, as when it rejected the application
of Mozambique for membership in the COMECON. While the Soviet

Union had its own agenda in Africa during the cold war, its policies were largely driven by its Western adversaries and aimed mainly at recognition of equal superpower status on the continent. The South African myth that the Kremlin was cunningly plotting to lay its hands on the treasures of the Cape nonetheless achieved wide credibility and helped to sustain the repression of democracy in the name of anticommunism.

Many African people were thus dragged into the superpowers' chess game. To be sure, many of the African leaders also manipulated the cold war to their own ends. They benefited from the rhetoric of anti-imperialism, as much as the apartheid ideologues benefited in presenting themselves as stalwarts of anticommunism resisting the "total onslaught" of the Soviet-sponsored ANC. All these master narratives, which forged strange alliances and designated imagined enemies, have now lost their guiding power. The "imagined war" has come to an end.

The cold war paradigm shaped America's understanding of Africa in ways that shut off domestic discourse as well as consideration of alternative policies. Africa's regional conflicts and their resolution were subsumed under the global competition. Revolutions in foreign countries were viewed as the great threat to the United States, and counterrevolutionary intervention became the hallmark of U.S. African policy.

The U.S.-Soviet collaboration in settling regional conflicts in Angola and Namibia in 1989 and the subsequent dissolution of the Soviet Union have deprived Western policy toward Africa of its former ideological lodestar and certainties. Ideas that had been rejected as infeasible or secondary in light of cold war ideological priorities now find a hearing on their merits. In consequence, nongovernmental organizations and special interest groups can be expected to exert a far greater influence in shaping foreign policy. The transnational environmental movement, as represented, for example, by Greenpeace, and global human rights organizations, such as Amnesty International, are two such forces that will make themselves increasingly felt in North American and Western European foreign policy. Other global lobbies that have attracted an international constituency include Medicine Without Frontiers, Oxfam, and various relief agencies. Responsiveness to such constituencies will invest Western policy on Southern Africa with both moral leadership and pragmatic good sense in making the global village a safer place for everyone.

Some critics dismiss the recent Western attentiveness to international human rights as another public relations exercise that aims at rehabilitating domestically unpopular governments. This overly functionalist interpretation, even if it were entirely correct, does not detract from the value of human rights advocacy, regardless of the mixed motives that may inspire it.

Human rights abuses are but one aspect of the Western public's prevailing negative image of Africa—an image that will have to be reversed if Western governments want to engender public support for new aid to Africa. For the dominant perception in the West is that Africa constitutes an unmitigated failure. In the years since the euphoria of independence in the 1950s and 1960s, most supporters of the anticolonial struggle have become thoroughly disillusioned with its outcome. Often cited are the economic stagnation and collapse in the countryside, the widespread human rights abuses, detentions without trial, torture, frequent coups in one-party states, the intercommunal massacres, civil wars, and the burgeoning graft and corruption of a government elite living in ostentatious luxury while paying lip service to humanist and socialist ideals. To this disastrous picture must be added the streams of refugees and more recently the devastating spread of the HIV virus, against which few African governments have taken serious measures. With the exception of Senegal, Botswana, and, arguably, one or two other countries, no sub-Saharan state can be held up as a democratic and economic success.

Thus the new Western emphasis on human rights as a precondition for development assistance constitutes a long overdue shift. Its skeptical reception and outright rejection by the majority of African regimes only confirms the correctness of the insistence. After the disappearance of apartheid as the Commonwealth's main raison d'être for the past decades, the spotlight will fall increasingly on its members' own domestic performance. Cold war allegiances will no longer serve to stifle criticism from embarrassed allies. Unless most Commonwealth members, particularly the African states, drastically reduce their infringement of human rights and democratic principles, the colonial club will marginalize itself further. With the emerging trilateral trading blocs, the Commonwealth will in any case lose importance as a sentimental alliance and contact arena for political elites. A strengthened United Nations increasingly substitutes for the colonial subsystems of cultural association. The same applies to la francophonie.

Future directions for Western policy toward Southern Africa can be discussed most sensibly in the context of four options for Western policy toward the Third World in general: militarization, abandonment, recolonization, and development.

Militarization comprises the acceptance of new security responsibilities for selected regions, such as the U.S.-led coalition in the Gulf War demonstrated for parts of the Middle East. The priority of this strategy lies in guaranteeing stability and access primarily through stepped-up policing, the formation of new military alliances, and security guarantees that provide for increased arms sales to and training of friendly local forces.

Abandonment would entail the gradual withdrawal of formerly involved outside forces. Regions would be left to fend for themselves as investment capital and government assistance are increasingly directed toward more economically attractive or politically promising states, such as the emerging democracies in Eastern Europe.

Recolonization defines the process of externally dictated economic policies, for example, through the so-called structural adjustment programs of the World Bank and the International Monetary Fund. While action of the World Bank has to be requested and the terms of the programs are formally negotiated and never unilaterally imposed, the bankruptcy of many Third World states and their dependency on further loans for vital imports leaves little leverage for bargaining. A stark choice of compliance or rejection is the only real option.

Development denotes the process of bilateral agreements on outside assistance with the goal of benefiting the mass of the population through broad economic empowerment. It differs from the World Bank's structural adjustment programs by offering substantial concessions on debt relief and investment in infrastructure and human resources (education, health care) of long-term benefit to the entire population, rather than short-term rewards only for an urban elite that has hard currency. Development policies can also include economic shock treatments, such as measures to correct an inflated currency, to increase export earnings, reduce government spending, privatize state enterprises, or cut subsidies. However, development policies do not primarily aim at paving the way for multinational profit-making but balance short-term investor interests with the long-term payoff of social investment in education and health care.

The four policy options sketched above are obviously not mutually exclusive; several could be pursued simultaneously with different emphases. Different Western countries will formulate their policies according to specific national interests and traditions. But the danger is that a strife-torn South Africa might be lumped together with other black African states as an unsalvageable proposition, a country best left to its own fate after all well-meaning outside efforts to secure a pluralist democracy are deemed to have failed as a consequence of a mixture of ingrained political violence and economic demise. An increased exodus of South African whites would vindicate those analysts, like Pierre van den Berghe (1979), who predicted the departure of most whites not only as the most likely development but also the most desirable solution to a colonial problem. An exodus would heighten the outside disillusionment with a noble experiment that went as sour as Tanzanian socialism or Zambian humanism.

This improbable doomsday scenario aside, Western policy toward the Southern African region is likely to be different from Western policy toward other Third World regions. In the United States and in Canada, the general public is largely indifferent to foreign developments, but South Africa—like Israel—is an exception. Because of the anti-apartheid movement, as well as the ease with which Western media can report from an English-speaking state, South Africa figures prominently in the North American public consciousness. Kith-and-kin relations in Britain, Canada, and Germany and bonds between African-American activists and South African blacks will continue to reinforce a high level of public interest in the former apartheid state. The possibilities for tourism could add to this public involvement. While the new South Africa does not possess the emotional support and clout of the Israeli lobby, the South African activist diaspora, so to speak, far supersedes any other Third World cause in influence and intellectual investment.

South Africa is unique among the decolonizing regions in having spawned a wide international lobby of knowledgeable partisans in the worldwide anti-apartheid movement, and the dismantling of apartheid is unlikely to obliterate the movement's legacy. While this network has traditionally been viewed as a committed enemy of the South African state, it could become an effective agent for the reconstruction of the new postapartheid nation. The idealism of a professional lobby that has connections in the governments and media in virtually every major country could sustain Western interest in South Africa long after apartheid. Unlike Zimbabwe or Namibia, where international interest faded with the day of independence, South Africa will not overnight appear to be a story that has been resolved.

During the likely fractious power-sharing period, the international lobby will take its cues from the ANC; how this latent support is activated will depend heavily on the word of Mandela. It may not be too farfetched to envisage the day when those who once lobbied for sanctions actively campaign for renewed investment as the duty of responsible business in assisting a fledgling democracy. The tragedy may well be that this day has been so long delayed, and the interim economic decline and social disintegration have grown so deep, that the new South Africa will be beyond even the most enthusiastic rescue efforts of its dedicated supporters.

If these assumptions are correct, then Western foreign policy toward Southern Africa will not follow the route of abandonment. Quite apart from increased economic ties and the importance of the modern South African sector for the development of the Southern African region as a whole, together with renewed South African membership in the UN, the Commonwealth, and the OAU, the tortuous past relationship has cemented rather than weakened future Western–South African ties and public involvement in shaping them.

Nor are the investment demands of Eastern Europe likely to channel all investment capital in an eastern rather than southern direction. Within the emerging trilateral trading blocs, Eastern Europe is increasingly viewed as the primary responsibility of Germany and the European Community. When North American and Japanese capital weighs the advantages and disadvantages of the two regions, South Africa has overwhelming attractions: a modern infrastructure, a functioning market, and a skilled business class—none of which exist or will soon exist in the former Soviet Union—as well as an English-language environment, scarce mineral resources, and an attractive climate. The great advantages of Eastern Europe in the form of location, an educated labor force, and a large pool of scientists are likely to be overshadowed for some time by the organizational deficits of a former command economy. Thus South Africa is unlikely to be abandoned by all risk capital in favor of Eastern Europe, though much will depend on the perceived political stability of the two regions. Once the transitional political violence has been overcome, South Africa may well score far better.

Decisions about economic investment also entail questions about whether the affluent North has the political will to pursue altruistic internationalist policies. Cranford Pratt (1990) has persuasively sketched the enormous obstacles that the application of cosmopolitan values faces in countries geared to neoprotectionism in order to avoid domestic deindustrialization. Pratt notes the often ignored friction between a social-democratic tradition of global solidarity and the simultaneous protection of domestic workers' interests against so-called unfair competition from low-wage countries. To date, narrow domestic definitions of national interests have won out against internationalism. The Third World's access to the affluent Northern markets, resource and technology transfer, debt relief, and constraints on transnational corporations have generally been offered only when the richer initiators have benefited themselves or have had little choice in avoiding worse and unmanageable conditions. The end of the cold war has removed another constraint on the pursuit of immediate national economic advantages. The North American–South African constellation, where a policy of global solidarity coincided with domestic advantage and relatively little cost, is unlikely to repeat itself in an ever more competitive world of emerging trading blocs. The humane global components of national cultures, the long-term objectives of international equity and development, are unlikely to survive in an atmosphere of global nationalist revival.

Therefore, Southern Africa, lying outside the major trading blocs, cannot realistically expect much assistance from its Western colonial mentors. The states of Southern Africa will have to fall back on their own regional cooperation and individual advantages in promoting interregional developments. Southern Africa may still be a priority for development assistance, but it will be competing for a shrinking pie.

TRAINING A NEW MANAGERIAL CLASS

Outsiders are now focusing on the training of a new civil service culture in South Africa. An excellent report by the Commonwealth's Expert Committee on Southern Africa sets out a detailed rationale for the training needs of the new South Africa together with imaginative and realistic proposals to finance and implement educational programs for postapartheid skills.[2] The magnitude and urgency of these needs are enormous. As has often been pointed out, the efforts to abolish apartheid pale in comparison with the task of coping with its legacy.

At present, only 2.2 percent of managers in South Africa's top companies are black (SAIRR, update, July 16, 1991). Although blacks constitute a majority of the civil service, including homeland bureaucracies, they generally occupy the very lowest positions. Official statistics record that 41 percent of the public service in South Africa (excluding the TBCV states) is African and 39 percent is white. However, of the 2,885 posts in the five top income categories in central state departments and provinces, only 14 were occupied by blacks in 1990 (*Sunday Times,* October 20, 1991). The upper echelons of the state bureaucracy are thoroughly dominated by an Afrikaner cultural ethos. The civil service elite is also almost exclusively male. For example, among the 141 permanent and 11 acting judges, in 1991 only one was a woman and one was black.

In Eastern Europe, as Marinus Wiechers has pointed out, the transition to a new order has meant both "doing away with the old policies" and "doing away with the people in government applying these policies." But, Wiechers concludes, "We cannot afford to do the same in South Africa" (*Sunday Tribune,* October 27, 1991). There simply are not enough well-trained people to replace all the old bureaucrats and administrators, no matter how soiled their hands are. Indeed, the dependency on the old civil service by any postapartheid government and the likely retention of tainted institutions and people will be one of the most striking dilemmas of the new order. The civil machinery that was created by the apartheid state and employed for implementing apartheid is now being asked to usher in the anti-apartheid polity.

The explanation for "the dearth of capacity to support leadership in the democratic movement by formulating coherent and viable perspectives on economic policy" lies not only in the legacy of apartheid education.[3] After all, thirty years of exile with hundreds of scholarships for those who sought asylum in the East and West should have produced a fair core of competent progressive economists, quite apart from the opportunities for black students at the liberal English-speaking universities.[4] The absence of economic skills in the opposition is also due to an internal "progressive" sentiment and a norm of exile education that dismissed studies of "bourgeois economics" as not only a waste of time but a sellout to the system. Now the ANC will have to pay the price of keeping such myths alive rather than preparing itself to administer the country.

Likewise, the internal opposition had demonized the state and capital to such an extent that any professional training in its method of operation smacked of treason. Braan Fleisch has aptly described the self-imposed distance from tainted skills: "For those who remained in the country for the intense years of the struggle, there was never even a thought about running, controlling and administering an advanced industrial society. The enemy was business, business methods and business mentality. The state was the enemy. No one wanted to understand how the state ran the country, the principal concern was how the state was used as a mechanism of repression. In place of the state, activists posited a romantic notion about popular participation" (*Searchlight South Africa*, July 1991). Victoria Brittain, in a nostalgic memorial to the socialist dream, has described the word *progressive* for Southern African activists as meaning "being led by nationalist governments organised on Marxist-Leninist models learned in the schools of eastern Europe, where students from both parties got an education way beyond the dreams of colonial Africa" (*Southern Africa Report* [Toronto], July 1991). As long as it is still not openly acknowledged within the ANC that this kind of education does not help to solve South Africa's problems, no well-meaning foreign economic expertise and training will make much of a difference. Political education within the ANC as well as other movements seems almost as important as the acquisition of managerial skills.

Unless effective affirmative action programs ensure a more representative managerial class, both in the public and private sectors, effective apartheid will continue as a nameless condition, despite the new constitution. Since the South African private sector can finance its own managerial needs in well-endowed business schools, it is the neglected area of public administration that needs most attention.[5]

To train black managers and administrators within South Africa rather than abroad seems both more cost-effective and appropriate. Granting scholarships for study abroad made sense when adequate educational facilities for blacks did not exist in South Africa. Apart from specialized graduate studies abroad, foreign educational assistance could now be spent inside the country far more beneficially, achieving a greater impact with limited resources and also reducing the brain drain, as fewer foreign students would be living abroad for long periods.

On the other hand, there is a case to be made for encouraging South African students to attend universities abroad for a period. The total change of environment, the experience of a new political culture, and the opportunity for renewed self-esteem, for black students particularly, are not inconsequential for their future leadership roles. Many prominent blacks speak about study abroad as having increased their self-confidence. The positive experiences of being in a new setting, free of the stigma of race and all its self-fulfilling expectations, and of being considered an authority on developments in one's country do have empowering effects. Those who argue the most loudly in favor of cost-effective approaches are all too often members of the privileged group who fail to appreciate such personal experiences.

The disbursement of educational assistance, however, takes place within an intense political contest inside South Africa. To receive foreign support or be left out of sponsorship affects the standing of competing black political organizations and their associated institutions and members. Individuals may even choose to join organizations not for ideological reasons but solely for individual advancement. Sheer survival coerces others to join, as when Black Consciousness adherents fled South Africa during the late 1970s and found to their surprise that they had to link up with the rival ANC if they wanted scholarships and opportunities for advancement. A similar informal coercion exists within Natal/KwaZulu, where often Inkatha membership remains a precondition for a career in the civil service or even for obtaining vital necessities.

FOREIGN ASSISTANCE FOR WHAT?

There has not yet been a serious discussion of how external funding has affected the democratic movement inside South Africa. At present 90 percent of the ANC's expenses are covered by funds from abroad.[6] This skewed cash flow creates its own problems. Obviously, external funding relieves leaders from having to cultivate close links with their constituency. It can also create leaders—by endowment as it were—and tempt them to be less scrupulous than they would be under the tight financial control of a grass-roots membership.

In one of the few self-critical assessments by an ANC sympathizer, Farid Moulana Essack argues along these lines that external funding "worked against" real democracy rather than ushering it in.

> External funding made it even less necessary for us to remain accountable to the local communities and interest groups on whose behalf we acted and spoke. Millions of rands flooded into the country—and are still flowing in—with little insistence upon strict accounting for their use. Suppression made it impossible to adhere to proper bookkeeping procedures. This absence of accountability worked against the development of organic bonds within our communities, and at the same time, gave rise to a multiplicity of small kingdoms.
>
> (*Die Suid-Afrikaan*, December 1990–January 1991)

Many a promising leader's downfall can be attributed to well-intentioned foreign support that created temptations, irresistible in a sea of poverty, to embark on corruption. With frequent invitations abroad—sometimes traveling first-class as people's representatives so as to escape South African second-class status—once popular spokespersons became even more alienated from their communities.

Foreign donors always make choices that have direct political implications. They can choose to be neutral by allocating assistance across the board to all contenders, or they can favor one movement over the other. They can use political criteria in awarding scholarships in order to discriminate against applicants with a particular orientation, or they can back one research group over another equally qualified team with different political sympathies.

Were they willing to commit sufficient resources, foreign donors could, theoretically, determine the winners and losers of the South African political contest. But such an undertaking would unwisely interfere with the free choice of South Africans. Rather than attempt to directly or indirectly influence the outcome of any free South African political contest by taking sides among the opposition groups, foreign donors should focus their efforts on leveling the playing field between the oppressed majority and the privileged establishment. If it is the goal of intervention to help establish the democratic process and secure competent administrators, then assistance for political development should be given across the board to all comers, regardless of their political affiliation. The task is to promote the process, not to select the winners.

Many Western initiatives are now biased toward the ANC and its allies. These efforts ignore the PAC and Azapo and recoil from the Inkatha Freedom Party. The secret funding of Inkatha during the Botha era and the ongoing political violence have reinforced international perceptions that Inkatha is part of an undemocratic apartheid system, "opposed to the democratic anti-apartheid forces" in the words of the Commonwealth Foreign Ministers.[7] This kind of labeling may well exacerbate political violence by marginalizing one group and elevating others, thereby reinforcing hegemonic temptations all round. If the cooperation of all significant political groups is necessary for a peace accord to last and a political settlement to be reached, Western policy, judged by its own stated goals of enhancing South African democracy, should not favor the presently strongest party as "a government in waiting."

In this respect, outside attitudes toward Inkatha or the nonviolent sections of the white ultra-right constitute a test case as to whether Western foreign policy primarily assists ideologically acceptable organizations or aims at achieving accommodation. A policy interested in reconciliation must communicate with ideological foes as well as favorites. If the primary aim of Western foreign policy is the peaceful democratization of South Africa, then undemocratic organizations need even more attention than the democratic parties.

To date, Western public opinion and activist groups have largely ignored or dismissed alternatives to the ANC-led opposition. Though the PAC's provocative sloganeering about "one settler, one bullet" is unpalatable to the nonracial sentiment of the West, rhetorical terrorism has potential mass appeal that should not be ignored.

The nonviolent sections of the white right wing pose an even sharper choice between pragmatic accommodation and moralistic rejection. Wisely, Mandela himself urges that the white right wing has to be accommodated in the new South Africa, irrespective of how repugnant its beliefs are to the ANC: "We do not want them to remain in the future South Africa as a Renamo-type force. Let us try to reach these people now and assure them that they have nothing to fear from majority rule."[8] Mandela's judicious attitude toward intransigent ideologues would be difficult to put into practice, since neither his constituency nor the militant right wing want to promote such an accommodation. The best that can be hoped for is that the ANC can engage the moral ideologues of Afrikaner self-determination, who still form the majority in the right-wing camp.

NEGLECTED AREAS
OF FOREIGN DEVELOPMENT ASSISTANCE

In addition to providing assistance for human resource development and emphasizing human rights, multiparty democracy, and peace-keeping as preconditions for good government, the West should focus on six specific priorities for aid to South Africa and, by extension, the region as a whole. These six neglected realms are professional policing, public works programs, low-cost housing, women's rights, AIDS education, and tourist development.

Professional Policing. The need to integrate MK and the South African Defence Force has been discussed at great length, but only recently has attention been given to the reform of the police in a postapartheid society. Yet the police remain the front line of state power in daily life, and political transformation will be meaningless unless accompanied by an institutional change in police culture. To merely exchange personnel, to gradually Africanize the police, as in Zimbabwe and Namibia, without redefining their role could be to substitute unprofessional black officers for unprofessional white ones.

A professional police force would be well trained, well educated, and well paid. Enhancing the prestige of the police and raising salaries to attract better candidates remain urgent tasks. The new police will also need to be carefully screened for psychological fitness and stability. Unsuitable officers should be retired or retrained; the cost would surely be less than the damage that could be done to the fragile social fabric by reckless so-called defenders. Citizens also need an independent complaints board that would hear grievances against unfair police treatment and refer complaints to the courts for prosecution and compensation.

In a comprehensive review of the intrawhite controversy about the proper role of the police force, Ronald Weitzer (1991) concluded that the few-rotten-apples approach does not address the lack of professional training, selection, and recruitment. The absence of citizens' control of the police through independent monitoring and complaints boards, according to this author, "inflate police morale, but they also help to perpetuate traditional attitudes and practices."

In her study of riot-control policing, Anthea Jeffery (1991) proposes that the present squads be replaced by a special multiparty "national peace guard" that together with a multiparty monitoring committee would ensure order during the transition. Adoption of this suggestion, combined with more representative recruitment, clearer legal guidelines and accountability, as well as professional training in communication skills and community involvement could transform the South African police from a partisan force into a more widely respected, impartial institution that served the entire community.

Despite the demonization of police and army officers, many in the ranks are proud professionals who carry out the orders of whatever legitimate government is in power. Most officers conceive of themselves foremost as technocrats rather than committed counterideologues. Therefore, the appeal to depoliticize the forces, instead of using them opportunistically to uphold unpopular policies, remains the most sensible approach.

The ANC's call to establish people's self-defense units under the guidance and control of Umkhonto could backfire if these private armies and power bases for local warlords exacerbate existing tensions. However, the units might also be the only way in which a moderate political leadership could direct and discipline its anarchic following and restore a semblance of order. This seems to have been the intent of the organizers; an ANC booklet exhorts: "Umkhonto cadres, particularly ex-prisoners and those due to return from exile, must play a leading and active role in the establishment of the defence structures."[9] The writers emphasize "firm political direction" and the rooting of units in their communities. An internal army under the control of exiles and former prisoners would obviously strengthen the ANC's tenuous hold over unfamiliar and often hostile terrain. As long as the ANC remains committed to ending the violence while tolerating opposing parties, such units may well be in the short-term interests of peace. On the other hand, the spread of weapons and training could well result in greater carnage and aggression toward dissenters. No state can afford to lose the monopoly of coercion without destabilizing itself. A well-qualified professional police force in which the ANC units were fully integrated would seem the less risky option. Moreover, private armies are easier to establish than to control. Should the ANC's self-defense units provoke other parties to mobilize militia, South Africa would be on the way to becoming another Lebanon.

Rather than blindly supporting the ANC's militarist wing, the international community could initiate and finance a buy-back weapons program. Since law enforcement remains ineffective in South Africa's radically politicized environment, material incentives may be the only way to reduce the proliferation of illegal guns. As land mines are cleared after a war, so other weaponry has to be collected and destroyed once peace has been negotiated.

Public Works Programs.   No society can achieve humane intergroup relations, security, and stability when crime rates are steadily rising. Social causes of anomie in South Africa have been amply documented: an unemployment rate of 40 percent, the disintegration of the traditional family under the migrant labor system and subsequent urbanization, the resistance strategy of ungovernability and the general brutalization under apartheid. Better professional policing, as necessary as it is, addresses the symptoms of crime but not the underlying causes. Most of the youths involved in criminal activities live beyond

the reach of traditional institutions or the discipline of political organizations. Such groups are unable to address the "crisis of masculin-
ity," which feminists have pointed to as a source of the problem, or
to offer the much-needed training and formal education, even if more
resources and trained teachers were available. Statistics show that
levels of interpersonal violence are highest among Coloureds, followed by Africans and whites; the rates for Indians are by far the
lowest. The degree of anomie reflects above all the poorer self-image
of Coloureds and the much higher self-confidence of Indians, despite
greater discrimination and social stigma against the latter. One explanation for this difference is that the Indian communities have emphasized cultural pride, educational achievements, and family honor,
while the more atomized Coloured communities lack civic and political leadership. Leadership is much stronger in African areas, despite
a higher degree of socioeconomic deprivation, but poverty has made
the African townships the focal point of interpersonal violence, which
increasingly affects everyone in the country.

Mandela noticed the time bomb in a remarkably frank and astute
observation, "The youths in the townships have had over the decades
a visible enemy, the government. Now that enemy is no longer visible,
because of the transformation that is taking place. Their enemy now
is you and me, people who drive a car and have a house. It's order,
anything that relates to order, and it is a grave situation" (*The Star,
International Weekly*, September 10–16, 1992, p. 12). The ANC's
mass action, the periodic channeling of resentment into well-
rehearsed demonstrations meant to discipline the youths' anger, always runs the risk of degenerating into looting and intimidation if not
carefully directed and controlled.[10]

One solution would be a two-year compulsory national service for
all sixteen- or eighteen-year-olds except those enrolled in institutions
of higher learning. Unlike the current military call-ups for whites, this
tour of duty would focus on training in the context of public works
programs, community service, and individual development. For example, the corps could work on providing electricity to the 70 percent
of African households that are not yet connected to the countrywide
grid; it could improve the roads and facilities in rural areas and build
proper houses in the vast shack settlements. Such a national service
program would thus simultaneously improve the quality of life in the
poorest areas, discipline and mold the essential individuals of the new
nation, and provide everyone with basic vocational training. Incen-

tives such as pay, housing, preferential employment for service veterans, and travel opportunities may be sufficient to entice older unemployed youth into the service on a voluntary basis, as happened during the New Deal in the United States and during the uplift programs for poor Afrikaners in the 1930s.

Of course, only a legitimate government could initiate such a scheme. However, the planning of the program should begin now, after the widest consultation. Unfortunately, the blueprints of all parties remain silent on how to deal with the urgently needed resocialization and rehabilitation of the young "lost generation."

Low-Cost Housing. The housing shortage in South Africa was estimated at 1.2 million homes in 1990, with a new demand of 174,000 homes against an actual supply of 25,000. Since 60 percent of black households cannot afford a home worth more than 12,500 rand ($4,500), they necessarily have to fall back on informal shack dwelling. Despite the demand for housing, successful social-democratic experiments and workers' self-help programs have yet to be emulated in South Africa. For example, Quebec's legendary labor leader Louis Laberge formed Corvée Habitation, a fund to which construction workers pay fifteen cents of their hourly wage, and which provides mortgages at 3 percent below the prime rate. So far more than fifty thousand workers have borrowed from the program to buy houses they built. In 1984 the Quebec Federation of Labor launched the Fonds de Solidarité, an investment fund that buys into business to ensure union jobs. To date, it is estimated that investments of $170 million in ninety projects have saved twenty thousand jobs. Successful union-controlled enterprises on a much larger scale include Germany's Neue Heimat, which has built houses in bomb-damaged areas, and Singapore's Provident Fund, which solved a massive housing crisis by a forced saving scheme under state auspices. The reluctance of South Africa's organized labor to engage in similar projects is only partly due to its organizational weakness and relative infancy. The flirtation with capitalism that all these endeavors, from credit unions to housing funds, represent is deeply resented in South Africa.

The planned housing subsidies by the Independent Development Trust Finance Corporation, a subsidiary of the Independent Development Trust (IDT), appropriately target the squatter sections of South Africa. Only low-income families qualify for a free serviced site for which individual title is transferred. In dispensing loans, the corporation relies on employers to administer the loans, inform workers about the program, and establish workers' loan committees that decide on the criteria for granting credit. Through this program, then, an individual without collateral can secure some cash to build a basic house. Like the saving associations (stokvels) that operate in the townships, the innovative scheme also uses peer pressure to ensure that creditors meet their commitments.

Although pilot projects for this program were several times oversubscribed, the sensible loan schemes did not receive full cooperation from the ANC or from state institutions or from private developers, the last of whom saw that their role would be undercut by the subsidies. The Independent Development Trust's attempt to borrow abroad encountered fierce initial opposition among anti-apartheid groups in Europe. Only Mandela's endorsement of the endeavor appeased the opposition.

Women's Rights. There are few so-called Western countries where the status of women is still locked into the traditional mold as much as in South Africa. Half-naked bodies adorn the front pages of even serious papers. Feminist debate is in its earliest stages. Child-care facilities are underdeveloped. A women's movement is confined to a few privileged university lecturers and other professionals. The few female executives in progressive organizations complain as intensely about chauvinist treatment as the lone female member of the National Party caucus. While some outstanding South African women have achieved worldwide reputations (Helen Suzman, Mamphele Ramphela, Winnie Mandela, and Nadine Gordimer come to mind) and while women's organizations have been in the forefront of political activism—witness the Black Sash and the independent initiatives of African women from the Durban beerhall boycotts in the 1950s through the strikes in the 1980s—the public realm remains a male domain. Only 3 of 170 working-group members at the first Codesa meeting were women. Among the advisors, the number of women was slightly higher, but no more than 5 percent. After five hours of heated debate in 1991 the ANC national conference scrapped a draft proposal that 30 percent of the 50 ordinary NEC posts be allocated to women. Ninety percent of the conference delegates were men, and the majority of them repeated the well-known arguments against affirmative action, although they all supported it in principle: Women elected in a quota system would have a diminished status if they did not win their seats in an open contest; to allocate posts by gender would entrench an undesirable form of "group rights" in the organization.

Thus far, widespread wife battering and sexual abuse are largely ignored. Only a few cases are reported, and few resources are committed to shielding and healing the victims. In black communities in particular, patriarchal customs reinforce the exploitation and submission of women. Abortion, for example, remains taboo and illegal, and most African men scorn birth control. Yet an empirical survey about leisure activities and opportunities of township youth yielded one surprising result: When asked to name the "major problems for young people," 65 percent of the respondents mentioned teenage pregnancy, compared to 37 percent who cited unemployment and 31 percent who named education and training.[11] Nonetheless, the consequences of unwanted children, unsafe abortions, and inadequate child care for the society at large and the emancipation of African women in particular remain unacknowledged.

Development assistance, at present, is not linked to population policies. But if a society lags so far behind in elementary preconditions for the social development of half of its population, foreign aid could be designed to encourage some changes, notwithstanding the political sensitivity and controversial nature of the issues. For example, foreign aid could be tied to progress in introducing modern birth control options. The ability to delay pregnancy would not only establish women's human rights to control their own bodies, but would help to free women from being the most exploited segment of African society. Moreover, a good case can be made that democratic rights at large are impossible to ensure when an ever-increasing population density exacerbates poverty and environmental destruction. Yet international donors remain indifferent toward population policies. One explanation, that under apartheid Pretoria politicized the demographic ratios,[12] will soon be moot. And the excuse of respect for indigenous traditions and sentiments seems misplaced when the consequences include the degradation of women and birthrates that portend societal disintegration.

Unfortunately, the underdeveloped feminist tradition in South Africa, together with the cultural and racial gender divide, hamper the trends that have elsewhere most effectively influenced birthrates. Witwatersrand sociologist Jacklyn Cock, a participant in the April 1989 Harare meeting of fifty-five women from inside South Africa with twenty-five exiles from ANC missions abroad, noted: "Throughout the meeting there was an emphasis on women's role as mothers. We women are the producers of children. We go through the nine months, the feeding period, the fears and anxieties." The needs expressed by mothers and the priorities of middle-class white progressive women were quite different, and Cock felt that "attempts to formulate a shared oppression often floundered on biologistic reasoning" (*Weekly Mail*, April 28, 1989). Indeed, given the different social backgrounds of the two groups, any dialogue about their common oppression would have been highly artificial, the shared abhorrence of apartheid notwithstanding.

Political tensions have also prevented an open debate on population control. Because birth control is generally frowned upon and also associated with state designs to suppress the black majority, most progressive organizations avoid offering family-planning assistance. Although South Africa is not now overpopulated by international standards, if the rate of population growth continues to exceed the rate of economic growth, all development efforts will remain futile. While it is true that high birthrates are the consequences of poverty and not its cause, it is also true that the lot of poor women and squatter women would be considerably improved if they were to have more control over childbearing. Moreover, the burgeoning population negatively affects the environment and inevitably destroys the natural habitat, unless state policies intervene. It is in this area that postapartheid South Africa could look to the successful development politics of South Korea, Singapore, or China. While South Africa will not want to adopt the repressive labor policies that facilitated the dramatic takeoff of the Pacific Rim countries, it could model its incentives for birth control on the Asian example.

AIDS Education.   Compared with Central and East Africa, South Africa had a lower incidence of AIDS cases in the early 1980s, but business research and medical evidence have indicated an alarming spread of the HIV virus since the mid 1980s, first among the white homosexual population and later—and more rapidly—among black heterosexuals. Virginia van der Vliet has summarized the available data: "Sober medical research findings suggest that given present levels of infection and the current eight to nine months doubling time, 6% of the black population aged 15–60 might be HIV positive by 1991 and this could rise to 18% by 1992" (*Frontline File,* April 1991). In other words, AIDS is likely to claim far more fatalities than apartheid did, yet both the domestic and international anti-apartheid campaigns have remained largely silent. Years after behavior modification programs and general awareness campaigns were launched elsewhere throughout the world, nothing had been done in South Africa. Not a single senior white or black politician publicly mentioned the subject until October 1990, when the minister of health, Rita Venter, announced cabinet approval of a committee to focus on prevention. A study conducted by Planned Parenthood in Khayelitsha in 1992 found that 79 percent of the respondents did not know that AIDS is transmitted by sexual intercourse and only 57 percent had ever heard of AIDS (*Cape Times,* December 3, 1992).

Like everything else, AIDS education in South Africa quickly fell victim to politics. Many blacks labeled AIDS a "white man's disease." The ANC journal *Sechaba* asked "why 'such a deadly virus should suddenly spring from nowhere' " and pointed to "the possibility of the viruses being developed in the secrecy of the laboratories of many imperialist countries" (van der Vliet, *Frontline File,* April 1991). Right-wing whites, on the other hand, privately welcomed the "natural" correction of differential growth rates or, at most, deplored the devastating impact on the labor force. Conservatives disseminated rumors that many of the returning ANC exiles were infected. When the mining companies introduced AIDS testing for migrant workers, the unions and the ANC did not go beyond the obvious by pointing out that South African social conditions facilitated the spread of the disease.

Despite increased awareness of AIDS in Southern Africa, and noble resolutions about AIDS education passed at special congresses and at political meetings, denial and silence are still widespread. For example, even the 1991 final Commonwealth Heads of Government Meeting communique does not mention AIDS, but vaguely lists "communicable diseases" among a host of other problems. Yet the World Health Organization estimates that six million adults on the African continent are infected with HIV, of whom a million have developed full-blown AIDS, and infant and child mortality rates are expected to rise. Nonetheless, safety tests for blood products have not yet been introduced everywhere in Southern Africa.

For South Africa alone, Jonathan Broomberg, Malcolm Steinberg, and Patrick Masobe predict 5.2 million cases of HIV and 666,000 cumulative deaths from AIDS by the year 2000; 7.4 million cases of HIV and 2.9 million cumulative deaths by 2005; and 8.2 million cases of HIV and 6.6 million cumulative deaths by 2010.[13] Grania Christie (1991) discusses contingent predictions with a 30 percent maximum infection rate in the total population, translating into a 60 percent rate among workers by 1995.

Not only the migrant workers' system but also traditional polygamy—which denies common-law wives any legal rights or control over their sexuality—encourages the spread of AIDS. Adelaide Magwaza has reported on a survey of black women in one of the squatter camps around Durban; 60 percent of the women interviewed were either the second or third common-law wife. "Although they were aware of the danger of AIDS, they were unwilling to discuss AIDS and protective sex with their husband for fear they would either lose financial support or lose the husband to his other common-law wives" (*The Condenser*, 1991).

Sex education is not compulsory in South African schools and is inhibited by the strictures of both the Calvinist Christian National Education and African traditions. Yet AIDS education, as part of a broader health and life skills training, must begin at the primary-school level if behavior and attitudes are to be changed. Among older students, peer counseling should be encouraged. Counseling, especially in black communities, must also include traditional healers (sangomas) since, by one estimate 80 percent of black patients first visit a traditional healer.[14] Similar education and peer counseling programs could be introduced into every factory and workplace.

The ANC's refusal to have its repatriated exiles from high-risk areas in Africa tested for HIV may have the unintended effect of further spreading the disease in South Africa. Mandatory testing would have been one of the few areas where an emulation of Cuba's management of its soldiers in Angola would have made eminent sense, but the politicization of AIDS precluded support for precautionary measures. For example, the pro-ANC weekly *New Nation* (July 12–18, 1991) published allegations by former police operative Ronald Bezuidenhout that he was instructed by the CCB—an undercover arm of the state defense force—to transport four AIDS-infected "askaris" (former MK soldiers who joined the police) to spread the virus in Soweto and East Rand townships. Even if the allegations are untrue, as the police maintained, they reinforced the perception among blacks that the state was responsible for the spread of the disease.

Tourist Development. The development of a green tourism belt from Kenya to South Africa could serve both broad economic and environ-

mental goals. The labor-intensive tourist industry could provide revenue and jobs, while protecting the world's largest and most diverse
chain of natural wildlife parks. Joint initiatives by the National Parks
Boards of Kenya, Tanzania, Botswana, Namibia, Zimbabwe, and
South Africa could link the Kruger National Park with the Okavango
Delta, the Etosha Pan, Victoria Falls, Serengeti Park, and Kenya's
Masai Mara Nature Reserve. As long as the considerable revenues
could be guaranteed to benefit the local population and not only the
tour operators, African tourism could be the most effective force for
environmental conservation in some of the last authentic large wilderness areas on the planet. By gradually extending the park system,
instead of increasing destructive cattle grazing and deforestation, the
African nations could embark on a course of sustainable development.
A precondition for the success of the plan would be not to resettle the
local population but to integrate them as beneficiaries with vested
interests in a restructured, self-sufficient environmental protection
zone in which national boundaries become as irrelevant for tourists as
they are for big game.

The development of high professional standards of wildlife conservation, as well as planning for the more problematic aspects of mass
tourism, could be facilitated by exchanges between North American
park rangers and African game wardens. Sound management would
also enable rural people to benefit from local wildlife through licensed
hunting and animal craft production, as is practiced in Botswana and
Zimbabwe. Licensing would also ensure optimal protection from
poaching and could prepare the way for repealing the ban on the sale
of ivory, a ban imposed in 1989 by the Convention on International
Trade in Endangered Species because of poor management of ele-
phants and rhinoceros herds in East Africa. To resume their business,
the ivory cartel of the better-managed Southern African countries will
have to prove that their controversial trade both protects wildlife and
also benefits the rural population.

In Southern Africa, the social problems are immense and complex,
but the potential to solve the six predicaments exists as well, particularly if foreign assistance can be geared to these priorities.

CHAPTER NINE

Regional Relations
and Development Policies

South Africa is no longer an uncomplicated source of
foreign policy options and economic relations.

F. van Zyl Slabbert, 1991

With the disappearance of apartheid as a moral reference point in the
international community, Southern Africa will be in danger of being
increasingly marginalized in world affairs and the global economy.
Already more Western capital is flowing into the former Soviet Union
and Eastern Europe than into the entire Third World. Should the West
turn its back on a region it no longer deems strategically valuable, the
forging of intraregional models of development will become even
more crucial. Whether the new South Africa can shed its subimperial
role and take its destabilized hinterland into a new development phase
without dominating it economically, whether a regional common
market can develop, whether South Africa will be exclusively preoccupied with its own restructuring, and which regional organizations
will be most effective in avoiding marginalization and providing access to other markets—all these unresolved questions bear directly on
the life chances of 120 million people in the eleven sovereign states
that comprise Southern Africa.

Relations between postapartheid South Africa and the ten members
of the Southern African Development Community (SADC) will follow
one of three courses: SADC will disintegrate and the domestic situation in each country will determine its relations with South Africa;
SADC will be strengthened by South Africa's membership without the
individual states losing their political sovereignty; or, a Southern African regional union will be established and far-reaching economic
integration will be followed by a shared sovereignty.

In the academic literature, judgments on SADCC (as the organization was known before its change of name in July 1992) differ.

Peter Vale (1991, 217) concludes, "Judged not only by African but by world standards, SADCC has been a remarkably successful experiment." This may be so, if one uses member cooperation as a yardstick. However, in terms of SADC's initial goal of delinking the region from the apartheid economy and achieving a greater degree of self-reliance, the project has been a dismal failure. Christopher Coker (1991, 286) correctly states, "SADCC's attempt to create an alternative system has not succeeded." Indeed the level of intraregional trade has fallen to a meager 5 percent. Dan O'Meara (1988), in an assessment of the costs and impact of destabilization in 1988, concluded that South Africa has achieved most of its aims in Mozambique: "SADCC's original vision of steadily reduced economic dependence on South Africa has been shattered." The alternative regional transport system on which this independence strategy was predicated, namely the outlets through Mozambique, were severely disrupted by the war, and the historical asymmetrical interdependency of the region has been maintained in its infrastructural links (roads, railways), trade, and patterns of labor migration and capital flows. With the balance of trade heavily running in South Africa's favor and South Africa's exports to Southern Africa and the rest of the continent increasing dramatically, the economic integration of the region into the industrial heartland of the South is proceeding apace. What the apartheid state only partially achieved through military and diplomatic coercion—the submission of nominally sovereign neighbors under its self-proclaimed regional power status—unrestricted economic penetration will finally seal.

South Africa already dominates the region militarily and economically. The relationship of SADC states with South Africa varies only in the degree of captivity: from a total captive like Lesotho to the relatively independent Angola, whose economy is nonetheless increasingly drawn into the South African orbit of mining expertise. Mozambique, on the other hand, has been so devastated by a South African–sponsored civil war that the once-thriving Portuguese outpost has become the poorest nation in the world, reliant on $1.6 billion a year in foreign aid, which constitutes 74 percent of its budget. Table 2 summarizes other indicators of South Africa's economic dominance.

This dependency is not entirely one-sided. The economic future of the Witwatersrand depends on the Lesotho Highland's water scheme. Electricity from the Cahora Bassa project offers a more ef-

TABLE 2.   SADC COUNTRIES AND SOUTH AFRICA:
POPULATION, AREA, AND BASIC ECONOMIC
INDICATORS (1989)

SADC countries	Population (millions)	Area (thousands of sq km)	GDP ($ billions)	GDP Per Capita	GDP Growth Rate
Angola	9.2	1,247	$ 4.32	$ 470	0.6%
Botswana	1.3	562	4.88	2,216	5.7
Lesotho	1.8	30	0.14	87	− 2.1
Malawi	8.4	118	1.31	160	4.1
Mozambique	14.3	802	1.89	136	5.3
Namibia	1.6	823	1.66	1,290	0.6
Swaziland	0.7	17	1.66	936	4.6
Tanzania	28.3	945	2.97	105	3.3
Zambia	7.2	753	1.80	250	0.1
Zimbabwe	10.0	391	5.80	580	4.5
SADC total	82.8	5,708	26.43	282	
South Africa	35.9	1,100	87.50	2,437	− 1.1*

Sources. *South Africa International,* April 1991, p. 219, and *SADCC Annual Progress Reports,* 1989–90.
*Rate in 1991.

fective supply than nuclear power stations. Above all, the South has long relied on foreign mine laborers; though their number has declined to 200,000, they still constitute 37 percent of the total mine force. Nevertheless, South Africa could largely dictate the terms of its outside involvement. It contributes 75 percent of the total GNP of Southern Africa, and its per capita GDP is more than seven times that of the average for the ten SADC countries; only Botswana, due to its mineral exports, has a per capita GDP that approaches South Africa's. In the four World Bank levels of development, determined mainly by per capita income, South Africa ranks among the "upper-middle-income developing countries" together with Algeria, Hungary, Argentina, and the former Yugoslavia.

The interdependence between South Africa and the Frontline States is now commonly recognized, if only in South Africa through its power to draw unwanted economic migrants from its neighbors and further afield. Economically motivated migration is no longer confined to miners or unskilled workers or refugees from Mozambique. The postapartheid state's higher wages and better working conditions already attract doctors from Ghana and teachers from Zimbabwe and Swaziland. Can a relationship that is so asymmetrical also be mutually beneficial? Or will the bigger partner insist on those measures that serve only its interests? For example, SADC proposals to create a single regional market with the "progressive removal of barriers to the free movement of people and capital in the region" would have to be implemented at the expense of South African jobseekers. For similar nationalistic versions, the region's scarce domestic investment capital will be needed in the productive sector of the South African economy. If foreign capital is interested at all, it will look to the industrial heartland rather than the periphery of the region.

The reconstruction of its own economy will undoubtedly preoccupy South Africa and overshadow development assistance to neighbors. Nonetheless, Mandela has repeatedly stated that South Africa will not forget that "these countries have paid heavily in human and material costs for their support of our struggle." Mandela's assurance that regional obligations will be taken into account when designing the development process, however, may turn out to be impossible to implement. Even if the ANC will be the dominant party in government, it cannot afford to neglect the interests of its own constituency. Illegal foreign Africans should expect to be as unwelcome in the new South Africa as illegal Mexican immigrants in the U.S. or Algerians in France. Skin color will not engender solidarity. Even the long support for the ANC by the Frontline States may not shield their governments from disillusionment about the treatment of their nationals or the evaporation of the expected South African concessions. Some Frontline States may even welcome restrictions on migration in order to prevent a massive brain drain.

F. van Zyl Slabbert (1991) has speculated that "South Africa is going to strive to be a major recipient, rather than donor, of aid" during the period of reconstruction. Thus, the poorer Southern African countries will compete for scarce assistance resources with the richer South. An argument can be made that the poorer countries are more deserving recipients and that poverty and underdevelopment within South Africa should be addressed by its privileged sector rather than by the outside world. Just as a unified Germany has assumed sole economic responsibility for the former East Germany, so the new nonracial government in South Africa, the argument runs, has both the resources and sole duty to realize its promise of a prosperous democracy. Donor agencies should invest in the struggling Polands of Africa and not in its Germany. Advocates of this approach consider their main duty completed: they have helped to defeat apartheid and lay the preconditions for autonomous development with minimal foreign assistance in the future. To prevent future South African economic domination and ensure mutually beneficial regional cooperation, they urge that foreign aid be used to boost the SADC countries.

Rather than adopt this reasoning, donor agencies should consider an alternative that could be called the common-market option. Under this scenario, the new South Africa would join SADC, whose infant industries would need protection from being swamped by the developed South. The comparatively higher labor costs in South Africa, due to strong unions, however, may well lead to an exodus of manufacturing industries, similar to the relocation of North American manufacturing to Mexico.

The common-market option views South Africa as the crucial platform for the rescue and development of the Southern African region as a whole. The engine of the industrialized South would propel the vast periphery out of poverty. But this engine will stall if South Africa becomes overwhelmed by its internal development problems. Instead of South Africa's affluent class pulling the poor up, the apartheid legacies of impoverishment and political instability could push the wealthy sector down. Unlike Germany, the ratio between the two sectors is unfavorably skewed, and therefore the new South Africa needs assistance in order to be able to play a vital development role in the region. Under this approach, South Africa holds the key to reversing the decline elsewhere.

This strategy clearly has the support of the private and public sectors in South Africa, both of which are eager to penetrate the markets to the north, to establish airline links, and to integrate power grids. Long before the impediments of apartheid and sanctions had been removed, South African capital quietly secured its footholds in "hostile territory." The Development Bank of South Africa (DBSA) has successfully financed projects in Mozambique, Lesotho, Swaziland, and Malawi. It established links with the eighteen-state Lusaka-based Preferential Trade Area (PTA), the African Development Bank, and SADC, whose own development fund never took off. Foreign donors are also likely to place their trust increasingly in the regional powerhouse rather than its dependent beggars. Douglas Anglin (1991, 20) has astutely pointed out that "in the past, much of the very substantial financial support accorded SADCC has been politically motivated conscience money intended to compensate for the reluctance of some donors to confront apartheid directly." In the absence of that motivation and given the lack of tangible progress, significant development assistance can be expected to be diverted to what Anglin calls "the latest trendy target for external aid."

Some members of the European Community argue that the policy of continued or accelerated Western involvement with South Africa could be confined to a transition period of five to ten years, until the worst economic scars of apartheid have healed. Urgent needs in the crucial areas of housing, education, and health care will require the commitment of outside resources and skills until South Africa has achieved a more equitable distribution for normal development.

Economic concessions by the international community are a vital precondition for economic growth in the new South Africa. Preferential access for South African agricultural products to European Community markets could be granted through South Africa's acceptance into the Lomé convention as an underdeveloped country. North American markets are less important for South Africa because of transport costs. However, Canada and Germany could play a crucial advocacy role within the G7 group, and with the United States in particular, by urging that some of the debts of the new South Africa be written off and others rescheduled on favorable terms. For the SADC countries, debt repayment should be strictly linked to the ability to pay. As a rule, no country can retain its economic autonomy if more than 20 percent of its export earnings are devoted to debt servicing.

Measures to address the debt crisis now feature prominently at most international meetings. But despite an abundance of suggested remedies—the Baker Plan of 1985, the Toronto Terms of 1988, and the Brady Initiative of 1989 on commercial bank debts—the African countries' obligations continue to grow. For the whole of Africa the debt burden of $228 billion in 1991 equals roughly the continent's entire gross domestic product. Many African countries spend about 30 percent of their export earnings on interest payments. Small in comparative global terms, the African debt nonetheless paralyzes development programs in most countries.

A meeting of Commonwealth Finance Ministers held in Trinidad and Tobago in September 1990 linked substantial debt relief to structural adjustment programs in twenty of the world's poorest countries, mostly in sub-Saharan Africa. The Trinidad terms, however, cover only $18 billion of the $228 billion owed by African countries. Some Western countries are committed to broadening the current eligibility criteria, which require per capita earnings of less than $600 a year and an allocation of at least 25 percent of export earnings to servicing debt. Africa's middle-income states also face serious debt problems, and declining terms of trade, little growth in export demand, and drought continue to hamper African development.

African trade liberalization programs have so far not been reciprocated with less protectionism and less trade discrimination among the industrialized countries. Abolishing trade barriers and opening access to Western markets remains the single most important measure of development assistance. Failure to gain access threatens to jeopardize the structural adjustment programs that are now carried out by more than forty African countries.

HUMAN RIGHTS

Many African states cited apartheid to divert attention from their own human rights abuses. Now the spotlight will increasingly fall on human rights abuses elsewhere on the continent. Large-scale external efforts to combat apartheid should serve as a precedent in further undermining the outdated thesis that how a state treats its citizens is solely its own affair. The once-sacred Western doctrine of nonintervention into the domestic affairs of a sovereign state has been increasingly challenged. The international community that confronted apartheid now seeks to protect the Kurds in Iraq, irrespective of the objections of the sovereign government.[1]

Once nongovernmental organizations and other foreign institutions become discreet allies of one party only, however, their cozy relationship militates against forceful human rights monitoring. Public criticism is viewed as betrayal by old friends, and the long-standing relationship is jeopardized. Thus foreign support groups have to choose their role carefully. Unconditionally supportive foreign partisans may increase their influence within the ruling elite, but this valuable influence often entails acquiescence to violations of wider moral principles.

A more universalistic, rather than a more pragmatic, approach toward democratic deficiencies could be a worthy reorientation for Western foreign policy. It would be the logical continuation of the strong moral stance adopted toward apartheid South Africa. The new approach could resemble the policy of Amnesty International in castigating violations regardless of ideological or political alliances. This universalistic focus on inviolate moral principles would also appeal to a Western public whose sense of justice has been sharpened by the debate on South Africa. It could draw on support from a wide political spectrum, including traditional conservatives and left-liberals alike. "No business with dictators" and "No aid to oppressive governments" would obviously be opposed by those who stood to benefit from the relations, but the overwhelming majority of citizens would applaud a universalistic civil rights policy that allowed only for the necessary pragmatic contact with dictators.

With the exception of Malawi, where a senile maverick dictator and his clique hold the country in thrall, all SADC countries have made some progress toward democratization. Zambia's one-party rule, which began at independence in 1972, was overthrown by Frederick Chiluba in free multiparty elections in November 1991. In Zimbabwe, Robert Mugabe's African National Union–Patriotic Front is wavering in its stated preference for one-party rule. Zimbabwe's problems do not lie in race relations, since the government has always courted the four thousand white commercial farmers who own almost half of the country's fertile land, although new legislation to confiscate land without proper compensation has jeopardized the harmony. Mugabe's response to his critics, however, is often characterized by heavy-handed measures. Dissident students and union leaders have suffered, and journalists of the few private weeklies and monthly magazines are accused of disloyalty and sabotage when they refuse to toe the line of the mainstream papers, controlled by the parastatal Mass Media Trust.

In Tanzania, President Ali Hassan Mwrinyi set up a presidential commission with a yearlong mandate to study the feasibility of a multiparty system, and the ruling party has opened itself to new organizations and participants from an emerging civil society. In Angola the democratization process was interrupted when renewed fighting broke out after national elections in October 1992, which the losing Unita considered fraudulent. In contrast, Namibia, always the political laboratory for Pretoria, seems committed to moderation and reconciliation. Successive military regimes in Lesotho exist at the mercy of South Africa but will have to liberalize as soon as a new South African government takes office. Botswana has always been a comparative democratic model and continues to prosper. Even Swaziland's young King Mswati III, after returning at the end of 1991 from an annual two-month seclusion demanded by custom, has declared that he is determined to forge ahead with a process that may strip him and his courtiers of absolute power. In addition to Angola, the exception to the emerging peace and political conflict resolution is Mozambique, where peace talks sponsored by Italian bishops and other interested parties have made only slow progress since 1990.

MOZAMBIQUE

Mozambique deserves closer attention because it was here that Pretoria's counterrevolutionary strategy and the commitment to alternative development clashed most decisively. Because of geographical proximity, Frelimo, more so than the Angolan MPLA ideologically challenged the apartheid state through its commitment to nonracial socialism as well as by providing transit facilities for ANC guerrillas. The destabilization provoked by South African–sponsored Renamo also forced other Frontline States to use South African harbors as outlets and tightened Pretoria's stranglehold on Zimbabwe through "transport diplomacy." The strategy proved a success: in the late 1980s South Africa captured 70 percent of inland traffic, compared with 20 percent in the 1960s (Anglin 1991, 9). By forcing Mozambique into the Nkomati accord in March 1984, Pretoria had hoped that its diplomatic acceptance by a self-declared Marxist-Leninist state would lead to South Africa's wider legitimacy across the rest of the continent, which in turn would enhance access elsewhere in the world.

Renamo, a movement without an ideology, has yet to be the subject of systematic analysis. It distinguishes itself from other peasant rebellions in that it was conceived and sustained from outside, initially by Rhodesia. In this respect Renamo differs from Unita. However, Renamo has now acquired a life of its own. Despite continued outside assistance from elements in South African military intelligence, Kenya, Malawi, and private Brazilian, Portuguese, and U.S. backers, Renamo would not have acquired a foothold in the countryside had Frelimo not engaged in forced resettlement and tried to abolish the system of traditional chiefs and "nonprogressive" rural traditions,

including religion. The errors of a socialist regime that builds its
vision on the subjugation of its subjects have been aptly described by
French ethnographer Christian Geffray.[2] In several areas, particularly
in Nampula, Renamo forces were invited by local chiefs as protection
against Frelimo's schemes.

Frelimo alienated large segments of its constituency by its attempts
to suppress religious instruction, which the state considered divisive.
Although many Muslims among the Ajawa people in Niassa had
initially joined the nationalists and most Protestants (Wesleyan Meth-
odists, Scandinavian Independent Baptists, the Swiss Mission, and the
Church of the Nazarene) were always opposed to the colonial regime,
since the early 1970s the Marxist-Leninist–inspired drive to create an
atheist "new man" deprived the regime of major segments of its rural
constituency. The Catholic bishops' opposition to reeducation camps,
corporal punishment, and public floggings and the Muslims' resentment of the prohibition of *azan* (the call to prayer from the mosques)
paved the way for domestic and foreign support of Renamo. During
his presidency Samora Machel had identified "Catholic ex-seminari-
ans" as the most influential elements in the Renamo leadership.

Under President Joaquim Chissano, Frelimo has tolerated religion.
In 1987 Chissano even visited the Vatican, and the next year he
welcomed Pope John Paul II to Mozambique. Frelimo returned confiscated church properties and asked the pope for assistance in ending
the civil war. But Chissano has also called the bishops traitors when
their pastorals urged a dialogue between Frelimo and Renamo.

At its Sixth Congress in August 1991, Frelimo corrected the underrepresentation of the central provinces of Manica and Sofala and of
the most populous provinces of Zambezia and Nampula, where 50
percent of the national population resides. Frelimo's current 160-
member central committee has 57 women, probably the highest proportion anywhere in Africa. It remains to be seen whether the increasingly dominant technocrats whom Chissano brought into government
can give concrete meaning to the new "social-democratic" policies of
the party in the face of continued opposition by old-line ideologues.
The arrests of prominent politicians for a planned coup d'état in June
1991 indicate resistance to the capitalist policies of Chissano, despite
his overwhelming reformist mandate.

Though the government labels all Renamo forces "bandits," evidence indicates significant measures of hierarchical control and disciplinary order among Renamo. A strata of *mujeebas* (policemen) man-

age the civilian population in the vicinity of a camp. In a Renamo zone, civilians and combatants alike are severely penalized if they disobey orders or attempt to escape the control area. In so-called tax areas, civilians are exploited through forced labor, while in control zones "civilians are used for farming, sexual favours and for meal cooking" (*SouthScan,* October 18, 1991). While most published reports highlight how thoroughly the movement terrorizes the population, there is also evidence of severe disciplinary action against combatants who commit unauthorized brutalities. Another sign of order is that Renamo has honored signed agreements, for example, the 1989 deal with Malawi not to attack the Nacala corridor. The large-scale atrocities carried out by Renamo therefore seem to have been planned—not the results of anarchic banditry. Observers point to banditry as a separate problem resulting from the general breakdown of law and order, very much as in South Africa. "Government soldiers, Renamo combatants and freelance looters have all been witnessed to participate in actions of banditry in recent years" (*South-Scan,* October 18, 1991).

More U.N. intervention is urgently needed to end a war that has killed nearly 900,000 people and created millions of refugees as well as causing unmeasurable material damage. Renamo's backers must pressure the organization to aim for a power-sharing deal and participate in U.N.-supervised elections. If the international community were to signal a tradeoff for South Africa's collaboration, Pretoria's interest in gaining international legitimacy would motivate it to urge Renamo to accept a lasting cease-fire and negotiations for a political settlement. Mandela's suggestion to enact legislation that makes support for Renamo a punishable offense could be adopted in South Africa but would have to be supplemented by intervention with Renamo's other supporters.

The removal of external sponsorship for Renamo's violence obviously remains a priority. However, if Mozambique has become a "desocialized society," one in which robbery and begging have become a way of life, then the resolution of the conflict may well be out of reach of any government or any conference of diplomats. In this respect Mozambique, like Somalia, Liberia, Peru, or Lebanon, may represent a model of extreme social disintegration that traditional mechanisms of conflict resolution cannot remedy.

The unresolved Mozambiquan war and the looming right-wing threat in South Africa would seem the only justifications left for military expenditures among the Frontline States. Thus once the South African threat of destabilization has been removed and internal strife resolved, the democratic Frontline States could enact major cuts in defense spending. For example, Botswana, whose tiny air force comprises fewer than two dozen old planes, would have no reason to spend nearly 20 percent of its GNP on a massive $350 million air base near Molepolole, 130 kilometers northwest of Gaborone—unless to serve as a U.S.-sponsored listening base. Similarly, the call by the first Swapo Congress in Namibia to increase the size of the defense force and to consider the establishment of an air force and navy for the country of 1.3 million makes little sense except for control of the rich fishing grounds off the Namibian coast. If countries insisted on keeping large armies, substantial defense cuts could be made a precondition for access to loans from the International Monetary Fund or the World Bank.

THE CAUSES OF FAILURE

Many of the international nongovernmental organizations and other Southern African support groups find themselves in the difficult process of redefining their role from an anti-apartheid stance to a constructive pro-development position. Particularly among the more socialist-inclined activists, the capitalist economic policies of erstwhile socialist comrades have strained solidarity. "This is not the future we aligned ourselves to ten or twenty years ago," bemoans Toronto academic John Saul in exasperation over the embrace of a "new entrepreneurial bourgeoisie," by Frelimo and MPLA officials (*Southern Africa Report* [Toronto], July 1991). Soon, an ANC-led government will be denounced by former supporters in similar terms as having abandoned a noble dream in favor of becoming a new parasitic ruling class.

The lament by international supporters who don't have to live the dream in the midst of poverty and social chaos smacks of condescending Eurocentrism. It implicitly denies the black leaders the wisdom to devise their own policies and to learn from the mistakes of others. Instead they are presented anew as victims, defeated by the International Monetary Fund and by World Bank structural adjustment programs against their will. The corruption, waste, and inefficiency of command economies in an underdeveloped environment is seldom blamed for their collapse. On the contrary, one reads in a Canadian

anti-apartheid journal (*Southern Africa Report,* July 1991), a conspiracy theory according to which the very success of the socialist model
made it a threat to the larger powers, which therefore destroyed it.
"We were never going to be allowed to succeed" is the new rationalization for dismal failures that cannot be attributed only to outside
destabilization.

Although no one can forget that the South African–inspired assault
on the infrastructure in the Frontline States caused an estimated $60
billion in damage, the unacknowledged point remains that the indigenous armies of destabilization would not have found such fertile
ground had the Frelimo and MPLA governments not alienated the
peasant population. A democratic order in Angola and Mozambique,
instead of the one-party Marxist-Leninist regimes, would have allowed the opposition space and influence and thus prevented the
accumulation of exploitable frustration. Thus the destabilization ef-
fected by South Africa through Renamo and Unita cannot solely be
blamed for all the failures in Mozambique and Angola. Tanzania,
which was not devastated by a counterrevolution, nevertheless ruined
its own anticolonial revolution, albeit with little direct loss of life,
despite massive outside assistance and worldwide goodwill towards
Nyerere's austere leadership.

Nor can unfavorable terms of trade and dependencies from a colonial economy explain the failures exclusively. For example, although
Zambia's dependency on copper played havoc with national economic planning when copper prices fell rapidly, Zambia's corrupt
one-party regime, with a well-intended but weak president, also attributed its own planning failures to the colonial legacy. But if South-
east Asian states were able to shake off their colonial yoke through
export-led growth in basic consumer goods, why did African states
outside apartheid's orbit fall so far behind? The cultural cohesion of
the Asian models does not explain the gap; nor can a differential
resource base be cited, since many Asian success stories took place in
resource-deprived countries. Rather, the explanation lies in the postindependence policies toward development that the Asian countries
adopted.

The daily misery and dire poverty that beset the masses of African
people in several bankrupt Frontline States have led some observers to
condemn the structural adjustment programs of the IMF and World
Bank as tools of recolonization. Among them, Canadian economist
John Loxley (1991) argues that "structural adjustment is a new form

of imperialism in Third World countries." Undoubtedly, stringent demands by the banks undermine the economic sovereignty of the borrowers. But real sovereignty for most of the African artificial entities called states—created around the export of a commodity within a colonial economy—was never more than symbolic. Nominally, they are sovereign states, but they have never been truly independent. The freedom to choose among themselves who would govern their affairs or the installations of indigenous elites were much celebrated. But the constraints on the freedom of the new leaders were enormous. Hoping to escape these constraints, several made the mistake of aligning themselves with the wrong side in the cold war. Their role as proxies in a larger conflict exacerbated their dependency on foreign sponsors and seriously fragmented their countries. The first fatal weakening occurred when the new Mozambiquan and Angolan ruling groups encouraged the departure of their 400,000 colonial residents, who took their skills with them. This self-destructive expulsion only compounded the Portuguese colonial crime of not allowing an educated indigenous professional class to emerge.

There now exists ample evidence, beginning with Zimbabwean independence in 1980 to the Namibian decolonization ten years later, that the anticolonial victors have learned the value of co-existence. Tragically, however, at the very time when African leaders attempt to democratize, the new order becomes discredited by the unpopular economic measures associated with the correction of past mistakes. Nonetheless, South Africa promises to be the crowning success of a remarkable turnaround toward a historic accommodation. The future of the sub-Saharan region as well as the prospects of racial conciliation worldwide depend on the opening of the apartheid mind and on its black and white beneficiaries making a success of the historic compromise.

CHAPTER TEN

The Future of South Africa

Scenario-planning exercises enjoy great popularity in a society beset by anxiety and ideological confusion. The Anglo-American exhortation for a Japanese high road (Sunter 1987) as well as the Nedcor–Old Mutual plea for an economic kickstart have impressed receptive audiences across the troubled land. Subsequently, left-of-center academics joined with the "Mont Fleur Scenarios," in which they used the images of the ostrich, lame duck, Icarus, and flamingo to stimulate debate about the future of South Africa.[1] All these were useful exercises in opening the apartheid mind among whites and blacks alike. Political scenarios can challenge frozen mental maps and stimulate alternative, innovative thoughts and policies for coping with apartheid's fallout. The informed speculations are based on the assumption that history is open-ended and not predetermined, at least to a certain extent; that key actors and collectivities are subject to self-fulfilling and self-negating prophecies. In the apt phrase of Pieter le Roux, "At crucial stages, ideas, which do not determine outcomes often, are of crucial importance in determining the collective future of a nation."[2]

Rather than reviewing the varied scenarios sketched by others, our assessment adopts a somewhat different and more analytical approach. We have selected three courses of development as played out in other countries and want to compare South Africa to these models. By exploring the similarities and differences between South Africa and Zimbabwe, Yugoslavia, and Germany, and by examining the reasons for these countries' successes or failures, we can draw lessons about desirable policies in the postapartheid era.

ANOTHER ZIMBABWE?

Under this scenario, South Africa descends into a pseudodemocratic patronage system, with changing state clients favoring shifting alliances of expediency. This clientelism is characterized by high levels of corruption and little democratic accountability. South Africa would resemble the "authoritarian populism" of many African states, particularly Zimbabwe, where the white minority remains economically privileged and oils a kleptocracy in which an indigenous black bourgeoisie dominates the political scene exclusively in the name of a victorious liberation struggle. Zimbabwe's burgeoning civil service increased from 60,000 at the time of independence to 180,000 twelve years later, despite a declining economy and an increasing national debt. Unions are severely restricted, and protest by students and other elements in a weak civil society is periodically clamped down. A strong central state retains the monopoly of coercion; violence has not been privatized, as in Somalia, Chad, or Liberia. An incipient ethnically based rebellion has been partly defeated and partly co-opted rather than accommodated after a cease-fire, as attempted in Mozambique, Angola, Sudan, and Ethiopia.

Of all the African states, South Africa most resembles Zimbabwe in the degree of economic development, ethnic ratios, and cultural outlook. Indeed, Zimbabwe almost became part of South Africa; the referendum favoring inclusion was only narrowly defeated. Nonetheless, the obvious differences are equally striking: Zimbabwe remained basically an agricultural society in which peasants fought a bitter war of liberation against an illegitimate and internationally unrecognized settler regime. At the time of the unilateral declaration of independence from Britain in 1965, the majority of adult whites had not been born in the country, and they were only 4 percent of the total population—too few to resist an inevitable process of political decolonization.

At least three major structural differences make a Zimbabwean course unlikely in South Africa. First, the failure of the new Zimbabwean civil service resulted largely from the departure of half of the country's white population (which was about 250,000) after independence. Relatively skilled incumbents had to be replaced by poorly

prepared African bureaucrats, whose lack of expertise was often cam-
ouflaged by claims of entitlement. Even with a similar pressure of
Africanization in postapartheid South Africa, a large-scale exodus of
skilled administrators to a receptive neighboring country is ruled out.
Any new government will have to rely on the existing civil service, and
Africanization is likely to take place more through attrition than
through replacement or expansion.

Second, the expansion of the Zimbabwean civil service resulted
from the absence of a strong private sector to absorb newly graduated
students. The graduates, with high expectations in the euphoria of
decolonization, could find employment only in the public sector. In
South Africa, however, a much stronger private sector is keen to
recruit qualified blacks and give itself an African image. In short, the
employment capacity and opportunities in private business for skilled
blacks will relieve the civil service from a wasteful expansion.

Third, even if the lobby for a quick Africanization for the sake of
political, rather than occupational, reasons were to build up in South
Africa, the strong role of the private sector in the governance of the
country would counteract the kind of corruption that befell Zimbabwe. Until outside pressure, in the form of the IMF, constrained the
bankrupt administration in Harare, the government was unhampered
by internal checks and balances; indeed, cynics now dub the IMF in
Zimbabwe the second chamber, which effectively approves or vetoes
all legislation. Because of the much greater dependence of the South
African state on its economy and its tax-conscious managers in Johannesburg, the postapartheid government will not be allowed to sabotage the prospects of economic growth through poor governance. The
realistic hope remains that mutual incentives remain strong enough to
prevent profligate overspending by the new government in South
Africa.

Peter Moll (1991, 134) makes the optimistic point that "it is of
major concern to every liberation movement that the economic policies it introduces in its first year of power do not undermine its
chances of succeeding at the polls at the next election." However, the
very opposite could be assumed with equal persuasiveness: the need
to win the next election in a climate of high expectations may well
tempt a liberation government to pursue reckless economic policies
for short-term gains, as politicians the world over have done, unless
constrained by independent central banks. Cynics even maintain that
in the absence of an entrenched democratic tradition, an unsuccessful

government may well cancel a second election, or rule as a one-party state. If such a course of unilateral partisanship in economic policies were attempted, however, it would be heavily penalized by strong countervailing forces in South African society and abroad. Inasmuch as neither side can achieve political stability without the cooperation of the other, so too economic success depends on compromise. To be sure, such rational calculations do not preclude ideologues or power-hungry individuals from trying to achieve their partisan goals at the expense of the common good—but they are unlikely to succeed in South Africa.

ANOTHER YUGOSLAVIA?

If black youths turn away from the liberal, compromising ANC, or if white right-wingers declare an independent Boerestaat that cannot be militarily defeated, or if Natal secedes under the banner of Zulu nationalism, then South Africa could disintegrate along racial and communal lines. The escalating violence and economic collapse could lead to the unraveling of the state, as in Yugoslavia, which has stunned the world by its regression into ferocious nationalism and chauvinism, long thought to have been laid to rest by the defeat of fascism and the rise of civilized modernity. South African state and business interests, together with international forces, want to prevent virulent civil strife at all costs. A right-wing breakaway or military coup, however, could be conceivable under extreme conditions of disorder, even if not successful in the long run.

Thus far, however, most of the massacres in South Africa are not linked to an ongoing ethnic, secessionist conflict, but amount to political killings during a transitional power struggle about the postapartheid order. Artificial ethnic client states, like Ciskei, lack the mass support for genuine ethnonationalism. Yugoslavia has fallen apart because separate nationalities had been forced together. In South Africa, synthetic ethnicities were coerced to be apart and now strive to rejoin in one nonracial state.

Nonetheless, the absence of heavy weapons and outside sponsors for ANC and Inkatha forces offers scant reassurance in a climate of extreme hostility, skillfully stimulated and manipulated by incorrigible right-wing advocates of a master race. After all, the old Group Areas Act amounted to an "ethnic cleansing" of formerly integrated city centers. Much of the violence in Natal and the Vaal townships results in "political cleansing," with opponents being driven from hostels and squatter camps.

Any analogies between aggressive Serbs and violence-instigating Zulu nationalists are clearly ahistorical and misleading, although there are some superficial similarities. Like the Serbs, Zulu speakers constitute the largest ethnic group in their nation's cultural mosaic, although both groups are politically divided; like the Serbs behind Milosevic, Zulu nationalists behind Buthelezi cultivate a warrior tra-dition of heroic resistance against alien conquerors; at the same time, Serbs and Zulus are economically and educationally disadvantaged, compared with more affluent and "westernized" competitors like the Slovenians and Croats or more urbanized Indians, Coloureds, and whites in South Africa. The historical mythologies and contemporary disadvantages make the quest for recognition and entitlement a vola-tile endeavor for Serbs and Zulus alike.

A closer historical parallel, however, can be drawn between the Serbs and Afrikaner nationalists. Both dominate a divided state and, above all, monopolize its army. In both countries there were pro-Allied and pro-Axis factions in World War II. Only in Yugoslavia, however, did this alignment lead to mutual pogroms, which further stimulated semi-independent republics in the old Yugoslav federation. And in South Africa, unlike Yugoslavia, none of the factions, with the exception of a small Afrikaner minority, strives for an expanded homeland—even the Boerestaat advocates do not envisage an area cleansed of outsiders. In short, in Yugoslavia artificial units of people were forced together and now aim at being apart. Under apartheid, people were coerced to live apart and now strive to unite in one state.

Moreover, there are no internal boundaries in South Africa that are considered as legitimate as those in the artificial Balkan federation. None of the South African provinces and Bantustans possesses an independent viable economy, as is the case in the Balkans. In fact, Bantustan independence was never recognized internationally, and most "homelands" are expected to be fully reintegrated into the new South Africa. The former apartheid state thus represents a much more politically, economically, and culturally integrated society. Unlike Yugoslavia, where the people are divided by shrines of historical battles dating back to 1389 in Kosovo, and where different religions, languages, and alphabets separate the territories, South Africa never belonged to rival empires with expansionist and irredentist designs on their neighbors.

The role of a sizable Muslim community in both settings further illustrates the differences. In 1971 Tito designated Muslims in Yugoslavia to be a separate people, a nationality. Both Croats and Serbs consider Muslims as having been forcibly converted by the Ottoman Turks and, therefore, really Croats and Serbs in an unfortunate disguise. In contrast, the half a million South African Muslims merely perceive of themselves as a religious community.

Despite the horrible massacres and several thousand deaths in political infighting during apartheid's dying years, the conflicts between the main contenders for political power are still conducted with some restraint, especially when compared to the brutality that is devastating Yugoslavia. In particular, the black-white conflict has remained relatively disciplined, though the struggle between the ANC and Inkatha is becoming more violent. Is it the lack of hostility on the part of the leadership that has prevented racial war? Is it the propagated nonracialism of the ANC that restrains the pent-up anger? Is it that the government has learned more sophisticated methods of control, as evidenced by the assignment of 75 percent of the old riot police to desk jobs after psychological testing? A foretaste of alternative developments was provided by the racist terror campaign carried out by units of the PAC's military wing Apla (Azanian People's Liberation Army) with bombings of restaurants in King Williams Town and Queenstown at the end of 1992. Countermeasures were difficult to enact, not only because of the vulnerability of civilian targets but also because the PAC's political leadership has no operational control over its military wing. For the first time, white South Africans began to grasp how much they owed to the nonracial disciplined opposition of the ANC.

The comparatively disciplined ways of conducting street politics in Cape Town or Pretoria, however, remain fragile and utterly dependent on a moderate political leadership retaining control over its militant following. That is the main purpose of mass action. Yet a few shots by a deranged activist on either side, or more assassinations of political figures, could easily ignite a bubbling volcano. So far, thousands of unemployed youngsters in tattered shoes toyi-toyi together with black students in fashionable clothing behind respectable leaders under the SACP and ANC flags. The unity of "mass action," however, remains fragile. Ideologically, the frustrated youth are much closer to the PAC, which boycotted the protests because they were aimed at restarting negotiations rather than replacing the regime. The most enthusiastically chanted refrain was "Tambo, give us guns!" Yet Tambo has finally suspended the armed struggle, and few see any prospects of resuming the romanticized guerrilla war, even if negotiations fail.

South Africa also differs from the Balkans in the paternalistic nature of its intergroup relations. In Bosnia and Herzegovina, as in Nazi Germany, the minority is considered the embodiment of evil, the source of a grand conspiracy, the historical enemy that has prevented others from realizing their rightful destiny. Parochial nationalism precludes co-existence with outsiders, who are defined as not belonging to the community of citizens. In South Africa, on the other hand, the ruling minority has treated blacks not as cunning enemies but as inferior children. The "white man's burden" imposed the task of educating and administering "uncivilized natives," not the elimination of irredeemable foes. Later, rational labor exploitation precluded the irrational hostility that characterized European conflicts between competing nationalisms. The colonial paternalism of the semifeudal setting in South Africa has allowed flexible adjustments according to shifting economic needs and changing power relations. An excluded majority strives for its rightful share of the state and economy, which the powerholders try to manipulate but cannot extinguish. Reform from above aims at preventing a class revolution from below. South Africa resembles the French Revolution except that the have-nots want to join the bourgeoisie rather than kill them off; they do not want to seize their assets, but share in them.

Ethnic and racial "cleansing" of a territory in which different groups are interspersed cannot be excluded as impossible for all times. However, the ethnic reorganization of an interspersed settlement would signal the failure of a common economy and thereby the source of minority profit and security. Unlike in Yugoslavia, or the former Soviet Union, where different people with separate histories and memories each see great economic advantages in secession, in South Africa separate economies would harm blacks and whites alike. Understanding of this interdependence remains widespread. Some consider it the result of colonial indoctrination, while others attribute it to a long learning process of mutual contact. However, as illustrated by events in Sarajevo, which was even more ethnically integrated, interdependence does not preclude extreme brutality.

Yet in South Africa no political movement deliberately aims at destroying the source of wealth and development in order to triumph over its adversaries. Quarreling elites may achieve economic decline by default but not as a matter of policy. To be sure, each side aspires to reorganize and restructure existing institutions in its own mold, but all have to take their opponents' strength into account. No party can impose its will by force alone; if any actor resorts to massive violence, it is clearly violence without victory. This consideration may not prevent escalating turmoil, but it motivates those strong counterforces that would lose from a descent into chaos. Thus international capital and local business are in the forefront of engineering stability. Such forces for negotiation and peace, in contrast, have little stake in Bosnia. Accommodation is also muted in the European interethnic conflicts because each side's wounded identity is bound up with victory. The South African conflict over power and privilege, on the other hand, allows a mutually satisfactory identity on the basis of sharing. Intergroup conflicts are confined to rugby games and soccer stadiums, where competing national anthems are roared and partisan flags are waved.

In Yugoslavia all sides resorted to the battlefield because a victory seemed possible and advantageous after the discredited political rules had broken down. In South Africa, mutually credible political rules are in the process of being established for the first time, because the beneficiaries of past illegitimate power realize the advantage of being legitimate political stakeholders. Even dissident members of the Conservative Party are talking about a nonracial right wing. The Boerestaat dreamers neither envision expelling outsiders nor establishing an irredentist home for all Afrikaners; they only hope to secure a safe fallback position should nonracialism turn sour.

Future conflict will arise if a dogmatic nonracialism denies or represses sizable groups who feel strongly about their ethnic or racial identity. In response, ethnicity or tribalism would reassert itself, claiming suppression of legitimate aspirations. Marginal groups, aware of minority persecution elsewhere, are already invoking the language of self-determination and minority protection in order to gain legitimacy. The irony lies in all sides viewing themselves as victims of the others: Inkatha as the target of MK; the ANC as the victim of Inkatha and colluding government forces alike; the National Party as the potential sufferer of majority tyranny. The ANC/Inkatha conflict over power and turf clearly contains the most explosive potential for a Yugoslavian-type civil war.

The possibility of secessionism makes the constitutional debate about federalism versus centralism particularly significant. Were South Africa to adopt a centralist constitution against the will of regional actors, even if they are a numerical minority, it would risk secessionist movements leading either to civil war or the eventual breakup of the country. If, on the other hand, a federal constitution guarantees meaningful regional autonomy to parties opposed to the national majority, civil war may be avoided. In this respect, Inkatha's power may lie not in numbers but in its ability to disrupt an imposed settlement.

So far, the bargaining has been bedeviled by simultaneous election-eering. For all parties to reach historic compromises is incompatible with each enhancing its election chances. At the same time, nothing demonstrates more clearly how the South African situation differs from communal conflicts elsewhere than the realistic conviction by all South African parties that they can deeply cut into their opponents' vote with the right strategies. Few Protestants or Catholics in North-ern Ireland are swayed by changing party politics; few Serbs would vote for Croats, and vice versa. In South Africa, however, persons of all racial groups have aligned themselves with the ANC and Inkatha, and more blacks can be expected to support formerly exclusive white parties. In this difference lies the realistic hope that South Africa can avoid becoming another Yugoslavia.

ANOTHER GERMANY?

The most rational and also the most likely scenario for South Africa is a social-democratic pact between business, labor, and key state bureaucracies, as practiced in postwar Germany. This pact would involve genuine co-determination in the private sector and negotiated wage constraints and limited price increases in order to make South Africa competitive in the world market and raise productivity. In return for the state's extended social investments in education, health, and housing, unions would abandon adversarial labor relations and class warfare. Labor and business would see themselves more as partners in rebuilding a new nation, not as adversaries engaging in regular trials of strength through strikes and mass action.

This third scenario does not presuppose high employment and high levels of welfare in order to work. An affluent economy with high social wages and stable industrial relations is the goal, not the precon-dition, of the social-democratic vision. Indeed, the much romanticized

Swedish model was introduced in the 1920s, when Swedish economic development was approximately at the level of current South African development.[3] Co-determination and industrial partnership in Germany came about after the complete destruction of the economic base. Nor does social democracy occur without intense political struggles. Social democracy does not promise industrial harmony, merely the minimization of conflict through sensible labor relations and rules of bargaining from which all sides benefit. Since the legalization of trade unions in the 1970s and mutually acceptable rules for settling labor disputes in the 1980s, South Africa has made considerable progress toward industrial democracy, an arbitration system, a labor court, and workplace jurisprudence, long before political democracy appeared on the horizon.[4] Yet the concept of a social pact is still interpreted quite differently by capital and labor. Business attempts to buy labor peace and productivity through some paternalistic largesse on the shopfloor, and unions view arbitration and bargaining as a prelude to higher forms of class warfare.

Unlike Europe and industrial democracies elsewhere, South Africa granted union rights before granting the political franchise. The ensuing struggle for political rights through industrial action has created one of the most militant union movements in the world. Its leaders are deeply suspicious of co-optation by capital and favor independent workers' control. A survey of Cosatu shop stewards (Pityana and Orkin, 1992) reveals a surpising profile of this key group. The typical activist is a male in his thirties who has some high school education and prefers to read in English, although he usually speaks an African language at home. Most are regular churchgoers, yet they display strong economic socialist leanings and union loyalty above a basic ANC predisposition. This profile led one reviewer to surmise that the Cosatu leadership "rests on a constituency with political positions considerably to the left of anything Cosatu has aired publicly" (*Business Day,* July 13, 1992). Compared with the more apolitical or even conservative outlook of union members in Western societies, unions in South Africa are characterized by a more moderate leadership but a militant grass-roots. The more the rank and file can make itself heard, the more uncompromising a stance is likely to emerge. During the decades when political opposition was banned, an informal culture of resentful militancy arose, untempered by the moderating influences of more farsighted leaders. The mythical stature accorded to the leaders in exile has gradually diminished after opposition was

legalized. The increasing dominance of Cosatu in the tripartite opposition alliance confirms these trends. On the other hand, a high degree
of unionization facilitates a social-democratic pact—which is impossible in the United States, where only a quarter of the work force is
unionized.

Another problem in reaching a social compact in South Africa
remains the skepticism of management toward union representatives
as full decision-makers from the shopfloor to the boardroom, lest their
participation be seen as management's abdication of responsibility on
the slippery road to socialism. Unions, in turn, "tend on the whole to
react negatively when employee participation schemes are introduced
by companies."[5] Unions dismiss the transformative capacity of industrial democracy as manipulative co-optation, and they are so steeped
in notions of class struggle that financial participation schemes are
viewed as fostering an alternative ideology. Thus they objected to the
unilateral launching of an innovative employee shareholding plan
introduced in the late 1980s by Anglo-American and its subsidiaries at
no cost to workers. But, in time, the unions are likely to see the
advantages of workers' participation, including shared responsibility
for quality and productivity in return for veto rights over managerial
decisions. Successful political negotiations may also pave the way for
alternative perceptions in industrial relations, as does the fledgling
"Economic Forum," promoted by farsighted forces in all three camps
against strong opposition from the unions, the cabinet, and employers.

No major South African company as yet stands as a successful
model of industrial democracy and economic performance. Most enterprises have not progressed beyond allowing workers to make
suggestions for improving their immediate area of responsibility; a
few have sought to create a climate of democratic paternalism in order
to make unions superfluous. The president of the South Africa Foundation, Warren Clewlow, writes that "the promotion of economic
growth requires a new relationship of partnership between business
and government" (SA Foundation Review, April 1992, p. 3)—without
ever mentioning the other vital actors for social peace.

Frank Horwitz has astutely pointed to a peculiar paradox: "South
African society has become highly politicized, yet many are politically
illiterate."[6] This politicized illiteracy is equally evident among business executives. South African capitalism, as articulated at cocktail
parties or dinner conversations, in chairman's reports or interviews in
the financial press, frequently displays liberal paternalism together

with a crude, unfettered free-market advocacy that lacks the sophisticated understanding of labor relations and international forces
found among management in Europe. It seems that the temptation to
become partisans in a divided society has blinded highly intelligent
people from recognizing their own long-term interests, let alone considering the merits of an antagonist's approach.

However, there are emerging forces that pursue a wider vision and
occasionally achieve a breakthrough. The launch of the tripartite
National Economic Forum at the end of 1992; the deal struck between
Cosatu and the government about unionization and social benefits for
farm and domestic workers, together with Cosatu's new say in controversial draft legislation for public-sector workers; and, above all,
the restructured National Manpower Commission, have been rightly
labeled "a watershed" in a dramatic new industrial relations system
(*South African Labour Bulletin*, November–December 1992, p. 1).
Duncan Innes (1992, 5) concludes his long-term observation of the
labor scene: "The era of outright conflict and open hostility between
management and organized labour, which characterized so much of
the decade of the 1980s, is now closing and in its place is emerging an
era where the old enemies must learn to deal with one another on a
new basis, building new forms of co-operation and participation in
the process." Such visions assume an essential rationality on the part
of class antagonists, but rational behavior has not always been the
hallmark of class and ethnic conflicts; ideological obsessions and
deep-seated historical hatreds have often carried the day. Nonetheless,
the end of the cold war and the experience of massive poverty in South
Africa have led even self-declared Leninists to reject Lenin's immiseri-
zation as advantageous for the revolution. Thus Joe Slovo openly
admits: "What must also feature in our calculation is the rapidly
deteriorating economic and social situation for the majority of our
people, *our ability to maintain mobilisation in this deteriorating situation* and the kind of economic base on which we hope the new
government will set about the national democratic transformation of
South Africa" (*New Nation*, November 20, 1992, p. 1). With such
remarkable pragmatic rationality on both sides of the continuing
ideological disagreement, there is no reason for South Africa to fail
in the quest for reluctant reconciliation. If a highly politicized and
better-organized labor movement can lead the way to stability and
rationality, suspicious competing political leaders will have to fall in
line.

In this process of forging cautious cooperation, many a utopian dream will be disappointed, particularly on the Left, but also among hardline advocates of an unfettered free market. Their capitalist vision nonetheless will survive in a modified form. The socialists will have to sacrifice most of their dream because they have the least real power, despite the mass sympathy for radical restructuring.

Whether social democracy and a social charter can be achieved depends ultimately on those still holding power in South Africa. The dismantling of apartheid has brought the ANC into the government, but it is unlikely that the formerly disenfranchised will hold power in the immediate postapartheid era.

Democracy or Elite Cartel?

The looming disaster in this country will result from the
distortion of a noble goal in favour of a short-cut route to
Parliament by a handful of individuals.

Winnie Mandela, January 7, 1993

Who exercises power in South Africa becomes less and less relevant
for two reasons. First, the economic decline and volatile security
situation have engendered widespread sentiment that anyone who can
ensure development and stability ought to be given an opportunity to
do so. Second, the process of negotiating the revolution has educated
and changed the leadership of both the political establishment and the
opposition. Increasingly, the negotiators have come to resemble each
other in their technocratic outlook and pragmatic cooperation, to
share a problem-solving mentality created by the accelerating crisis.

For the ANC-SACP socialism has been reduced to antitrust legislation and affirmative action. Lenin may still be quoted, but the World
Bank, it seems, exerts a stronger pull. For Afrikaner nationalists racial
obsessions have given way to co-optation at any cost. Even the Broederbond is now ready to admit black Afrikaners, though, significantly, not women, regardless of color. The more farsighted sections
of the business elite, like Lonrho's Tiny Rowland, ingratiate themselves with any political leadership, regardless of its democratic record, showering favors ranging from free trips in Lear jets to gifts of
luxurious houses, invitations to corporate retreats and conferences in
Bermuda or Davos, seats on company boards, lavish fees for speaking
engagements, and preferential admission of relatives to educational
institutions. Mandela's attendance at the wedding of a daughter or the
presence of a high-profile ANC executive at a birthday party becomes

a status symbol of the true corporate insider. Dozens of diplomats and foreign NGO representatives wait in the wings with advice and funding of projects. It is remarkable how readily many of the once-stigmatized exiles and harassed activists have been tempted by the new access to power, though few can afford an ostentatious consumerism on meager ANC salaries. In this atmosphere of consensual lifestyles and reciprocal obligations, fundamental dissent about governing the country can hardly be expected, despite the different constituencies that corporate South Africa and the ANC represent. Ideologues deplore this informal elite cooperation as "obscuring the fundamental antagonism between our liberation movement and the apartheid regime,"[1] but this criticism is more nostalgia and posturing than real opposition. The *new* South Africa is a misnomer; only more color has been added at the top of the old stratification.

Who exercises power in the "new" South Africa also becomes irrelevant in light of looming anarchy. Any power that can guarantee order and safety is better than descent into barbarism à la Yugoslavia, Angola, or Somalia. If a new suppression of white and black violent extremism were perceived as essential, a multiracial emergency coalition could crush opposition even more effectively than the old racial minority regime. After all, the ANC has tortured its dissidents and spies almost as gruesomely as the apartheid police. The reluctant partners in joint domination may both conclude that they can afford only limited democracy. Already the Nationalists and the ANC agree that their bilateral agreements cannot be undermined by third parties in multilateral negotiations—a questionable but seemingly necessary authoritarianism that lies at the root of Inkatha's ire. The bilateral understandings, ironically, are a precondition for successful multiparty negotiations.

A pessimistic outlook views a political settlement as a necessary but entirely insufficient condition for reversing the social disintegration and economic decline. While the political leadership of the two major parties is galvanized into a negotiated compromise—driven both by recurrent crises and by the violent extremes lurking as alternatives to their own entitlement—the ultimate determinants of a successful transition are economic and social. The legacy of decades-long conflict could reach a point where even the most determined government of national unity lacks the capacity to reconstruct ravaged communities. So far, all the peace accords have been associated only with further violence, and all the well-intentioned efforts at development have failed to bridge the gulf between a growing mass of outsiders and an increasingly multiracial but still comparatively small sector of middle-class insiders. It is the magnitude of reconstruction—economically, institutionally, and especially ethically—which more optimistic analysts of political transition overlook. The culture of corruption, moral bankruptcy, and ethical decay, the pessimists assert, has so undermined the social fabric that it would be naive to expect a democratic culture of accountability and integrity to replace the social degeneracy, regardless of the government in power. There is, this view holds, little difference between the looting of the public treasury by an ethnic civil service during a half-century of exclusive political power and the sharing in the spoils of a decadent lifestyle by an alternative movement that merely wants to have its people on the public payroll. In short, these skeptics argue, a mere exchange of political administrations or, worse, an enlargement of the civil service can hardly succeed in reducing a 50 percent illegitimate birth rate or a spiraling crime rate in the absence of moral renewal and the discipline of an alternative ideology.

Moreover, high expectations, together with already relatively high labor costs, make South Africa uncompetitive in the world market, especially if expectations are further raised by a populist party in power. South Africa is therefore seen as unable to afford a genuine democracy, in which the pent-up demands would destroy the delicate balance of antagonistic forces. Given the widespread malaise, a new multiracial oligarchy may even succeed in legitimating itself democratically through referenda and media manipulation.

Yet, even though a few ANC activists break up meetings of political opponents, just as the early National Party of P. W. Botha did thirty years ago, the new rulers at least hold out the promise of democratic accountability. The knowledge of atrocities in the ANC camps notwithstanding, the newcomers can be taken at their word on human rights and accountability that a strong civil society will insist on retaining. Above all, they can claim a much broader mandate; they do represent the aspirations of the deprived majority. Deviating from the promised course would jeopardize a precious legitimacy on which the ANC depends more than its discredited partner in domination.

The prospects of South African democracy will depend heavily on the economic performance of the new regime. This does not, however, imply favoring business interests over labor at all costs, as many authors now argue. In the comparative literature on transitions, democracy is principally cherished as a means to protect human rights rather than to achieve material gains for disadvantaged groups. "In the interests of democratization, the corporate demands of business and the state may have to take precedence over those of labor," writes Giuseppe Di Palma, author of *To Craft Democracies*.[2] A reviewer of this work concludes: "In the U.S. social science literature, arguments for the feasibility of combining political reform and redistributive economic policies are increasingly difficult to find."[3] It is doubtful that such narrow definitions of democracy can be applied to South Africa.

Democracy without material gain would surely delegitimate a liberation movement that not only fought for symbolic equality but also raised expectations for greater wealth and material equality. Yet the democratic dilemma lies in the fact that a "democratic oligarchy"—an authoritarian order with a semblance of popular participation—is likely to perform better economically and to attract more foreign capital at lower labor costs than a genuine institutionalization of the popular will. The accumulated demands that real "people's power" would attempt to answer would at the same time drive away manifold vested interests on whose cooperation the performance of the new order depends. That predicament does not bode well for the prospects of genuine democratizers beyond the ritual of manipulated popular endorsement.

The elites of the newly enfranchised will face their real test when they are unable to satisfy the heightened expectations. Do they cancel the accord and join the dissatisfied masses in renewed struggle? Do they join in a new multiracial clampdown in the name of restoring law and order as a precondition for economic growth? Or do they patiently explain their predicament and educate their constituency in the political art of the feasible, as the ANC attempted to do in selling power-sharing? A split in the fragile movement is most likely when some of its acclaimed leaders conclude that liberation has been won while others assert that liberation has been betrayed. South Africa promises to remain an intense political battleground well beyond the clear-cut front lines of the apartheid days.

Within the ANC-SACP-Cosatu coalition, the new faultlines divide those who, not being part of the new deal, view transitions as "mass-driven," with permanent people's mobilization, and those who practice normal elite politics with minimal dependence on grassroots support. Even within the SACP the old contradiction between a guiding vanguard and people's choices has not been resolved. While all pay lip-service to *democratic* socialism, following the disaster with the East European *bureaucratic* version *The African Communist* now also cautions against "a lazy left-wing opportunism telling the people what they want to hear."[4] Already oppositional civics, an alienated youth, frustrated union leaders, township warlords, tribal and religious authorities, oppressed women, and several other dissatisfied constituencies vie for more influence.

Similar new faultlines characterize the establishment camp. The loose alliance between white and black separatists against a centralized state runs counter to traditional lineups. With roughly 25 percent of national support for the NP, 45 percent for the ANC, and 10 percent for Inkatha in 1993,[5] the NP made the pragmatic choice to abandon a losing anti-ANC coalition with Inkatha and instead aim at establishing a strong center with the ANC, against traditional ideological leanings. Only in the Western Cape does the NP command a clear majority, while in Natal a combined Inkatha-NP coalition would hold majority support, with the ANC securing less than 25 percent of the vote in both regions. Should these regional interests not be accommodated in a federal constitution, breakaway movements could well gain ground. Natal, with its highly successful but vulnerable 20 percent Indian minority and the "European" Western Cape, with a 56 percent Coloured population, could emerge as the Croatia and Slovenia of South Africa. Rapidly increasing regional differences, however, could be accommodated in a federal system through equalization payments and revenue sharing. Otherwise, booming high-security enclaves of residual capital and tax benefits, such as Cape Town's world-class waterfront or obscene fantasies like the "Lost City," would thrive more and more uncomfortably in a sea of surrounding poverty.

Regardless of the future political faultlines, there remain some fundamentals that allow a far more optimistic outlook for South Africa than can be ventured for other divided societies. While South Africa will remain a largely multiracial rather than nonracial society, it has good prospects of relatively harmonious race relations and even some minimal nationhood. Although twice as many whites (77 percent) as black Africans (37 percent) express support for the South African flag and Springbok emblem in international sporting events, an almost equally high percentage in both groups (87 percent blacks versus 93 percent whites) feel proud of being South African.[6] It should not be too difficult to find common national symbols and to forge a common identity for South Africans when pride in the land is already shared. Large majorities of over 70 percent in all groups, including ANC and NP supporters, agree on foreign policy: that a democratic South Africa should rejoin the Commonwealth (77 percent), that the international community can play a role in the transition (74 percent), that South Africa should become a peacemaker in the region (72 percent), and that the country must cooperate with its neighbors (83 percent).[7] In 1992, South Africans of all groups even shared old myths born out of successful indoctrination: 62 percent overall and 53 percent among ANC supporters respond with "no" to the statement, "The communist threat against South Africa is over," with some of the ANC-SACP supporters probably implying that the battle for socialism has not yet been won. The political consensus extends into the common consumerism of a modern Western industrial culture, where middle-class ideals predominate as much among blacks as whites. For instance, black parents stress "good manners," "tolerance and respect," and "neatness" as the most important values to be encouraged in children.[8] Despite largely separate and unequal schooling, the identical values inculcated, the authoritarian modes of instruction, and the rote learning, as well as the use of English in black higher education, further reinforce a common outlook, at least for the educated. Amazingly, even the mode of standardized universal testing in countrywide matriculation examinations has been accepted, despite an average African pass rate of less than 50 percent, compared with over 95 percent in other ethnic groups. From all these indicators an adherence to common values can be deduced, in contrast to the cleavages in other divided societies. A shared political middle ground has emerged at the elite level, in contrast to the kind of divided society that led Judge Richard Goldstone to comment, "Take Israel, you couldn't find a single Jewish judge, or Arab lawyer, who would be acceptable to the other side."[9]

The fundamental cleavages in South African society, therefore, do not concern issues of culture or race and identity, but social equity and increasing intraclass divisions, particularly in black society. In all surveys blacks and whites differ markedly in their assessment of their economic life chances, their grievances about unfair treatment, their hopes or anxieties about their material security, and hence their satisfaction with their quality of life. Rather than ethnicity, it is "class" (jobs, income, property) that matters most to blacks and whites. In an index of twenty-four policy issues with conflict potential compiled by

Schlemmer, the greatest discrepancies between the racial groups occurred in affirmative action with regard to job replacement in the civil
service, land redistribution, and higher taxation to support the poor.[10]
Symbolic issues such as official languages, flags and anthems, change
of place names, school integration, or black retribution for mistreat-
ment (Nuremberg trials) ranked low in conflict potential. Schlemmer
diagnoses black rank-and-file attitudes as inclined toward compromise on symbolic issues about which whites feel strongly, particularly
Afrikaans as an official language. However, there is greater adamancy
for demands on economic equality. Schlemmer concludes that the
"results suggest that culture and identity may not be as divisive in
South Africa as the current experience in Eastern Europe would lead
one to expect."[11] Our analysis confirms this finding and suggests that,
paradoxically, in a society with the most open racial oppression, race
relations may be far more harmonious under certain conditions than
in the United States, Israel, or other divided societies. The reasons for
this optimistic assessment of the promise of relative nonracialism lie
mainly in a different psychological predisposition of the colonized in
an industrial settler society.

American and European socio-psychological research findings
about the psychic scars of oppression have often been uncritically
applied to South Africa. It has been assumed that the victims of a legal
system of racial domination would show its marks, such as self-hatred
and low self-esteem, and that the "identification with the aggressor"
Bettelheim diagnosed among some inmates of Nazi concentration
camps would characterize the marginalized objects of decades-long
apartheid domination. Yet in many ways apartheid has had the opposite effect, serving as a protective buffer against the psychological
damage in discriminated minorities observed elsewhere. In legally
equal societies the victims easily blame themselves as individuals for
failure; in an institutionalized apartheid order of collective discrimination, the "system" was clearly at fault. Because the apartheid state
lacked worldwide legitimacy, its victims responded with resistance
rather than identification. Where "passing" was legally excluded, it
made no sense to strive for assimilation and to choose the oppressor
as the reference group.

The dominant mindset of active, resilient protest rather than passive acceptance of subordinate conditions was further reinforced by
numerical majority status. It makes a crucial difference for self-per-
ception whether the discriminated constitute an indigenous majority

or an imported minority. Moreover, numbers and self-reliant institutions enforce relationships of objective interdependence, which minorities dependent on goodwill or their special skills lack. A sense of confident self-legitimacy is enhanced by the retention of pre-colonial language in South Africa. Unlike African-Americans, all South African blacks speak an indigenous mother tongue through which they retain a vital link with the land of conquest, which New World slavery destroyed. South African subordinates therefore show little of the ambivalent identity that characterizes minorities elsewhere, who are made to feel that they do not belong. South Africans of all races lack such self-doubts and confront one another as equals. This perception of equality remains an important precondition of successful negotiations and pacting, and perhaps even a minimal sense of common nationhood. The chances of a future South African democracy and stability do not falter on incompatible identities but depend mainly on the promise of greater material equality in a common economy.

Notes

INTRODUCTION

1. Paul M. Sweezy and Harry Magdoff, "The Stakes in South Africa," *Monthly Review*, April 1986.

CHAPTER ONE

1. Quoted in Samuel Decalo, "The Process, Prospects and Constraints of Democratization in Africa," *African Affairs* 91 (1992): 7–35.
2. See Ulrich Menzel, *Das Ende der Dritten Welt und das Scheitern der Grossen Theorie* (Frankfurt: Edition Suhrkamp, 1992).
3. Hermann Giliomee, "Broedertwis: Intra-Afrikaner Conflicts in the Transition from Apartheid," *African Affairs* 91 (1992): 339–64.
4. Albie Sachs, "Perfectability and Corruptability—Preparing Ourselves for Power," University of Cape Town Inaugural Lecture no. 172, May 20, 1992, p. 8.
5. Leo Kuper, "Political Change in White Settler Societies: The Possibility of Peaceful Democratisation," in Leo Kuper and M. G. Smith, eds., *Pluralism in Africa* (Berkeley: University of California Press, 1969) pp. 169–209. Kuper's seminal piece remains one of the most insightful contributions on the topic.
6. For an elaboration of this point regarding Israel-U.S. relations, see Heribert Adam, "Ethnic Politics and Crisis Management," in Heribert Adam, ed., *South Africa: The Limits of Reform Politics* (Leiden: E. J. Brill, 1983) and also Heribert Adam, "Comparing Israel and South Africa: Prospects for Conflict Resolution in Ethnic States," in Pierre L. van den Berghe, *State Violence and Ethnicity* (Boulder: University Press of Colorado, 1990), pp. 113–42.
7. See the formulation of the 1955 Freedom Charter to this effect.
8. See Hermann Giliomee, ed., *The Elusive Search for Peace* (Cape Town: Oxford University Press, 1991) for an insightful comparative overview of the

three settler states—South Africa, Israel, and Northern Ireland—by a variety of area specialists.

9. Julie Frederikse, *The Unbreakable Thread: Non-Racialism in South Africa* (Bloomington: Indiana University Press, 1990).

10. On the various techniques used for state-reinforced ethnicity, see Leroy Vail, ed., *The Creation of Tribalism in Southern Africa* (Berkeley: University of California Press, 1989).

11. Rose (1971, 248) and other pollsters report that virtually all respondents accepted the label of either Catholic or Protestant.

12. Gerry Adams, *The Politics of Irish Freedom* (Dingle: Brandon, 1986), p. 64. For a more philosophical and comparative treatment of political violence, see the excellent collection edited by N. Chabani Manganyi and André du Toit, *Political Violence and the Struggle in South Africa* (Johannesburg: Southern Books, 1990).

13. The principal of individual and collective compensation has been practiced in the United States and Canada, where the governments have officially and belatedly recognized the injustices they committed against their citizens of Japanese origin during World War II, as well as in Europe. The South African government's expropriations are documented in land registries and alive in the memories of the victims.

14. The discussion of the fundamental contents and purposes of democracy in terms of regulating conflicting class interests remains underdeveloped in the vast literature on democratizing. Brief references to "economic democracy" and a potential process of "socialization" following phases of "liberalization" and "democratization" in O'Donnell and Schmitter's (1986, pt. 4, 11) analysis of transition are overshadowed by formalistic and constitutional considerations. Nor does their ambiguous term *socialization* capture the quest for economic equalization that necessarily follows political enfranchisement, particularly in a country with a legacy of apartheid inequality.

15. For a good introduction to the South African debate by pragmatic economists writing in nonspecialist language, see Peter Moll, ed., *Redistribution: How Can It Work in South Africa?* (Cape Town: David Philip, 1991). For a conclusion that nationalization can work if carried out correctly, see Keith Coleman, *Nationalisation: Beyond the Slogans* (Johannesburg: Ravan Press, 1991). For a controversial collection of essays by academics of the Economics Trends Research Group associated with Cosatu, see Stephen Gelb, ed., *South Africa's Economic Crisis* (Cape Town: David Philip, 1991).

16. For a practical proposal to solve the land question, involving a land tax, a land bank and a land court, see the plan outlined by Basil Moore in *Indicator,* Autumn 1991.

17. Quoted in Alan Gregor Cobley, *Class and Consciousness: The Black Petty Bourgeoisie in South Africa, 1924–1950* (New York: Greenwood Press, 1990), p. 229.

CHAPTER TWO

1. For an account of how the conservative de Klerk himself underwent the metamorphosis that led to his support for an anti-apartheid policy, see the

biography by his brother: Willem de Klerk, *F. W. de Klerk: The Man in His Time* (Cape Town: Jonathan Ball, 1991).

2. Hermann Giliomee, *Weekend Argus,* February 24, 1990.

3. *Sechaba,* February 1989, p. 27.

4. Magnus Malan, quoted in *The Economist,* March 21, 1992.

5. James Barber, "Smuts House Notes," *International Affairs Bulletin* 14, no. 1, 1990.

6. Thomas Ohlson, "The Cuito Cuanavale Syndrome: Revealing SADF Vulnerabilities," *South African Review* 5 (Johannesburg: Ravan Press, 1989), p. 182.

7. Personal interview, May 5, 1989.

8. The Swapo incursion on April 1, 1989, seemed to strengthen the South African militarists, who had argued all along that one could not rely on negotiations and agreements. Again it was the pressure by Swapo's sponsor that put the Namibia agreement back on track.

9. Given the strong sentiment against abandoning the armed struggle, the leadership also had to reinterpret "suspension" to mean a preparatory pause prior to renewed action. As SACP leader Raymond Mhlaba put it in February 1991: "The suspension of military activities does not mean that MK as such is disbanded. It is there intact, and there are MK members in military camps. Some have gone for refresher courses so that by the time we tell them to go into action, they are mentally and physically equipped and well versed in the use of modern weapons at their disposal." At the same time, however, in a new accord with Pretoria the ANC committed itself to cease military training and the setting up of underground structures. Therefore, the sooner MK combatants are integrated into existing SADF units or Bantustan armies, the better for peace on this front.

10. John Saul, *Southern African Report* (Toronto) May 1989, p. 7.

11. Deon Geldenhuys, *South Africa International Quarterly,* July 1991, p. 50.

12. See Anthony Sampson, *Black and Gold: Tycoons, Revolutionaries and Apartheid* (London: Hodder & Stoughton, 1987) on the excuses that South African corporate leaders made for refusing such a liaison.

13. Ann Bernstein and Jeff McCarthy, "Opening the Door," in *Opening the Cities,* Indicator S.A. Issue Focus, September 1990.

14. Some influential Afrikaner corporate executives, such as the late Sanlam Chief Fred du Plessis, favored defaulting on South Africa's debt and relying on growth through import substitution. These siege economists believed that South Africa could never satisfy the outside world, regardless of its normalization policies—that every time South Africa made a concession, the sanctions ante would simply be upped. Under this assumption, debt repayment would be a fruitless drain on resources. Merle Lipton (1990, 28–29) attributes the defeat of this strategy to the wise imposition of partial sanctions, which had the advantage of "leaving open the possibility that South Africa could 'claw its way back' into the international community."

15. For example, Minister Wim de Villiers said that South Africa's economic growth rate would be three to four times greater if sanctions were dropped and that "sanctions had reduced the growth of employment oppor-

tunities in the industrial sector to just 1% a year" (*Cape Times*, February 6, 1990).

CHAPTER THREE

1. George M. Fredrickson, "The Making of Mandela," *New York Review of Books*, September 27, 1990.
2. One independent African commentator remarked wryly of the ANC constitutional draft: "I have no problems with it whatsoever. It looks like it has been faxed straight from London. It lacks any peculiar South African idiosyncrasies, such as the quaint tricameral parliament displayed" (personal interview, July 27, 1991).
3. Hermann Giliomee, "The Leader and the Citizenry," unpublished manuscript, 1991.

CHAPTER FOUR

1. Editorial in *Sechaba*, October 1990, p. 1.
2. Cyril Ramaphosa, *City Press*, July 21, 1991.
3. For the same reason the vague 1955 Freedom Charter is elevated to sacred status because no other more specific platform could fulfill the function of uniting divergent views and interests. The Charter is the minimalist common denominator.
4. R. W. Johnson, "The Past and Future of the South African Communist Party," *London Review of Books*, October 24, 1991.
5. For a well-informed, although personalized, account of the ANC-SACP alliance by the editor of *Africa Confidential*, see Stephen Ellis and Tsepo Sechaba, *Comrades against Apartheid: The ANC and the South African Communist Party in Exile* (Bloomington: Indiana University Press, 1992).
6. Jeremy Cronin, *Work in Progress* 76, July–August 1991, p. 49.
7. Francis Fukuyama, "The End of History," *The National Interest*, no. 3, Summer 1989.
8. Michael O'Dowd, "Yes, Mr. Slovo, Modern Socialism Has Indeed Failed," *Business Day*, February 14, 1990.
9. Joe Slovo, "Has Socialism Failed?" *The African Communist*, no. 121, 1990, 21–51.
10. Mac Maharaj, *New Nation*, July 6, 1990.
11. A summary of this interview, conducted by Hermann Giliomee at an Idasa conference in Leverkusen, Germany, October 1988, was published in *Die Suid-Afrikaan*, February 19, 1989.
12. *The African Communist*, 3d quarter, 1989, p. 118.
13. In a fascinating study, Frederick Johnstone has pointed to the phenomenon of "racial bracketing," of "putting the racial problem into a special category of irrational evil. This permits a double standard; the old double standard of the Leninist Left (fascism as dictatorship is bad, communism as dictatorship is O.K.). Domination could be condemned by domination: racial domination (fascism) by rational domination (Leninism), irrational evil by a rationalist Marxism sitting in judgement on the privileged throne of Enlight-

enment reason and truth" ("Apartheid and the Gulag," unpublisheed manuscript, 1989).

14. George M. Fredrickson, "The Making of Mandela," *New York Review of Books,* September 27, 1990.

15. Unsigned editorial, *South African Communists Speak, 1915–1980* (London: Inkululeko Publications, 1981), p. 151.

16. A. Lerumo, *Fifty Fighting Years* (London: Inkululeko Publications, 1971), p. 79.

17. Slovo, "Has Socialism Failed?" All subsequent quotations from Slovo in this chapter are taken from this article.

18. Aryeh Neier has perceptively pointed to a reverse personality cult at work in the personalized blame of Stalin. "According to current official pronouncements, virtually all the evils of the past can be attributed to a single villain in much the same way that Stalin was once credited with every achievement in the Soviet Union. The effect is to promote a cult of personality in reverse" ("What Should Be Done about the Guilty?" *New York Review of Books,* February 1, 1990, p. 32).

19. Johnstone, "Apartheid and the Gulag."

20. Mervyn Frost, "Opposing Apartheid: Democrats against the Leninists," *Theoria,* no. 71, May 1988, pp. 15–22.

21. The January 8, 1989, ANC National Executive Committee Annual Policy Statement.

22. See Heribert Adam, *Modernizing Racial Domination* (Berkeley: University of California Press, 1971).

23. *Africa Confidential,* January 12, 1990.

24. Pallo Jordan, "The Crisis of Conscience in the SACP," *Transformation,* no. 11, 1990.

25. Albie Sachs, inaugural lecture at the University of Cape Town, May 20, 1992.

26. *The African Communist,* no. 123, 1990.

27. Pierre van den Berghe, "South Africa after Thirty Years" (unpublished manuscript, 1989).

28. *The African Communist,* no. 122, 1990.

29. Josef Skvorecky, "The Theater of Cruelty," *New York Review of Books,* August 16, 1990.

30. Harry Gwala, "Let Us Look at History in the Round," *The African Communist,* no. 123, 1990.

31. Dave Kitson, "Is the SACP Really Communist?" *Work in Progress* 73, March–April 1991.

32. *The African Communist,* no. 124, 1991.

33. Ibid.

34. This section of this chapter was published as an opinion column in many South African English-language dailies in August 1992.

CHAPTER FIVE

An earlier, briefer version of this chapter was presented by Kogila Moodley at the conference "The Legacy of Steve Biko" in Harare, Zimbabwe,

June 17–21, 1990, and was published in *Journal of Modern African Studies*, 29, no. 2 (1991): 237–51 and in Barney Pityana et al., eds., *Bounds of Possibility* (London: Zed Books, 1991), pp. 143–52.

1. Sam C. Nolutshungu, *Changing South Africa* (Manchester: Manchester University Press, 1982) pp. 147–48.

2. Aelred Stubbs, ed., *Steve Biko: I Write What I Like* (London: Penguin, 1988), p. 32.

3. B. S. Biko, ed., *Black Viewpoint* (Durban: Black Community Programmes, 1972), p. 7.

4. Mikhail Heller and Aleksandr Nekrich, *Utopia in Power: The History of the Soviet Union from 1917 to the Present* (New York: Summit Books, 1988), p. 9.

5. B. A. Khoapa, ed., *Black Review 1972* (Durban: Black Community Programmes, 1973), p. 64.

6. Heribert Adam, "The Rise of Black Consciousness in South Africa," *Race* 15, no. 2 (October 1973): 155.

7. Stubbs, *Steve Biko,* p. 39.

8. George M. Fredrickson, "The Making of Mandela," *New York Review of Books,* September 27, 1990, p. 27.

9. Robert Fatton, *Black Consciousness in South Africa* (New York: State University of New York, 1986), p. 66.

10. G. J. Gerwel, "Coloured Nationalism" in T. Sundermeier, *Church and Nationalism in South Africa* (Braamfontein: Ravan Press, 1975).

11. SASO, *Newsletters* [vols. 1 and 2, 1971–1977] (Durban: SASO), p. 7.

12. R. Miles, *Racism* (London: Routledge, 1989), pp. 73–76.

13. Nolutshungu, *Changing South Africa,* p. 149.

14. Ibid., pp. 155–57.

15. Mokgethi Motlhabi, *Black Resistance to Apartheid* (Johannesburg: Skotaville Publishers, 1985), p. 115.

16. Asha Rambally, ed., *Black Review 1975–6* (Durban: Black Community Programmes, 1977), p. 143.

17. Ibid., p. 135.

18. Dorothy Driver, "Women, Black Consciousness and the Discovery of Self," unpublished paper, 1990.

19. Khoapa, *Black Review 1972,* pp. 25–26.

20. Ibid., p. 66.

21. Gail Gerhart, *Black Power in South Africa: The Evolution of an Ideology* (Berkeley: University of California Press, 1979), pp. 291–92.

22. M. Seleoane, "The Black Consciousness Movement," *South African Foundation Review,* December 1989.

23. E. Baartman, "Education as an Instrument for Liberation" in H. W. van der Merwe, *African Perspectives on South Africa* (Cape Town: David Philip, 1978), pp. 273–78.

24. Kogila Adam, "Dialectic of Higher Education for the Colonized" in Heribert Adam, ed., *South Africa: Sociological Perspectives* (London: Oxford University Press, 1971).

25. Heribert Adam, "The Rise of Black Consciousness," p. 154.

26. Richard Turner, *The Eye of the Needle: Toward a Participatory Democracy in South Africa* (Maryknoll, N.Y.: Orbis Books, 1978).

27. Patrick Lawrence, *S.A. Foundation News,* January 1991.

28. The PAC has repeatedly criticized the ANC's decision to negotiate as "appeasement." "You cannot appease de Klerk, he is a Nazi," declared PAC leader Zeph Mothopeng (*Cape Times,* February 19, 1990). The decision to enter into negotiations under certain conditions is likely to further strain relations within the PAC.

29. Benny Alexander, interview, *Monitor,* June 1991.

30. More thoughtful members of the movement, such as returned exile Barney Desai, clearly realize the danger of radical counterracism: "I wish also to caution my brothers and sisters that the slogan of 'one settler one bullet' is inconsistent with our stated aims. No mature liberation movement has ever had as its stated policy an intention to drive the white people into the sea" (*Argus,* March 13, 1990). Presumably in good South African humor, another PAC adherent explained the macabre slogan by saying: "The PAC is a poor organisation and can't afford more than one bullet per settler." The disavowed slogan, which originated during the bush war in Zimbabwe, is nonetheless popular among the PAC grass-roots. White right-wingers have responded with bumper stickers that make the converse point: "One settler—one thousand bullets."

31. David Hirschmann, "The Black Consciousness Movement in South Africa," *Journal of Modern African Studies* 28, no. 1 (March 1990): 1–22.

CHAPTER SIX

1. John Kane-Berman, *Race Relations News,* December 1991.

2. A vast literature now exists on political violence in South Africa, though mostly of the propagandistic kind. Among the noteworthy academic works are Brian McKendrick and Wilma Hoffman, eds., *People and Violence in South Africa* (Cape Town: Oxford University Press, 1990), and N. Chabani Manganyi and André du Toit, eds., *Political Violence and the Struggle in South Africa* (Johannesburg: Southern Books, 1990). The Natal conflict is perceptively analyzed by Herbert Vilakazi, "Isolating Inkatha—A Strategic Error?" *Work in Progress 75,* June 1991, pp. 21–23, and by Mike Morris and Doug Hindson, "South Africa: Political Violence, Reform and Reconstruction," *Review of African Political Economy* no. 53, 1992.

On Inkatha and Buthelezi, the published accounts are almost unanimously hostile. See, for example, Gerhard Maré and Georgina Hamilton, *An Appetite for Power: Buthelezi's Inkatha and South Africa* (Bloomington: Indiana University Press, 1987), and Mzala (pseudonym for a deceased ANC activist), *Gatsha Buthelezi: Chief with a Double Agenda* (London: Zed Books, 1988). Empirical work is rare but see, for example, John Brewer, "The Membership of Inkatha in KwaMashu," *African Affairs* 84, January 1985.

On the malleable nature of ethnicity as a mental construct, juxtaposed to its endurability and primordiality, see Leroy Vail, ed., *The Creation of Tribalism in Southern Africa* (Berkeley: University of California Press, 1989), particularly the contribution by Shula Marks, "Patriotism, Patriarchy and Purity: Natal and the Politics of Zulu Ethnic Consciousness." Gerhard Maré, *Brothers Born of Warrior Blood* (Johannesburg: Ravan Press, 1992) writes with a similar perspective, as do, from a more general viewpoint, E. Hobsbawn and T. Ranger, *The Invention of Tradition* (Cambridge: Cambridge University Press, 1983). Against this literature stands an equally adamant body of writing on the primordial and sociobiological nature of ethnicity, perhaps best exemplified by Pierre van den Berghe's *The Ethnic Phenomenon* (New York: Elsevier Press, 1981).

Matthew Kentridge's *An Unofficial War* (1990), like most other journalistic efforts, describes the impact of the war on people's lives but does not analyze the forces that have caused and sustained the conflict. Most of these "verbal snapshots," as reviewer John Wright (*Transformation* 13, 1990) accurately describes this genre, implicitly blame Inkatha warlords, backed by the South African state, as if their one-sided aggression were self-evident. Indeed, the most puzzling question remains: "What possesses them to go to war against fellow blacks with such ferocity?" (Phillip van Niekerk, *Globe & Mail*, April 3, 1991). Yet as soon as the perceptive *Globe* correspondent asks the relevant question, he capitulates: "No one—not sociologists, psychologists or political analysts—can provide an explanation of what it is really about."

3. Lawrence Schlemmer, "Violence—What Is to Be Done?" *South Africa International*, October 1992, pp. 60–64.

4. Anthea Jeffery, *Spotlight* [South African Institute of Race Relations], October 1992.

5. Amanda Gouws, "Political Intolerance," and Lawrence Schlemmer, "The Mind of the Townships," in *Quarterly State of the Nation Report* [published by *Vrye Weekblad* and *Sowetan*], Winter 1991. Compare these figures with the widespread impression among Western conservatives that Buthelezi represents some six million Zulus, one quarter of the population.

6. P. W. Botha, personal interview, March 7, 1990.

7. Inkatha is also supported by conservative foundations around the world. For example, during the 1980s Inkatha received more than $9.6 million in public funds from the Konrad Adenauer Foundation in Germany. The ultraconservative Heritage Foundation claims Buthelezi as its favored black ally, and in 1991 the U.S. Agency for International Development granted Inkatha 7 million rand (versus 12.5 million to the ANC).

8. Peter Tygesen, *Africa Report*, January–February 1991, pp. 50–56.

9. M. G. Buthelezi, speech at Enhlalakahle, Greytown, September 29, 1991.

10. For a descriptive account of unofficial state violence by a well-known South African political journalist, see Patrick Lawrence's *Death Squads: Apartheid's Secret Weapon* (Johannesburg: Penguin Forum Series, 1991). In light of these atrocities against ANC activists, it is remarkable that the ANC has absorbed some of the chief perpetrators into its ranks. Cold-blooded murderers who now pose as legitimate ANC members have been accepted after professing a change of mind and exposing their masters.

11. The clashes between police and right-wing elements in Ventersdorp

during a speech by de Klerk in July 1991 resulted in the deaths of three AWB protesters; dozens were injured. Despite their ideological sympathy with the demonstrators, sixteen hundred Afrikaner police officers let loose with Alsatian dogs, tear gas, and live ammunition. Here, institutional loyalty and discipline outweighed ideological affinity. Many of the younger Afrikaner officers were confused, but their hesitation evaporated when they were attacked by half-drunken hordes wielding steel rods and led by respected elders. The scene deteriorated into a brawl, with the police claiming to defend de Klerk's right to speak and the right wing citing its freedom to protest.

12. The Goldstone Commission has been informally criticized by the ANC as "a captive of the structures of the state and the security forces" (*SouthScan* 10, July 1992, p. 208). The implied denial of the independence of a forthright judge as well as most of the commission's officials seems hardly justified. Obviously, some of the staff had to be recruited from government departments and universities. However, the fair-minded commission risked its legitimacy by being an almost entirely all-white and all-male affair.

13. "ANC units running wild, says Chris Hani," *Sunday Times,* August 2, 1992, p. 1.

14. In contrast to most activists, particularly those in the Transvaal, Nelson Mandela has always kept in polite contact with Buthelezi, both on the phone and by mail. "Obviously, my fervent hope," he wrote to Buthelezi from prison, "is to see, in due course, the restoration of the cordial relations which existed between you and OR [Oliver Reginald Tambo] and between the two organizations in the Seventies" (*Sunday Tribune,* April 16, 1989).

15. The ANC has courted and been courted by the military rulers of the Transkei (birthplace of Mandela, Hani, Mbeki, and many other top leaders) and also by sympathetic smaller Bantustans like Kwa Ndebele and Venda. Venda's military chief addressed an MK conference in August 1991 at the local university to wild cheers from former guerrillas now in search of jobs and recognition. Transkei's Holomisa is frequently mentioned as the possible future defense minister.

16. M. Roth, "Zulu and Xhosa—A Different Historical Consciousness," presented at the Conference on Ethnicity, Society, and Conflict, University of Natal, September 14–16, 1992.

17. Steven Friedman had astutely predicted that the well-intentioned "phasing out" of the hostels might well trigger greater violence if the hostel dwellers were not part of the agreement (*Weekly Mail,* May 10–16, 1991). In authoritarian fashion, the accord on the upgrading of the hostels was concluded without anyone having asked the inmates "whether they wanted the hostels to be phased out," according to Friedman.

18. The ploy of forged leaflets has been used extensively by secret agencies at different times and locations to fan intercommunal antagonism or to discredit activist groups. For example, in early 1990 pamphlets distributed widely in Natal maintained that Indian women carried an antidote to AIDS. Mandela repeatedly denounced this pernicious incitement to racial rape. Port Elizabeth seems to have been the center of fomenting anti-ANC sentiment during the 1980s when agents provocateurs issued forged UDF and Cosatu leaflets that

demanded financial contributions to the struggle from each household. Usually, the products could be easily identified by the false "struggle-language" they attempted to imitate. Over time, however, the products of the hatemongers have become more sophisticated and successful.

CHAPTER SEVEN

1. The figures seem to support the argument that even if the private wealth of whites, who constitute 13 percent of the population, was to be equally shared among the total population, it would not make any great material difference in the living standards of the impoverished majority. On the other hand, South Africa does have one of the most skewed income distributions in the world (Gini coefficient 0.68). Stellenbosch economist Servaas van den Bergh has pointed out that if recorded income were distributed as it is in the United States "the income of the poorest 15 million people in South Africa (40% of the population) would be about 70% higher than it is" (*EPSG Occasional Paper*, no. 3).

2. Due to his weapon thefts, underground activities, and imprisonment, the militant Rudolph assumed an almost Mandela-like mythical role among sectors of the ultra-right for a while.

3. The media's misperceptions led almost all pundits to predict an uncertain outcome for the referendum, with the *New York Times*, for example, forecasting a result "too close to call" (March 16, 1992). Even the Johannesburg *Weekly Mail* participated in painting the doomsday scenarios of both the English and Afrikaans press. The beneficial effect was that the press coverage mobilized the voters, and an unprecedented 85 percent turned in a ballot.

4. Denis Becket, "Leading the Right to Reason," *Die Suid-Afrikaan*, October–November 1991.

5. Pierre du Toit and Willie Esterhuyse, eds., *The Mythmakers: The Elusive Bargain for South Africa's Future* (Johannesburg: Southern Books, 1990).

6. Theo Hanf, *Koexistenz im Krieg: Staatszerfall und Entstehung einer Nation im Libanon* (Munich: Nomos Verlag, 1990).

CHAPTER EIGHT

1. This analysis has been inspired by the stimulating assessment of U.S. foreign policy in the post–cold war period by Michael Clough (1992); we thank him for generously providing us with a copy of his manuscript.

2. See Commonwealth Expert Group, *Human Resource Development for a Post-Apartheid South Africa* (London: Commonwealth Office, 1991) and International Development Research Council (IDRC), *Economic Analysis and Policy Formulation for Post-Apartheid South Africa* (Ottawa: IDRC, August 1991).

3. IDRC, *Economic Analysis,* p. 35.

4. It is overstated to assert, as the IDRC report does, that "under the Apartheid system of separate education, access to training in economics for blacks was confined to so-called ethnic universities" (p. 33). These exclusion-

ary practices have been defied by all English-language universities since the early 1980s.

5. The Graduate School of Business at the University of the Witwatersrand introduced a public administration speciality only in 1991, and the University of Cape Town has yet to decide where to locate the training of top civil servants. The Graduate School of Business at the University of Cape Town, however, has introduced an innovative Associate in Management program, largely financed by future employers. The enrollment reflects approximately the racial composition of the general population and creates a genuinely integrated interracial learning experience, particularly for Afrikaner and white students not accustomed to being in the minority in a classroom. Because the training of the civil service in South Africa traditionally took place at Afrikaans institutions, not at English universities, the latter were unprepared for the task of training a new, predominantly black civil service.

6. The confidential "Report of the Office of the Treasurer General," ANC National Congress, Durban, July 1991, gives the first detailed accounting of all ANC assets and liabilities at home and abroad. Membership fees cover 5.3 percent of ANC income, donations 3.7 percent, and grants 86.6 percent. The total ANC budget in 1990 amounted to 79,731,300 rand (approximately $27 million).

The South African Council of Churches (SACC) also relies on foreign grants, which finance almost 90 percent of its annual budget (*SouthScan*, November 1, 1991). The free-spending council was forced to cut its staff from 120 to 80 after a deficit of 26 million rand in 1990–91. Observers expect further cutbacks once foreign interest in South Africa declines.

7. Commonwealth Foreign Ministers Meeting, New Delhi, September 13–14, 1991.

8. Southern African Research and Documentation Centre, Harare, September, 30, 1991.

9. ANC, *For the Start of Our Lives: Guidelines for the Creation of People's Self-Defence Units,* 1991.

10. Yet political demonstrations remain one of the few tools to educate and to inculcate legitimate behavior among a heterogeneous constituency. Here is a concrete example, observed by Sindile Dikene, a poet who participated in the march on Cape Town on August 3, 1992: "A blonde policewoman turns colour, from pink to red and then to white at the whistles and finger salutes of the obscene and disgusting variety directed at her. And again I hear a voice from the 1980s, pleading, nearly on the verge of breaking down: 'Comrades, sexism is a vulgarity that belongs to the apartheid regime, not to us' " ("The Streets Are Alive with the Codesa Shuffle," *Die Suid-Afrikaan,* October–November 1992, p. 29).

11. Valerie Moeller, "Lost Generation Found," *Indicator South Africa,* May 1991.

12. It is probably for this reason that Mamphela Ramphela and Francis Wilson's comprehensive study *Uprooting Poverty* (Cape Town: David Philip, 1989) does not discuss birth control in South Africa. Yet while there is a slow decline in the African birthrate due to delayed urbanization and slow material

improvements in South Africa, birthrates remain high in the rest of the continent.

13. Cited in R. W. Johnson, "AIDS in South Africa," *London Review of Books,* September 12, 1991. See also Mary Crewe, *AIDS in South Africa: Myth and Reality* (Johannesburg: Penguin 1992).

14. M. V. Gumede, *Traditional Healers* (Johannesburg: Skotaville, 1990).

CHAPTER NINE

1. For a useful overview of this debate by authors who could not then envisage the post–cold war constellation, see R. O. Matthews and C. Pratt, eds., *Human Rights in Canadian Foreign Policy* (Kingston and Montreal: Queens University Press, 1988), particularly chapter 3 by Kim Richard Nossal.

2. Christian Geffray, *La Cause des Armes au Mozambique* (Karthala: Credu Press, 1990).

CHAPTER TEN

1. See Pieter le Roux, *Indicator South Africa* 9, no. 4, Spring 1992.

2. Ibid., p. 110.

3. The advantages of social democracy and the Swedish model for South Africa are most eloquently argued by Cape Town economist Pieter le Roux. See, for example, his "Economics of Conflict and Negotiation" in Peter L. Berger and Bobby Godsell, eds., *A Future South Africa* (Cape Town: Human & Rousseau, 1988). Le Roux has concluded that "the different groups and classes in South Africa are condemned either to fight each other to the death or make a social-democratic type of compromise" (*Weekly Mail,* July 12, 1991).

4. For a comprehensive comparative discussion of these issues in the South African context by the country's leading labor relations experts, including Douwes Dekker, Duncan Innes, Frank Horwitz, and Charles Nupen, see Mark Anstey, ed., *Worker Participation: South African Options and Experiences* (Cape Town: Juta, 1990) and Duncan Innes et al., eds., *Power and Profit: Politics, Labour and Business in South Africa* (Cape Town: Oxford University Press, 1992).

5. Johann Maree, *Social Dynamics,* 17, no. 2, (1991): 183.

6. Frank Horowitz, *Managing Resourceful People* (Cape Town: Juta, 1991), vii.

CONCLUSION

1. Editorial, *The African Communist,* no. 131, 1992, p. 6.

2. Giuseppe Di Palma, *To Craft Democracies: An Essay on Democratic Transitions* (Berkeley: University of California Press, 1990).

3. Nancy Bermeo, "Shortcuts to Liberty," *Journal of Democracy,* Spring 1991, p. 116.

4. *The African Communist,* no. 131, 1992, p. 6.

5. Johann Mouton, "Support for Political Parties and Leaders: Patterns and Trends in 1992," *Information Update* (HSRC, Pretoria), December 1992, 7–23.

6. Valerie Moeller, "A Place in the Sun: Quality of Life in South Africa," *Indicator South Africa*, Spring 1992, 101–8.

7. Anthoni van Nieuwkerk, "South Africa's Relations with the World: From Confrontation to Cooperation," *Information Update*, Spring 1992, 39–47.

8. Moeller, "A Place in the Sun," p. 105.

9. *Weekly Mail*, January 15, 1993, p. 19.

10. Lawrence Schlemmer, "Conflict in the New South Africa: Class Culture and Power," *Information Update*, Spring 1992, 4–6.

11. Ibid., p. 6.

Select Bibliography

Abedian, I. and B. Standish, eds.
   1992.   *Economic Growth in South Africa: Selected Policy Issues.*
              Cape Town: Oxford University Press.
Adam, Heribert.
   1971a.   *Modernizing Racial Domination.* Berkeley: University of Cali-
              fornia Press.
———, ed.
   1971b.   *South Africa: Sociological Perspectives.* London: Oxford Uni-
              versity Press.
Adam, Heribert, and Hermann Giliomee.
   1979.   *Ethnic Power Mobilized: Can South Africa Change?* New
              Haven: Yale University Press.
Adam, Heribert, and Kogila Moodley.
   1986.   *South Africa without Apartheid.* Berkeley: University of Cali-
              fornia Press.
———.
   1992.   *Democratizing Southern Africa: Challenges for Canadian Pol-
              icy.* Ottawa: Canadian Institute for Peace & Security.
Alexander, Neville [No Sizwe, pseud.].
   1979.   *One Azania, One Nation.* London: Zed Press.
———.
   1985.   *Sow the Wind: Contemporary Speeches.* Johannesburg: Skota-
              ville.
———.
   1989.   "Aspects of Non-Collaboration in the Western Cape, 1943–
              1963." In *The Angry Divide: Social and Economic History of
              the Western Cape,* ed. Wilmot G. James and Mary Simons.
              Cape Town: David Philip.

Anglin, Douglas G.
   1989.   "The Frontline States and Sanctions against South Africa." In
                Sanctioning Apartheid, ed. Robert E. Edgar. Trenton, N.J.:
                Africa World Press.

   ———.

   1990a.   "Ripe, Ripening or Overripe? Sanctions as an Inducement to
                Negotiations: The South African Case." *International Journal*
                45 (Spring), 360–85.

   ———.

   1990b.   "Southern African Responses to Eastern European Develop-
                ments." Paper presented at the 2d Soviet-Canadian Sympo-
                sium, Institute of African Studies, Moscow. June.

   ———.

   1991.   "South African Relations with Southern Africa: Continuity or
                Change?" Paper presented at the 20th Annual Conference of
                the Canadian Association of African Studies, York University.
                May 16–18.
Baker, Pauline.
   1989.   *The United States and South Africa: The Reagan Years.* New
                York: Ford Foundation.
Barber, James, Jesmond Blumenfeld, and Christopher R. Hill.
   1982.   *The West and South Africa.* London: Routledge & Kegan
                Paul.
Barrell, H.
   1990.   *MK: The ANC's Armed Struggle.* London: Penguin.
Baskin, Jeremy.
   1991.   *Striking Back: A History of Cosatu.* Johannesburg: Ravan
                Press.
Becker, C., and H. A. Khan.
   1990.   *The Impact of Sanctions on Incomes in South Africa and in the
                Frontline States.* Washington: IRRC.
Blumenfeld, J.
   1992.   *Economic Interdependence in Southern Africa: From Conflict
                to Cooperation.* Cape Town: Oxford University Press.
Bond, Patrick.
   1991.   *Commanding Heights and Community Control: New Eco-
                nomics for a New South Africa.* Johannesburg: Ravan Press.
Brecher, Irving, ed.
   1989.   *Human Rights, Development and Foreign Policy: Canadian
                Perspectives.* Halifax: The Institute for Research on Public
                Policy.
Brewer, John D.
   1987.   *After Soweto: An Unfinished Journey.* Oxford: Clarendon
                Press.

   ———.

   1989.   *Can South Africa Survive? Ten Minutes to Midnight.* London:
                Macmillan.

Buchanan, Allen.
1991.   *Secession: The Morality of Political Divorce from Fort
             Sunter to Lithuania and Quebec.* Boulder, Colo.: Westview
             Press.
Bundy, Colin.
1987.   "Street Sociology and Pavement Politics: Aspects of Youth/
             Student Resistance in Cape Town, 1985." *Journal of Southern
             African Studies* 13, no. 3.
Burman, S. and E. Preston-Whyte, eds.
1992.   *Questionable Issue: Illegitimacy in South Africa.* Cape Town:
             Oxford University Press.
Buthelezi, M. G.
1990.   *South Africa: My Vision of the Future.* London: Weidenfeld &
             Nicolson.
Cawthra, Gavin.
1992.   *The State of the Police: The South African Police and the
             Transition to Post-Apartheid Society.* London: Zed Books.
Charney, Craig.
1991.   "Vigilantes, Clientelism and the South African State." *Trans-
             formation* 16, pp. 1–28.
Chidester, D.
1992.   *Shots in the Streets: Religion and Violence in South Africa.*
             Cape Town: Oxford University Press.
Chikane, Frank.
1988.   *No Life of My Own.* London: Catholic Institute for Interna-
             tional Relations.
Christie, Grania.
1991.   "AIDS in South Africa." *South Africa International* 22, no. 1
             (July).
Christie, Pam.
1992.   *The Right to Learn: The Struggle for Education in South
             Africa.* Johannesburg: Ravan Press.
Clark, Andrew.
1991.   "An Overview of Canadian Policy toward Sub-Saharan Africa
             in the 1980s." Ottawa: North-South Institute.
Clough, Michael W.
1988.   Southern Africa: Challenges and Choices." *Foreign Affairs* 66,
             no. 5.
———.
1992.   "Free at Last? U.S. Policy toward Africa and the End of the
             Cold War." Unpublished manuscript.
Cobbett, William, and Robin Cohen, eds.
1988.   *Popular Struggles in South Africa.* London: Zed Books.
Cock, J.
1992.   *Colonels and Cadres: War and Gender in South Africa.* Cape
             Town: Oxford University Press.

Cock, Jackie, and Laurie Nathan, eds.
   1989.   *The Militarisation of South African Society.* Cape Town:
             David Philip.
Cohen, Stephen Philip.
   1991.   "Conflict Resolution: Principles in Practice." Paper presented
             at the Institute for the Study and Resolution of Conflict, Uni-
             versity of Port Elizabeth. July 29.
Cohin, Robin, Yvonne Muthien, and Abebe Zegeye.
   1990.   *Repression and Resistance: Insider Accounts of Apartheid.*
             London: Hans Zell.
Coker, Christopher.
   1985.   *NATO: The Warsaw Pact and Africa.* New York: St. Martin's
             Press.

——.

   1987.   *South Africa's Security Dilemmas.* New York: Praeger.

——.

   1991.   "Experiencing Southern Africa in the Twenty-first Century."
             International Affairs, April.
Cole, Josette.
   1987.   *Crossroads: The Politics of Reform and Repression, 1976–
             1986.* Johannesburg: Ravan Press.
Coleman, Keith.
   1991.   *Nationalisation: Beyond the Slogans.* Johannesburg: Ravan
             Press.
Collins, Peter.
   1991.   "Pigs, Farmers and Other Animals." In *The Watershed Years.*
             Cape Town: Leadership Publication.
Connor, Walker.
   1984.   *The National Question in Marxist-Leninist Theory and Strat-
             egy.* Princeton: Princeton University Press.
Davies, Rob, Dan O'Meara, and Sipho Dlamini.
   1988.   *The Struggle for South Africa: A Reference Guide* (new ed.).
             2 vols. London: Zed Books.
Davis, Stephen M.
   1987.   *Apartheid's Rebels: Inside South Africa's Hidden War.* New
             Haven: Yale University Press.
Debray, Regis.
   1974.   "Marxism and the National Question." *New Left Review* 105
             (September–October), pp. 25–41.
Degenaar, Johan.
   1991.   "The Myth of a South African Nation." Idasa occasional
             paper. Cape Town: Idasa.
De Klerk, Michael, ed.
   1991.   *A Harvest of Discontent: The Land Question in South Africa.*
             Cape Town: Idasa.
De Villiers, Marq.
   1987.   *White Tribe Dreaming.* New York: Viking.

Diamond, Larry, Juan J. Linz, and Seymour Martin Lipset, eds.
   1988.   *Democracy in Developing Countries.* Boulder, Colo.: Lynne
              Rienner Publishers.
Dugard, John et al.
   1992.   *The Last Years of Apartheid: Civil Liberties in South Africa,*
              New York: Ford Foundation.
Edgar, Robert E., ed.
   1989.   *Sanctioning Apartheid.* Trenton, N.J.: Africa World Press.
Ellis, Stephen, and Sechaba Tsepo.
   1992.   *Comrades against Apartheid: The ANC and the South African
              Communist Party in Exile.* Bloomington: Indiana University
              Press.
Everett, David, and Elinor Sisulu, eds.
   1992.   *Black Youth in Crisis: Facing the Future.* Johannesburg:
              Ravan Press.
Filatova, Irina.
   1991.   "One, Two or Many? Aspects of the South African Debate on
              the Concept of Nation." Unpublished manuscript.
Fine, Robert, with Dennis Davis.
   1991.   *Beyond Apartheid: Labour and Liberation in South Africa.*
              Johannesburg: Ravan Press.
Frankel, Philip, Noam Pines, and Mark Swilling, eds.
   1988.   *State, Resistance and Change in South Africa.* Johannesburg:
              Southern Publisher.
Frederikse, Julie.
   1990.   *The Unbreakable Thread: Non-Racialism in South Africa.*
              Johannesburg: Ravan Press.

————.

   1992.   *All Schools for All People: Lessons for South Africa from
              Zimbabwe's Open Schools.* Cape Town: Oxford University
              Press.
Fredrickson, George M.
   1991.   "African Americans and African Africans." *New York Review
              of Books,* September 26.
Freeman, Linda.
   1989.   "All But One: Britain, the Commonwealth and Sanctions." In
              Sanctions against Apartheid, ed. Mark Orkin. Cape Town:
              David Philip.

————.

   1986–1991. "Annual Comments on Canadian Policy towards South
              Africa." *Southern Africa Report* [Toronto]. December.
Friedman, Steve.
   1986.   *Building Tomorrow Today.* Johannesburg: Ravan Press.
Furtado, Celso.
   1970.   *Obstacles to Development in Latin America.* New York:
              Doubleday.

Garner, Jonathan, and J. Leape.
1991.   "South Africa's Borrowings on International Capital Markets:
             Recent Developments in Historical Perspective." London:
             Centre for the Study of the South African Economy and Inter-
             national Finance, London School of Economics.
Gastrow, Shelagh.
1992.   *Who's Who in South African Politics* (4th ed.). Johannesburg:
             Ravan Press.
Gelb, Stephen, ed.
1991.   *South Africa's Economic Crisis.* Cape Town: David Philip;
             London: Zed Books.
Giliomee, Hermann.
1992.   "The Last Trek? Afrikaners in Transition to Democracy."
             South Africa International 22, no. 3 (January): 111–20.
Giliomee, Hermann, and Jannie Gagiano, eds.
1990.   *The Elusive Search for Peace: South Africa, Israel and North-
             ern Ireland.* Cape Town: Oxford University Press.
Giliomee, Hermann, and Lawrence Schlemmer, eds.
1989a.   *Negotiating South Africa's Future.* Johannesburg: Southern
             Book Publisher.
———.
1989b.   *From Apartheid to Nation-Building.* Cape Town: Oxford Uni-
             versity Press.
Greenberg, S.
1980.   *Race and State in Capitalist Development: South Africa in
             Comparative Perspective.* New Haven: Yale University Press.
Hanlon, Joseph.
1991.   Successes and Future Prospects of Sanctions Against South
             Africa." London: Centre for the Study of the South African
             Economy and International Finance, London School of Eco-
             nomics.
Hanlon, Joseph, et al.
1990.   *The Sanctions Report.* Report prepared for the Common-
             wealth Committee of Foreign Ministers on South Africa. Har-
             mondsworth: Penguin.
Hansson, D., and D. van Zyl Smit, eds.
1990.   *Towards Justice? Crime and State Control in South Africa.*
             Cape Town: Oxford University Press.
Haysom, N.
1986.   *Mabangalala: The Rise of Right-Wing Vigilantes in South
             Africa.* Johannesburg: Centre for Applied Legal Studies.
Heard, Tony.
1991.   *The Cape of Storms: A Personal History of the Crisis in South
             Africa.* Johannesburg: Ravan Press.
Hermassi, Elbaki.
1980.   *The Third World Reassessed.* Berkeley: University of Califor-
             nia Press.

Horowitz, Donald L.
1991.   *A Democratic South Africa? Constitutional Engineering in a Divided Society.* Berkeley: University of California Press.

Howard, R.
1988.   "Black Africa and South Africa." In *Human Rights in Canadian Foreign Policy,* ed. Robin Matthews and Cranford Pratt. Kingston, Ont.: Queen's University Press.

Indicator Project South Africa.
1989.   *An Overview of Political Conflict in South Africa: Data Trends, 1984–1988.* Durban: University of Natal.

Innes, D., M. Kentridge, and H. Perold.
1992.   *Power and Profit: Labour, Politics and Business in South Africa—Innes Labour Brief.* Cape Town: Oxford University Press.

International Development and Research Council (IDRC).
1991.   "Economic Analysis and Policy Formulation for Post-Apartheid South Africa." Ottawa: IDRC mission report. August.

James, Wilmot.
1992.   *Our Precious Metal. African Labour in South Africa's Gold Industry.* London: James Curry; Cape Town: David Philip.

Jeffery, Anthea.
1991.   *Riot Policing in Perspective.* Johannesburg: SA Institute of Race Relations.

Johns, S., and R. Hunt Davis.
1991.   *Mandela, Tambo and the African National Congress: The Struggle against Apartheid, 1948–1990.* Cape Town: Oxford University Press.

Johnson, R. W.
1991.   "What Buthelezi Wants." *London Review of Books.* December 19.

Johnson, Shaun, ed.
1989.   *South Africa: No Turning Back.* Bloomington: Indiana University Press.

Kahn, Brian.
1991.   "Capital Flight and Exchange Controls in South Africa." London: Centre for the Study of the South African Economy and International Finance, London School of Economics.

Kallaway, Peter, ed.
1984.   *Apartheid and Education: The Education of Black South Africans.* Johannesburg: Ravan Press.

Kenney, Henry.
1992.   *Power, Pride and Prejudice.* Johannesburg: Jonathan Ball.

Kentridge, Matthew.
1990.   *An Unofficial War: Inside the Conflict in Pietermaritzburg.* Cape Town: David Philip.

Leape, Jonathan I.
1991.   "South Africa's Foreign Debt and the Standstill, 1985–1990."

London: Centre for the Study of the South African Economy and International Finance, London School of Economics.

Lee, R., and L. Schlemmer, eds.
1991.   *Transition to Democracy: Policy Perspectives.* Cape Town: Oxford University Press.

Legge, Garth, Cranford Pratt, Richard Williams, and Hugh Winsor.
1970.   *The Black Paper: An Alternative Policy for Canada towards Southern Africa.* Toronto.

Lelyveld, Joseph.
1985.   *Move Your Shadow.* New York: Penguin.

Lijphart, Arend.
1985.   *Power-sharing in South Africa.* Berkeley: Institute of International Studies, University of California.

Lipton, Merle.
1986.   *Capitalism and Apartheid: South Africa, 1910–1986.* London: Gower Press.

———.
1990.   "The Challenge of Sanctions." London: Centre for the Study of the South African Economy and International Finance, London School of Economics.

Lodge, Tom, Bill Nasson, et al.
1991.   *All, Here, and Now: Black Politics in South Africa in the 1980s.* New York: Ford Foundation.

Louw, Leon, and Francis Kendall.
1986.   *The Solution.* Bishop: Amagi Public.

Loxley, John.
1991.   "Deeper in Debt. What Are Our Alternatives?" *Southern Africa Report* [Toronto], July, pp. 10–15.

McCormick, Shawn.
1991.   "Angola: The Road to Peace," *CSIS Africa Notes.* Washington: Center for Strategic and International Studies. June 6.

McKendrick, B., and W. Hoffman, eds.
1990.   *People and Violence in South Africa.* Cape Town: Oxford University Press.

Malan, Rian.
1990.   *My Traitor's Heart.* London: Bodley Head.

Mallaby, Sebastian.
1992.   *After Apartheid: The Future of South Africa.* New York: Random House.

Maller, Judy.
1992.   *Conflict and Co-operation: Case Studies in Worker Participation.* Johannesburg: Ravan Press.

Manganyi, N. Chabani.
1991.   *Treachery and Innocence: Psychology and Racial Difference.* Johannesburg: Ravan Press.

Manzo, Kathryn.
1992.   *Domination, Resistance and Social Change in South Africa.* New York: Praeger.

Maré, Gerhard.
1992.   *Brothers Born of Warrior Blood: Politics and Ethnicity in
            South Africa.* Johannesburg: Ravan Press.
Maré, Gerhard, and Georgina Hamilton.
1987.   *An Appetite for Power: Buthelezi's Inkatha and the Politics of
            Loyal Resistance.* Johannesburg: Ravan Press.
Marks, S., and P. Anderson.
1990.   "The Epidemiology and Culture of Violence." In *Political Vio-
            lence and the Struggle in South Africa,* ed. C. Manganyi and A.
            du Toit. London: Macmillan.
Marx, A.
1992.   *Lessons of Struggle: South African Internal Opposition
            1960–1990.* Cape Town: Oxford University Press.
Mbeki, Thabo.
1991.   "South Africa's International Relations—Today and Tomor-
            row." *South Africa International* 21, no. 4 (April): 231–35.
Meer, Fatima.
1988.   *Nelson Mandela, Higher than Hope: Rolilahla We Love You.*
            Johannesburg: Skotaville.

———.
1989.   *Resistance in the Townships.* Durban: Madiba.
Moll, Peter, ed.
1991.   *Redistribution: How Can It Work in South Africa?* Cape
            Town: David Philip.
Murray, Martin.
1988.   *South Africa: Time of Agony, Time of Destiny.* London:
            Verso.
Mzala [pseud.].
1988.   *Gatsha Buthelezi: Chief with a Double Agenda.* London: Zed
            Books.
Nasson, Bill.
1989.   "Opposition Politics and Ideology in the Western Cape."
            South African Review, vol. 5, ed. Glen Moss and Ingrid Obery.
            Johannesburg: Ravan Press.
Nattrass, Nicoli, and Elizabeth Ardington, eds.
1990.   *The Political Economy of South Africa.* Cape Town: Oxford
            University Press.
O'Donnell, Guillermo.
1988.   *Bureaucratic Authoritarianism: Argentina 1966–1973 in Com-
            parative Perspective.* Berkeley: University of California Press.
O'Donnell, Guillermo, and Philippe C. Schmitter.
1986.   "Resurrecting Civil Society." In *Transitions from Authoritar-
            ian Rule: Prospects of Democracy,* ed. Guillermo O'Donnell,
            Philippe C. Schmitter, and Laurence Whitehead. Baltimore:
            Johns Hopkins University Press.
O'Donnell, Guillermo, Philippe C. Schmitter, and Laurence Whitehead, eds.
1986.   *Transitions from Authoritarian Rule: Prospects of Democ-
            racy.* Baltimore: Johns Hopkins University Press.

O'Dowd, Michael.
    1991.   "The New National Party and the Politics of Negotiation." In *Democracy and the Workplace: Politics, Labour and Business in South Africa*, ed. D. Innes, M. Kentridge, and H. Perold. Cape Town: Oxford University Press.

———.
    1992.   *The Growth Imperative*. Johannesburg: Jonathan Ball.
O'Meara, Dan.
    1988.   "Destabilization of the Frontline States of Southern Africa, 1980–87." Ottawa, Canadian Institute of International Peace and Security, Background Paper.

———.
    1992.   "The New National Party and the Politics of Negotiation." In *Power and Profit*, ed. Duncan Innes, Matthew Kentridge, and Helene Perold. Cape Town: Oxford University Press.
Orkin, Mark, ed.
    1986.   *The Struggle and the Future: What Black South Africans Really Think*. Johannesburg: Ravan Press.
———, ed.
    1989.   *Sanctions against Apartheid*. Cape Town: David Philip.
Owen, Ken
    1992.   *In Our Times*. Johannesburg: Jonathan Ball.
Pampallis, John.
    1992.   *Foundations of the New South Africa*. London: Zed Books.
Patel, Leila.
    1992.   *Restructuring Social Welfare: The Options for South Africa*. Johannesburg: Ravan Press.
Pauw, J.
    1991.   *In the Heart of the Whore: The Story of Apartheid's Death Squads*. Johannesburg: Southern Publisher.
Payne, Richard J.
    1990.   *The Nonsuperpowers and South Africa*. Bloomington and Indianapolis: Indiana University Press.
Pityana, Barney, et al., eds.
    1991.   *Bounds of Possibility: The Legacy of Steve Biko and Black Consciousness*. London: Zed Books.
Pityana, Sipho Mila, and Mark Orkin, eds.
    1992.   *Beyond the Factory Floor: A Survey of Cosatu Shop-Stewards*. Johannesburg: Ravan Press.
Pratt, Cranford, ed.
    1989a.   *Internationalism under Strain: The North-South Policies of Canada, The Netherlands, Norway and Sweden*. Toronto: University of Toronto Press.

———.
    1989b.   "The Limited Place of Human Rights in Canadian Foreign Policy." In *Human Rights Development and Foreign Policy: Canadian Perspectives*, ed. Irving Brecher. Halifax: Institute for Research on Public Policy.

—————, ed.

1990. *Middle Power Internationalism.* Montreal and Kingston: McGill-Queen's University Press.

Pratt, Renate.

1990. "From the Gold Mines to Bay Street: In Search of Corporate Social Responsibility." In *Canadian Churches and Foreign Policy,* ed. B. Greene. Toronto: James Lorimer.

Preston-Whyte, E., and C. Rogerson, eds.

1992. *The Informal Economy of South Africa: Past, Present and Future.* Cape Town: Oxford University Press.

Price, Robert T.

1990. *The Apartheid State in Crisis.* New York: Oxford University Press.

Przeworski, Adam.

1986. "Some Problems in the Study of the Transition to Democracy." In *Transitions from Authoritarian Rule: Prospects of Democracy,* ed. Guillermo O'Donnell, Philippe C. Schmitter, and Laurence Whitehead. Baltimore: Johns Hopkins University Press.

Robertson, M., ed.

1991. *Human Rights for South Africans.* Cape Town: Oxford University Press.

Rose, Richard.

1971. *Governing without Consensus.* London: Macmillan.

Sachs, A.

1990. *Protecting Human Rights in a New South Africa.* Cape Town: Oxford University Press.

Saul, John.

1986. "South Africa: The Question of Strategy." *New Left Review* 160 (November–December).

—————.

1988. "Mysteries of the Dark Continent." *This Magazine* 22, no. 4, 18–22.

—————.

1990. *Socialist Ideology and the Struggle for Southern Africa.* Trenton, N.J.: Africa World Press.

—————.

1991. "South Africa: Between 'Barbarism' and 'Structural Reform.' " *New Left Review* 188 (July–August): 3–44.

Schlemmer, Lawrence.

1991. "Negotiation Dilemmas after the Sound and Fury." *Indicator South Africa* 8, no. 3, 7–10.

Schrire, Robert.

1992a. *Adapt or Die: The End of White Politics in South Africa.* New York: Ford Foundation.

—————, ed.

1992b. *Wealth and Poverty: Critical Choices for South Africa.* Cape Town: Oxford University Press.

Seekings, J.
1991.   "Inkatha and the Origins of 'Hostel' Violence on the Witwa-
               tersrand, 1990–91." Unpublished paper. University of Cape
               Town.
Segal, Ronald, ed.
1964.   *Sanctions against South Africa*. Harmondsworth: Penguin.
Simpson, G., et al.
1991.   "Political Violence in 1990: The Year in Perspective." Unpub-
               lished paper. Johannesburg, Project for the Study of Violence.
Sitas, A.
1981.   "The Making of the Comrades Movement in Natal, 1985–91."
               Unpublished paper. Oxford University.
Sparks, Allister.
1990.   *The Mind of Africa*. London: Heineman.
Stavrou, S., and L. Shongwe.
1989.   "Violence on the Periphery: The Greater Edendale Complex."
               Indicator South Africa 7, pp. 53–57.
Suckling, John, and Landeg White, eds.
1988.   *After Apartheid*. London: James Currey.
Sunter, Clem.
1987.   *The World and South Africa in the 1990s*. Cape Town: Human
               & Rousseau.
Swilling, M., R. Humphries, and K. Shubane, eds.
1992.   *Contemporary South Africa Debates Series—The Apartheid
               City in Transition*. Cape Town: Oxford University Press.
Taylor, Rupert.
1991.   "The Myth of Ethnic Division: Township Conflict on the
               Reef," *Race and Class* 33, no. 2, 1–14.
Thompson, Leonard.
1985.   *The Political Mythology of Apartheid*. New Haven: Yale Uni-
               versity Press.
Unterhalter, Elaine, et al., eds.
1991.   *Apartheid Education and Popular Struggles*. Johannesburg:
               Ravan Press.
Vale, Peter.
1991.   "Points of Re-Entry—Prospects for a Post-Apartheid Foreign
               Policy." *South Africa International* 21, no. 4 (April): 214–30.
van den Berghe, Pierre L., ed.
1979.   *The Liberal Dilemma in South Africa*. London: Croom Helm.
———, ed.
1990.   *State Violence and Ethnicity*. Niwot: University of Colorado
               Press.
van Zyl Slabbert, F.
1991.   "Political Implications of Post-Apartheid South Africa with
               Emphasis on Southern Africa." Address delivered to the Africa
               Leadership Forum, Windhoek. September.

————.
1992. *South Africa's Quest for Democracy: Problems and Possibilities in Transition.* Johannesburg: Penguin Books.

Webster, Eddie.
1985. *Cast in a Racial Mould.* Johannesburg: Ravan Press.

Weitzer, Ronald.
1991. "Elite Conflicts over Policing in South Africa: 1980–89." *Policing and Society,* pp. 257–68.

Wood, Bernard.
1990a. "Canada and Southern Africa." *The Round Table,* no. 315, pp. 280–90.

————.
1990b. "Towards North-South Middle Power Coalitions." In *Middle Power Internationalism,* ed. Cranford Pratt. Montreal and Kingston: McGill-Queen's University Press.

Selected Southern African Journals and Newsletters

ACAG Update (P.O. Box 261096, Excom 2023). Monthly bulletin of the anticensorship action group of South Africa, mainly recording assaults on freedom of speech and media censorship.

AFRA Newsletter of the Association for Rural Advancement (170 Berg Street, Pietermaritzburg 3201). Provides moving accounts of forced resettlements and the struggle to reclaim African land.

Africa Analysis (167 Kensington High Street, London W8 6SH). A fortnightly, and rather expensive, bulletin on financial and political trends in the whole of the African continent. Particularly useful to stockbrokers, trade analysts, and authors of risk studies.

Africa Confidential (Computer Posting, 120/126 Lavender Avenue, Mitcham, Surrey CR4 3HP). Probably the most widely read and best-informed fortnightly newsletter on Africa, albeit with an unfortunate tendency to focus on personalities rather than on the interests and social forces they represent.

Africa Insight (P.O. Box 630, Pretoria 0001). The quarterly of the Pretoria Africa Institute. Often contains useful articles on countries in sub-Saharan Africa, which are only now receiving closer attention in the South.

Africa Report (833 UN Plaza, New York, NY 10017). A readable, bi-monthly journalistic magazine of commentary on African events for American taste.

Africa Research Bulletin (Blackwell Publishers, 108 Cowley Road, Oxford OX4 1JF). The most authoritative summary of press reports, speeches, statistics, and events throughout the continent. Published monthly since 1964.

African Affairs (18 Northumberland Avenue, London WC2N 5BJ). Published quarterly for the UK Royal African Society. A thorough, somewhat eclectic and anthropologically focused academic journal that offers solid and esoteric articles as well as a substantial book review section.

The African Communist (P.O. Box 1027, Johannesburg 2000). The theoretical quarterly of the SACP, billed as "a forum for Marxist-Leninist thought," mostly of the orthodox kind.

Agenda (29 Ecumenical Centre Trust, 20 St Andrews Street, Durban, 4001). A journal about women and gender, and the triple "exploitation and oppression" of South African women "on the basis of their class, race, and gender." It aims to reach a wide audience through accessible style, but the resulting selection often lacks depth and is beset by sloganeering.

Canadian Journal of African Studies (Canadian African Studies Association, Innis College, University of Toronto, 2 Sussex Ave., Toronto, M5S 1A1). This journal has established a reputation for solid (if sometimes rather academic) refereed articles and reviews. Bilingual (English and French).

CSIS Africa Notes (Center for Strategic and International Studies, Suite 400, 1800 K Street N.W., Washington, D.C. 20006). A monthly briefing paper on a topical African issue, ably selected by veteran Africanist Helen Kitchen, of interest to American policy makers.

Democracy in Action (Idasa, Hill House, 1 Penzance Road, Mowbray 7700). A bimonthly newsletter of the Institute for a Democratic Alternative that has increasingly developed into a jargon-free yet sophisticated forum for political education. It strives to present accessible debates about South African political problems of the day.

Development and Democracy (Urban Foundation, P.O. Box 1198, Johannesburg 2000). A new irregular journal by the develoment lobby of big business with comparative contributions by high-powered academic experts.

Development Southern Africa (Box 784433, Sandton 2146). The quarterly of the Development Bank of Southern Africa, in which traditionally oriented economists, social workers, and public administration specialists dominate the discussion.

Die Suid-Afrikaan (Breestraat 215, Cape Town 8001). An influential mouthpiece of liberal Afrikaner intellectuals, founded by Hermann Giliomee and now edited by André du Toit. High analytical quality combined with a keen sense of the burning issues of the day.

Fast Facts (SA Institute of Race Relations, P.O. Box 31044, Braamfontein 2017). A monthly update of Institute members of current issues for busy readers.

Front File (37 Fairhazel Gardens, London NW6 3QN). One of the better of several London-based monthly commentaries on South African developments, written by veteran journalist Stanley Uys. Often reprinted crucial information from obscure sources but unfortunately ceased publication in 1992.

Frontline (Box 32219, Braamfontein 2017). An unpredictable and generally entertaining monthly presided over by maverick editor Denis Becket, who sometimes hits on little-noticed contradictions in South African life.

Indicator South Africa (Centre for Social and Development Studies, University of Natal, Durban 4001). An informative, nonpropagandistic, and jargon-free quarterly monitor of South African political, urban and rural, and economic trends. A good source for up-to-date statistics and pithy analyses.

Information Update (HSRC, P.O. Box 9086, Pretoria 0001). A quarterly

HSRC expensive publication to keep decisionmakers up to date on the latest survey results. Although the same material is more cheaply and, frequently, more concisely presented by the various publications of the Institute of Race Relations, *Information Update* is valuable for its in-depth empiricism.

The Innis Labour Brief (The Innis Labour Brief Co., P.O. Box 91070, Auckland Park 2006). A manual on current economic, political, and industrial developments. Highly informative on trends in the labor field; by a former Wits sociology lecturer turned successful business consultant.

Journal of Contemporary African Studies (Africa Institute of South Africa, P.O. Box 630, Pretoria 0001). A biannual interdisciplinary journal, previously published by the Pretoria Africa Institute and now by Rhodes University. A more voluminous emulation of the reputable *Journal of Modern African Studies* containing thorough, scholarly articles.

Journal of Modern African Studies (Huish, Chagford, Devon, TQ13 8AR). One of the best and up-to-date academic journals, with a broad range of contributors, under the able editorship of David Kimble.

Land Update (Box 16858, Doornfontein [Johannesburg] 2028). The journal of the National Land Committee is a valuable source of news and commentary on resettlements and the debate about a new land policy.

Leadership (P.O. Box 1138, Johannesburg 2000). A glossy advertisement for a more enlightened corporate culture. Superb photographs and a good nose for trendy politics and lifestyles.

Mayibuye (P.O. Box 61884, Marshalltown 2307). The monthly journal of the ANC and successor of *Sechaba,* which was published in exile. The contributions, through which the ANC leadership tries to keep its bewildered constituency on course, are mainly aimed at mobilization.

Monitor (P.O. Box 13197, Humewood 6013, 19 Clyde Street, Central Port Elizabeth, 6001). Edited by Rory Riordan; publishes three editions a year on glossy paper with stunning photographs. A poorer but more political version of *Leadership,* with a heavier focus on human rights issues, more in-depth interviews, and fewer corporate topics.

New Nation (P.O. Box 10674, Johannesburg 2000). A weekly ANC-supporting tabloid of atrocities and continued struggle, edited by Zwelakhe Sisulu. Includes a useful educational supplement that, together with documents and commentary on internal ANC debates, provides a unique source of insights into urban black thinking in the PWV region.

Politikon (PSASA, Box 1040, Florida 1710). The journal of the South African Political Science Association featuring solid academic analyses of both South African problems and issues pertinent to political science in general.

Race Relations News (P.O. Box 31044, Braamfontein 2017). The quarterly official journal of the liberal South African Institute of Race Relations. Written in an easily accessible style, it defends the traditional liberal values of pluralism and democratic tolerance and is equally critical of human rights abuses whether perpetrated by the government or by liberation movements. Summaries of the Institute's research and the text of speeches by Institute members generally convey a valuable nonpartisan overview of the South African conflict.

Race Relations Survey (South African Institute of Race Relations. P.O. Box 31044, Braamfontein 2017). The annual authoritative book-length compendium of intelligently organized facts, figures, and commentary, mainly gleaned from the South African press. The survey has established a high reputation as a meticulous and indispensable overview for any serious student of South Africa.

Reality (P.O. Box 1104, Pietermaritzburg 3200). The combative and refreshing voice of the handful of moral liberals left in South Africa. Not shy to criticize the regime and the ANC alike on the basis of a genuine commitment to individual freedoms and human rights.

Review of African Political Economy (P.O. Box 678, Sheffield, S1 1BF). A provocative, critical analysis of the political economy of the Third World by authors of the unorthodox Left.

RSA Policy Review (SA Communication Service, Private Bag X745, Pretoria 0001). A monthly journal of interviews with government ministers and articles by bureaucrats with the aim of elaborating National Party policy.

S.A. International Affairs Bulletin (Jan Smuts House, University of the Witwatersrand, Wits 2050). South African foreign policy issues and international relations are analyzed by the academics of John Barratt's institute.

S.A. Journal of Economic History (Economic History Society of Southern Africa, c/o Division of Economic History, University of the Witwatersrand, Wits 2050). A biannual academic publication with a focus on economic history.

SA Labour Bulletin (P.O. Box 3851, Johannesburg 2000). The only consistent account and analysis of union struggles since the emergence of independent unions in the early 1970s. More oriented toward praxis than theory, it is nevertheless not an in-house organ but a sympathetic, factual observer of and commentator on the plurality of trends and events in the labor sphere.

Searchlight South Africa (14 Talbot Ave., London N2 0LS). A little-known Trotskyite journal founded by Baruch Hirson, who not only knows the activist history from the inside but crusades against the shortcomings of the ANC and its ally, the SACP.

Social Dynamics (Centre for African Studies, University of Cape Town, Rondebosch 7700). An academic social science journal, typical of the genre with the occasional brilliant article or book review tucked amidst dull, esoteric, and jargon-laden treatises.

South Africa International (P.O. Box 7006, Johannesburg 2000). The quarterly of the South Africa Foundation, the big business lobby. It has become ever more sophisticated in its broad range of authors and coverage of topics pertinent to South African socioeconomic development. The journal, together with the Foundation's newsletter, comes free to interested subscribers, who are mostly business professionals.

South Africa in the Nineties (HSRC, Private Bag X41, Pretoria 0001). A new quarterly published by the Social Dynamics section of the Human Sciences Research Council with analytical contributions on the progress towards a democratic social order written by academics across the political spectrum.

South African Defence Review (Institute for Defence Politics, P.O. Box 4167, Halfway House 1685). Generally useful and pertinent working papers to facilitate the transition to a democratically accountable and national defense force in a postsettlement South Africa, edited by Jakkie Cilliers.

South African Journal of Human Rights (Juta Ltd., P.O. Box 14373, Kenwyn 7790). Thorough academic discussions of the legalism of the apartheid nightmare by the best legal minds of South Africa in the liberal tradition.

South African Sociological Review (Editor: Jeff Lever, University of the Western Cape, Bellville 7530). Like *Social Dynamics,* the academic journal publishes a wide spectrum of research and reviews mostly by South African academics.

Southern Africa Report (427 Bloor Street W., Toronto, M5S 1X7). The strident, bimonthly Canadian voice of John Saul, deploring capitalist-racist collusion in the world and longing for the days of the original Frelimo. Well-informed on Mozambique but predictable on South African events.

Southern Africa Report (P.O. Box 261579, Excom 2023). A weekly airmail bulletin compiled by veteran liberal journalist Raymond Louw. It contains perceptive summaries of selected events, along with separate commentaries by the editor that adhere to liberal principles similar to those of *SouthScan.* Weak on economic trends but strong on human rights issues.

Southern African Review of Books (Centre for Southern African Studies, University of the Western Cape, Bellville, Capé). An excellent bimonthly paper in the format of the *New York* or *London Review of Books* that not only focuses on South African debates about literature and art but is equally valuable for its treatment of avant-garde political controversies. Edited by historian Rob Turrell from London.

SouthScan (P.O. Box 724, London N16 5RZ). One of the most informative and comprehensive newsletters; also among the least expensive for individual subscribers. Focuses about equally on economic and political issues, and is slightly biased toward ANC interpretations.

Spotlight (South African Institute of Race Relations, P.O. Box 31044, Braamfontein 2017). Bimonthly dispassionate analysis of a particular topical issue, such as educational reform, violence, negotiations, or political strategies.

Theoria (University of Natal Press, P.O. Box 375, Pietermaritzburg 3200). A scholarly, non-disciplinary journal in the humanities, arts, and social sciences. It encourages reflection on important intellectual currents and social, artistic, and political events.

Towards Democracy (Institute for Multi-Party Democracy, 85 Field Street, Durban 4001). A new in-house journal by Oscar Dhlomo's non-partisan Institute with useful analysis and exhortations for political tolerance and national reconciliation.

Transformation (Economic History Department, University of Natal, Durban 401). A quarterly, rather modest, semi-academic journal of the broad independent left, covering similar ground as *Work in Progress* but with more careful selection of in-depth articles and commentary. Essential reading for understanding intraleft debates.

Vrye Weekblad (P.O. Box 177, Newton 2113). The Afrikaans equivalent of the *Weekly Mail,* with much more in-depth contributions that cover a broad spectrum of political, cultural and human interests, under editor Max du Preez.

The Weekly Mail (P.O. Box 260425, Excom 2023). Probably still the most lively, though not unbiased, source of rich details about the darker and lighter sides of living in the land of apartheid.

Work in Progress (Southern African Research Service, P.O. Box 32716, Braamfontein 2017). A fine example of radical leftist but jargon-free analysis in the tradition of critical democratic socialism. Like *Transformation,* crucial to understanding the intricacies of debates on the Left.

Index

(1982) / 33. *Soldiers without Politics: Blacks in the South African Armed Forces,* by Kenneth W. Grundy (1983) / 34. *Education, Race, and Social Change in South Africa,* by John A. Marcum (1982) / 35. *The Land Belongs to Us: The Pedi Polity, the Boers and the British in the Nineteenth-Century Transvaal,* by Peter Delius (1984) / 36. *Sol Plaatje, South African Nationalist, 1876–1932,* by Brian Willan (1984) / 37. *Peasant Consciousness and Guerrilla War in Zimbabwe: A Comparative Study,* by Terence Ranger (1985) / 38. *Guns and Rain: Guerrillas and Spirit Mediums in Zimbabwe,* by David Lan (1985) / 39. *South Africa without Apartheid: Dismantling Racial Domination,* by Heribert Adam and Kogila Moodley (1986) / 40. *Hidden Struggles in Rural South Africa: Politics and Popular Movements in the Transkei and Eastern Cape, 1890–1930,* by William Beinart and Colin Bundy (1986) / 41. *Legitimating the Illegitimate: State, Markets, and Resistance in South Africa,* by Stanley B. Greenberg (1987) / 42. *Freedom, State Security, and the Rule of Law: Dilemmas of the Apartheid Society,* by Anthony S. Mathews (1987) / 43. *The Creation of Tribalism in Southern Africa,* edited by Leroy Vail (1989) / 44. *The Rand at War, 1899–1902: The Witwatersrand and Anglo-Boer War,* by Diana Cammack (1990) / 45. *State Politics in Zimbabwe,* by Jeffrey Herbst (1990) / 46. *A Democratic South Africa? Constitutional Engineering in a Divided Society,* by Donald L. Horowitz (1991) / 47. *A Complicated War: The Harrowing of Mozambique,* by William Finnegan (1992) / 48. *J. M. Coetzee: South Africa and the Politics of Writing,* by David Attwell (1993) / 49. *A Life's Mosaic: The Autobiography of Phyllis Ntantala,* by Phyllis Ntantala (1992) / 50. *The Opening of the Apartheid Mind: Options for the New South Africa,* by Heribert Adam and Kogila Moodley (1993)

About the Authors

HERIBERT ADAM is Professor of Sociology at Simon Fraser University, Vancouver, and also holds a regular visiting appointment at the University of Cape Town. His books include *Modernizing Racial Domination* (California, 1971), *Ethnic Power Mobilized: Can South Africa Change?* (with Hermann Giliomee, Yale, 1979), and *South Africa without Apartheid* (with Kogila Moodley, California, 1986). Address communications to: Department of Sociology, Simon Fraser University, Burnaby, B.C., Canada V5A 1S6. FAX: 604-291-5799 (Canada) or 27-21-4061911 (South Africa).

KOGILA MOODLEY is Associate Professor in the Department of Social and Educational Studies at the University of British Columbia. Born and raised in the Indian community of Durban, South Africa, she is the editor or coauthor of *Race Relations and Multicultural Education* (UBC Press, 1984), *South Africa without Apartheid* (California, 1986), and *Beyond Multicultural Education: International Perspectives* (Detselig, 1992). Address communications to: Department of Social and Educational Studies, 2044 Lower Mall, University of British Columbia, Vancouver, B.C., Canada V6T 1Z4. FAX: 604-822-4244 (Canada) or 27-21-4061911 (South Africa).

Compositor: ComCom, Inc.
Text: 10.7/13 Sabon
Display: Sabon
Printer: Haddon Craftsmen, Inc.
Binder: Haddon Craftsmen, Inc.